**Richard Bateman, Peter Humphries, Sim...
Sue Jenkinson and D...**

geography@work 1

© Folens Limited, on behalf of the authors.

United Kingdom: Folens Publishers, Waterslade House, Thame Road, Haddenham, Buckinghamshire HP17 8NT.
www.folens.com

Ireland: Folens Publishers, Greenhills Road, Tallaght, Dublin 24.
Email: info@folens.ie

Folens publications are protected by international copyright laws. All rights are reserved. The copyright of all materials in this publication, except where otherwise stated, remains the property of the publisher and author. No part of this publication may be reproduced, stored in a retrieval system, or transmitted, in any form or by any means, for whatever purpose, without the written permission of Folens Limited.

Richard Bateman, Peter Humphries, Simon Howe, Sue Jenkinson and Dawn Price hereby assert their moral rights to be identified as the authors of these works in accordance with the Copyright, Designs and Patents Act 1988.

Series designer: Fiona Webb
Illustrations: Celia Hart and Tony Randell
Cover design: Design by Form (www.form.uk.com)
Back cover photos: Back cover photos (from l to r): © ABC Ajansi/Corbis Sygma; Mark Boulton/Alamy; Digital Mapping Solutions from Dotted Eyes © Crown Copyright 2008. All rights reserved, licence number 100019918; WaterAid/Caroline Irby

Every effort has been made to trace the copyright holders of material used in this publication. If any copyright holder has been overlooked, we should be pleased to make any necessary arrangements.

British Library Cataloguing in Publication Data. A catalogue record for this publication is available from the British Library.

ISBN 978 1 85008 302 3

Contents

Why are South America and Africa two pieces of the same jigsaw? 4–63

Do you really know where you live? 64–123

What does my area need? 124–151

Why are some countries dry whilst others flood? 152–179

Glossary 180–187

Index 188–191

Contents

Richard Bateman

1	What are oceans and continents and what lies below them?	6–9
2	What power do Earth movements have?	10–11
3	Where do earthquakes happen?	12–15
4	Why do earthquakes happen and how do we measure them?	16–19
5	What was the biggest earthquake ever recorded?	20–21
6	How do earthquakes cause tsunamis?	22–23
7	What types of volcanoes and eruptions are there?	24–27
8	Where do we find volcanoes in the world?	28–29
9	Do South America and Africa fit together like two jigsaw pieces?	30–33
10	Why are there earthquakes and volcanoes in the middle of oceans?	34–37
11	What are tectonic plates and where do they start and end?	38–41
12	What happens when one continental plate meets another continental plate?	42–45
13	How is the power of the Earth showing through in North and South America and Africa?	46–49
14	Why do people continue to live in earthquake zones and near volcanoes?	50–51
15	Can we protect ourselves against earthquakes?	52–53
16	Can we predict hazards from volcanoes?	54–57
17	What are 'hot spots' and 'supervolcanoes' and should we worry?	58–59
18	How do emergency services work after earthquake and volcano disasters?	60–63

What are oceans and continents and what lies below them?

South America and Africa are both continents. A continent is a large area of land on the surface of our planet, Earth. An ocean is a huge body of salt water. In this lesson we will explore the oceans and continents and discover what they are made of. We will also learn how to add names to a map of the world and how to explain something using clues.

FACT FILE
Seas are shallow parts of oceans near continents, such as the North Sea off the east coast of the United Kingdom.

CHALLENGE

1. Do you think we should have:
   a) five continents or seven?
   b) one ocean or five?
2. Using an atlas name the oceans 1, 2, 3, 4 and 5 and the continents A, B, C, D, E, F and G.

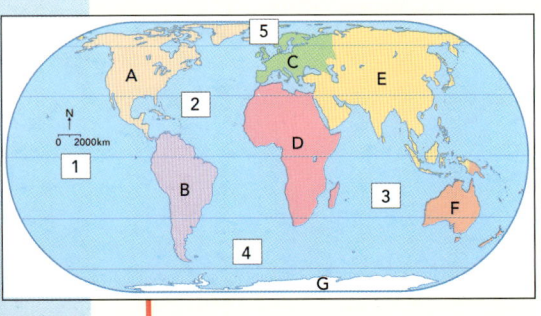

The continents

Everyone says there are seven continents, but in fact there are only five. These are, from biggest to smallest:

- Eurasia (54.9 million square km)
- America (42.5 million square km)
- Africa (30.3 million square km)
- Antarctica (12.1 million square km)
- Australia (7.7 million square km).

We say there are seven continents because in the past Asia was thought to be very different from Europe. It was cut off from Europe by mountains and deserts, so that it seemed like a different continent. What we know as Asia is 45 million square km, while Europe is just 9.9 million square km. These are now combined to form the continent Eurasia.

North and South America are regarded as two continents because the strip of land connecting them is so thin, but in fact they are the same land mass. North America is 24.7 million square km and South America is 17.8 million square km.

The oceans

The continents make up only 29% of the surface of our planet. Most of it (71%) is covered with one ocean. However, we choose to say there are five oceans. These are, from biggest to smallest:

- Pacific Ocean (156 million square km)
- Atlantic Ocean (77 million square km
- Indian Ocean (69 million square km)
- Southern Ocean (20 million square km)
- Arctic Ocean (14 million square km).

What are oceans and continents and what lies below them?

Digging deeper

Planet Earth is so big that even the deepest ocean is like a shallow puddle on its surface. Under the water of every ocean is the solid rock of the Earth's **crust**. The deepest hole ever drilled went 19km through the crust. As the drill went down, it bored through rocks which grew hotter and hotter, while the pressure of the rocks around the drill increased.

If we could drill deeper, we would eventually drill into a zone called the **mantle**, where the rock is not solid. The great heat and pressure have made the rock plastic, like Blu-tack or playdough. The centre of the Earth is called the **core**.

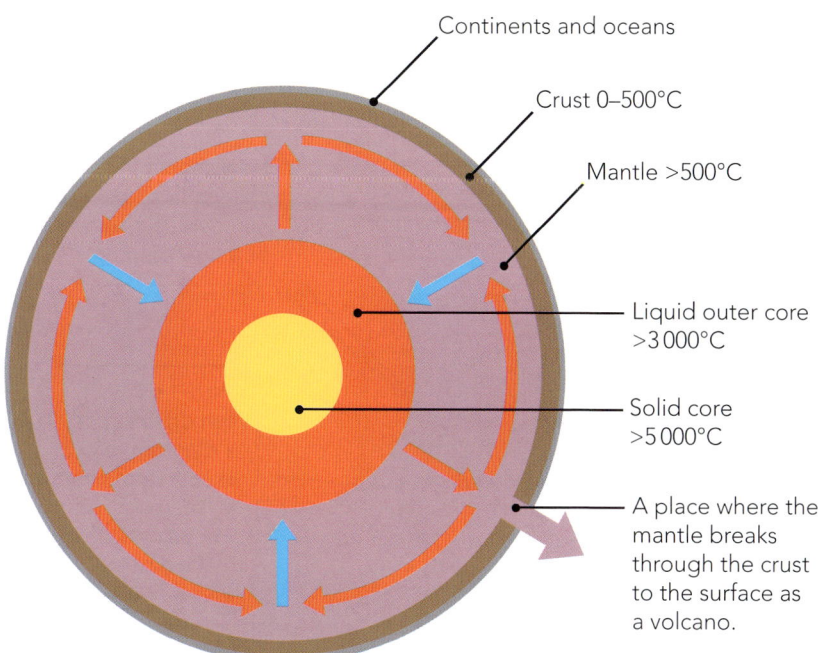

b The structure and movements of the Earth

This is what the Earth would look like if it was cut in half. The oceans, continents and crust are too thin to show up as any more than a line, like the shell of an egg. The heat and pressure increase as you move towards the core. In the core, radioactivity creates great energy and this causes movement of the mantle (shown by the red arrows). Where the mantle moves sideways, it drags the solid rock of the crust with it, causing earthquakes, volcanoes and mountains to form. Cooler bits of mantle sink back towards the core (blue arrows). Most of this goes on slowly, although often dramatic earthquakes and volcanoes give us a tiny idea of the immense power of the Earth.

CHALLENGE

3 From clues given so far, have you any idea why South America and Africa might fit together like jigsaw pieces?

What are oceans and continents and what lies below them?

'MyPlace': Extended research enquiry into the power of the Earth

Throughout your work into the power of the Earth you will carry out enquiries and complete activities. While you are working, imagine that you are a geographical writer, researching anything and everything about this topic that YOU find interesting and collecting it all together. This includes illustrations (like maps, photos, diagrams and graphs), writing (like quotes, opinions, descriptions and explanations) and sounds. You could stick everything into a scrapbook or use a computer to create a record of your thoughts and feelings like a MySpace™ page.

The mind map below may give you some ideas.

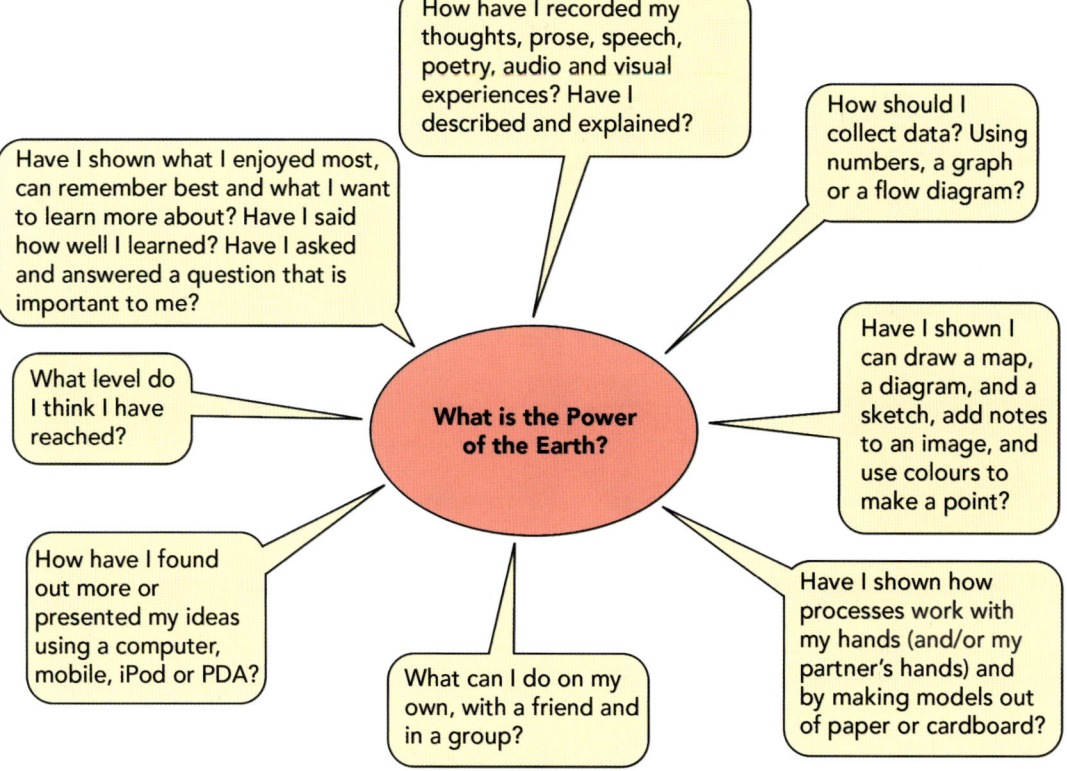

Success criteria levelling grid

Study the levels on the grid on the next page. The squares show how you can build your achievements from the top row (Level 3) down to the bottom row (Level 8+). If you can show that you are able to do all of the tasks in the squares along the row well, you can award yourself or your partner that level. Your teacher will then let you know whether he or she agrees.

What are oceans and continents and what lies below them?

Geographical enquiry and skills	Knowledge and understanding of places	Knowledge and understanding of patterns and processes	Knowledge and understanding of environmental change and sustainable development	Level
I can find information from more than one source. I can answer questions when they are set. I can design titles and can draw maps.	I know some places where earthquakes have happened and where some volcanoes are.	I can point out earthquakes and volcanoes on maps and talk about how they are formed.	I can say how earthquakes and volcanoes affect the environment of places and make them different from other places.	3
As 3, plus I can find information from other textbooks and the Internet. I can draw graphs, diagrams sketches and sketch maps.	As 3, plus I can understand and describe what these places look like in different parts of the world.	As 3, plus I can describe where earthquakes and volcanoes are. I can also describe how they happen.	As 3, plus I can understand why people want to continue to live in these dangerous places.	4
As 4, plus I can explain why I select sources. I can add my own notes to illustrations. I can set myself some tasks.	As 4, plus I can explain how these places are similar to or different from each other.	As 4, plus I can explain how earthquakes and volcanoes affect people.	As 4, plus I can begin to explain how people can live sustainably with earthquakes and volcanoes.	5
As 5, plus I can use sources and illustrations effectively.	As 5, plus I can explain how these places are caused by movements of the Earth.	As 5, plus I can explain complicated ideas like subduction and sea floor spreading.	As 5, plus I can explain different ways of managing such environments sustainably.	6
As 6, plus I can show which sources and illustrations are most useful. I can come to well argued conclusions.	As 6, plus I can explain how these places are changing because of movements of the Earth.	As 6, plus I can show how people have different ways of making decisions about how to live in such places.	As 6, plus I can explain how sustainability affects the ways that people manage environments.	7
As 7, plus I can ask my own questions and evaluate sources before I use them. I can say why my argued conclusions are sensible ones.	As 7, plus I can show how places change because Earth movement processes change over time.	As 7, plus I can show how levels of wealth can influence these decisions.	As 7, plus I can show a personal understanding of sustainability.	8
As 8, plus I can independently create other lines of enquiry.	As 8, plus I can explain how to predict change.	As 8, plus I can explain how wealth can influence decisions on quality of life.	As 8, plus I can compare ways of sustainably managing environments.	8+

What power do Earth movements have?

Earth movements can generate fantastic amounts of power, putting 500 million people (one in 12 people in the world) at risk. **Geologists** (who study rocks) know a lot about the spectacular power that lies within the Earth, but have only scratched the surface of this topic. In this lesson we will find out more about the incredible power of earthquakes and volcanoes and the effect this power has on our environment and us as individuals.

Studying the events

The photographs on the next two pages show a glimpse of the damage that can be caused by the Earth moving.

The power of volcanoes

A **volcano** (note: two volcanoes) is a mountain where molten rock and gas come out of the Earth onto the surface. People who study volcanoes are known as **volcanologists**. The captions around Photo a show what just one volcano did in 1991.

a

1 3 August 1990: The first volcanic activity in 500 years started in this part of the Republic of the Philippines, a country of islands in the South-West Pacific Ocean. Volcanologists put extra equipment on the volcano to monitor its activity.

2 2 April 1991: A plume of steam and ash exploded from a 1.5km long fissure in Mt Pinatubo. People 0–10km from the volcano were told to evacuate (move away).

3 13 May 1991: There were 30–180 earthquakes per day under the volcano.

4 7 June 1991: 1 500 earthquakes were recorded under Mt Pinatubo. A tephra – an eruption of gas, steam and rocks – sent up a cloud 8km high. People 1–20km from the volcano were told to evacuate the area.

5 15 June 1991: The main eruption of tephra (boulders ash and dust) rose 34km hig and travelled 400km. Dust blew away over the wh of the Earth.

6 16 June 1991: Heavy rai cased mudflows 'like runny concrete' to race down the mountain at 50km per hour

7 1991–2: The volcano los 260m from its summit. 740 people who did not move away were killed. Temperat around the world went dow by 0.5°C. Damage was £200 million.

What power do Earth movements have?

The power of earthquakes

An **earthquake** is a sudden movement within the Earth that can be felt at the surface. It might be so slight that people are not aware of it – or it may be so severe it causes damage. A scientist who studies earthquakes is called a **seismologist**. Photo b shows just a small amount of the devastating damage caused by an earthquake in Ismit, in North-West Turkey, on 18 August 1999.

- Accidents can be caused where roads are damaged.
- Bare soil shows where the Earth has torn apart.
- Traffic jams form where cars cannot pass.
- The road has been broken where the Earth moved and tore it apart.
- Roof tiles slide off with the vibrations.
- The Earth can become soft so buildings may sink.
- People move into the streets for safety from falling buildings.
- Some buildings can seem to be undamaged.
- Whole buildings fall down because their walls are broken by the shock.
- Walls fall down and break into rubble.
- Diggers are brought in to lift broken rubble to find buried people.

CHALLENGE

1 Study the photograph of Mount Pinatubo erupting (photo a). Decide which of these enquiry words: What? Why? When? How? Where? and Who? you would put to each caption. (You can use more than one for each caption.)

2 Study the photograph and the captions of the earthquake at Ismit (photo b). Decide which information you are most interested in and explain why you are particularly interested.

3 Imagine you were near Mount Pinatubo or Ismit when the alarm sounded. Write a 100 word account of:
a) What might you notice.
HINT: Look at the captions around the photographs and use some quotes from them.
b) How you might feel.
HINT: Think about using words like scared, fascinated and puzzled.

Where do earthquakes happen?

Earthquakes happen all over the world all the time, but the really powerful earthquakes tend to happen in certain areas. In this lesson, we will learn about the Earth's most powerful earthquakes and the pattern of earthquake zones.

The United States Geological Survey is a government organisation in the USA. It surveys the rocks of the nation and other events in the Earth's crust, including every earthquake which is measurable.

Its scientists say there are 500 000 earthquakes every year in the world. Only one in five of these (100 000) can be felt by us on the surface of the Earth. And only 100 earthquakes per year cause major damage in the world.

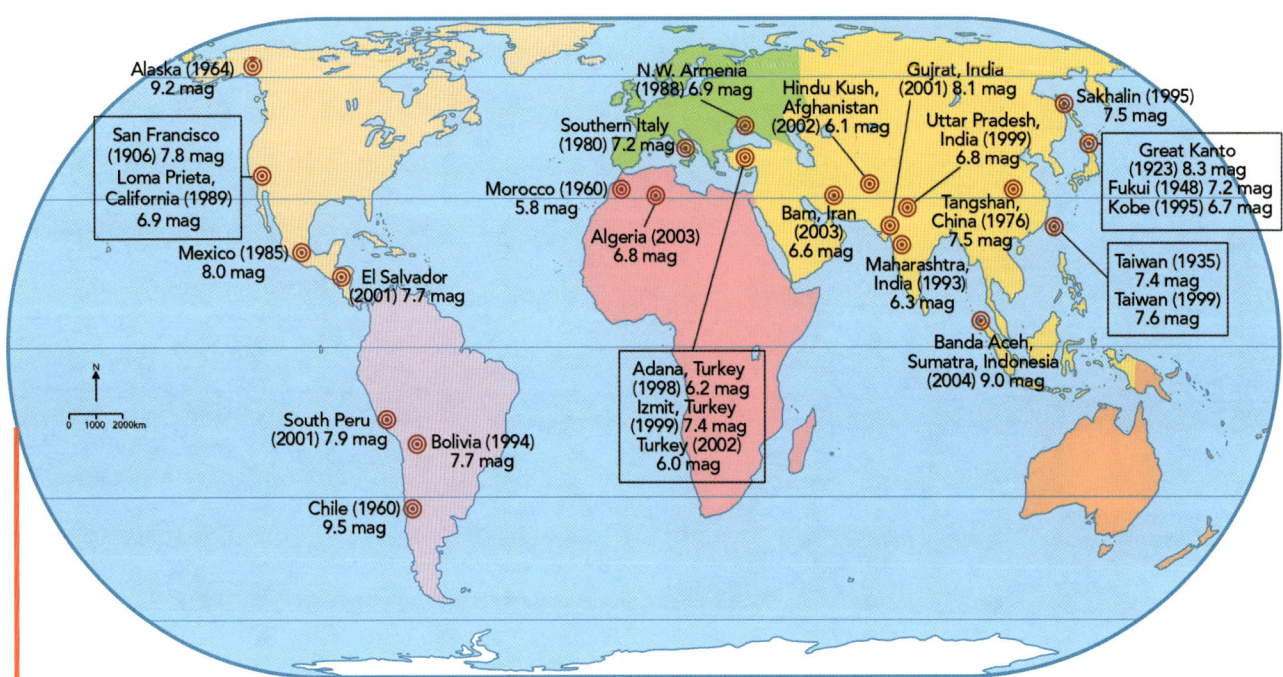

a The 28 biggest earthquakes in recorded history. Note that 'mag' means '**magnitude**', which describes how powerful the earthquake was. For example an earthquake of 7.0 mag is not as powerful as one measuring 9.0 mag

CHALLENGE

Map a shows that some countries can be hit by huge earthquakes more than once.

1 a) Which two countries have had three major earthquakes?
   b) Which two countries have had two major earthquakes?
   c) Which country has had the biggest earthquake of all?
   d) When did it happen?
   e) How powerful was it?

Where do earthquakes happen?

Where are earthquakes most likely to happen on land?

Map b shows which areas of the world are at the greatest **risk** of earthquakes. The higher the risk, the more likely it is that an earthquake will happen.

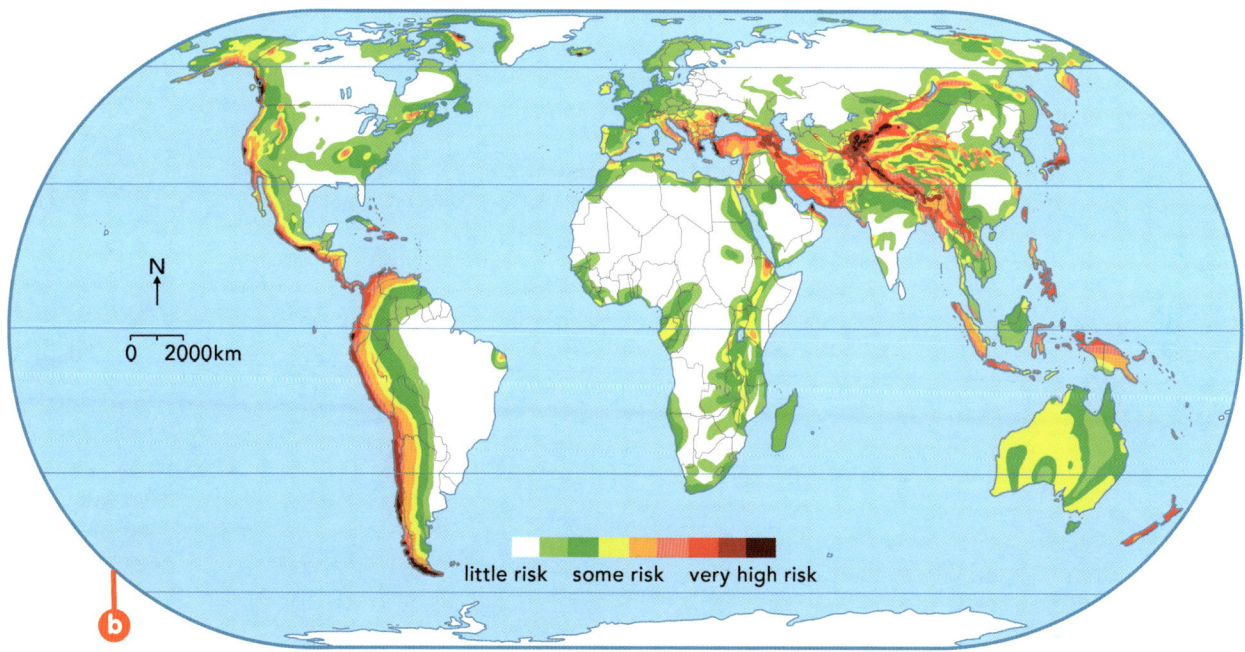

b

CHALLENGE

2 Use an atlas to identify the areas and countries in the table below on map b.
3 Copy and complete the table and, using map b, decide which of the countries are:
   a) at very high risk of experiencing an earthquake.
   b) at some risk of experiencing an earthquake.
   c) at little risk of experiencing an earthquake. The first one has been done for you.

Country	Very high risk	Some risk	Little risk
Eastern USA		✓	
Western USA			
Central Canada			
UK			
Turkey			
Eastern Brazil			
Chile			
Central Russia			
Western China			
Indonesia			
South Africa			
Australia			

Where do earthquakes happen?

What is the pattern of where earthquakes happen?

The pattern of earthquakes is how they are spread out over the Earth. Map d shows where modern equipment has recorded earthquakes between 1963 and 1998. Most of these earthquakes were so small that only sensitive instruments could pick them up. Only a few caused damage.

- Alpine Mountains of Southern Europe and Atlas Mountains of Northern Africa
- Mountains of Western North America
- Mountains of Hawaii
- Mountains of Central America and the Caribbean Island Arc
- The South-East Pacific Ocean Ridge
- Andes Mountains of South America

C This fly-over road has been toppled by an earthquake

Where do earthquakes happen?

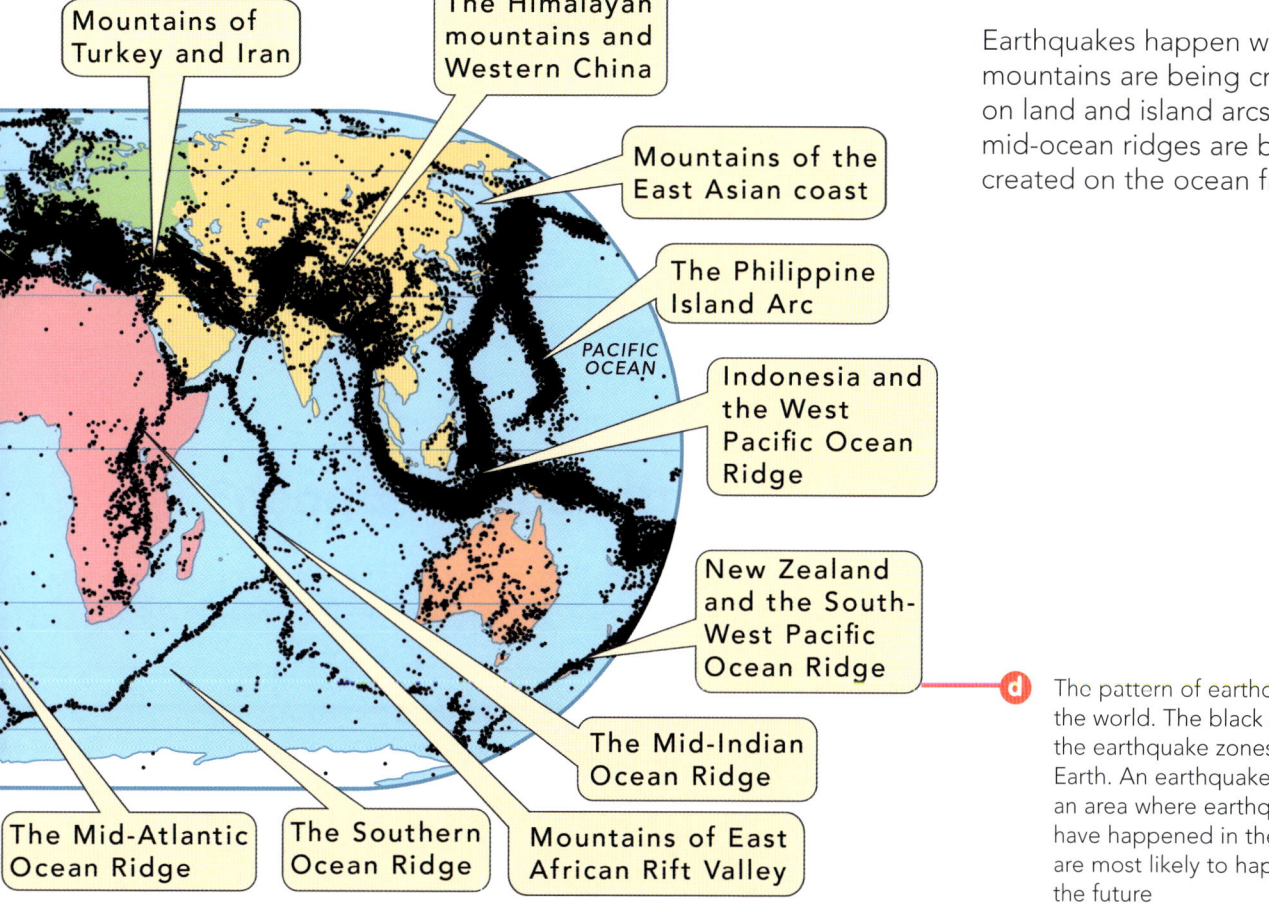

Earthquakes happen where mountains are being created on land and island arcs and mid-ocean ridges are being created on the ocean floor.

d The pattern of earthquakes in the world. The black areas are the earthquake zones of the Earth. An earthquake zone is an area where earthquakes have happened in the past and are most likely to happen in the future

CHALLENGE

4 Look at map d.
   a) What patterns can you see?
   b) Which of these statements do you think are true and which are false? Copy and complete the True or False activity.

Descriptions of the patterns of the world's earthquakes	True	False
1. The pattern is made up of lines.	✓	
2. The lines on land are mainly thinner and those in the oceans are thicker.		
3. The lines run through the centre of the oceans.		
4. The pattern of dots is evenly spread out.		
5. There is a thin line running from Western Europe, through Turkey to the Himalayan mountains and south to Malaysia and Indonesia.		
6. There are thick lines down the western coasts of North, Central and South America.		
7. All around the Pacific Ocean the lines almost join up to make what is known as the 'Pacific Ring of Fire'.		
8. There is a ring of earthquakes around the Caribbean Sea.		
9. There is a ring of earthquakes in the Western Pacific Ocean.		
10. There is a ring of earthquakes in the Eastern Pacific Ocean.		

Why do earthquakes happen and how do we measure them?

We think of our homes, the grass we play on and the paths, pavements and roads we travel on as being solid and dependable. But in many parts of the world they aren't. The earth below us is slowly moving and in some parts of the world it suddenly moves with a jolt, causing an earthquake. In this lesson, we will learn how earthquakes happen and how scientists measure their magnitude.

Why do earthquakes happen?

Deep down in the earth, hot rock under great pressure in the mantle is slowly moving. As it moves it puts the rock on the surface of the earth under great pressure to move. Most of the time friction stops the rock on the surface moving. But, after a while, the rocks do move, in quick jolts that send shockwave vibrations through the rocks nearby. These vibrations are earthquakes. Sometimes they can be felt all over the Earth.

Maps a–d show four different ways in which the surface rock moves and causes earthquakes.

CHALLENGE

1. Use two small pieces of sandpaper. Put one over the other with the rough sides facing each other and with a weight such as a block of wood on top, which you then hold down (as in the diagram below). Try to move the sandpaper slowly in the directions shown in the diagram. You should find that at first the sandpaper resists movement because of the friction between the two sheets, then they move suddenly with a jolt. This resistance followed by a sudden movement simulates what happens in an earthquake.

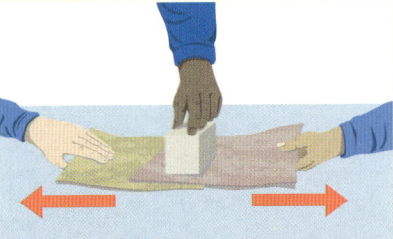

HEALTH AND SAFETY NOTE

Be careful not to cut your hands on the sharp edges of the sandpaper.

CHALLENGE

2. Study maps a–d opposite. In threes, choose one map and see if you can show how moving rocks create earthquakes, volcanoes and mountains. Then demonstrate and explain this to another group.

3. Copy and complete the following True or False activity:

Statement	True	False
1. Earthquakes happen in Japan because the Pacific Ocean floor is moving towards Asia.		
2. Earthquakes happen under Iceland because the Pacific Ocean floor is splitting.		
3. Earthquakes happen in California because the ocean is moving southwards and the continent is moving northwards.		
4. Earthquakes happen near the Mediterranean Sea because Asia is moving towards Europe.		
5. Earthquakes are shockwave vibrations caused when rocks move suddenly.		

Why do earthquakes happen and how do we measure them?

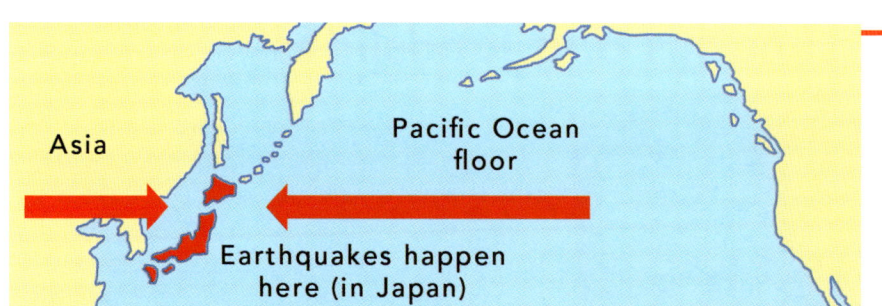

a The Pacific Ocean floor is moving towards Asia. Where they collide, earthquakes occur

b The Atlantic Ocean floor is moving apart. Where it splits, earthquakes occur

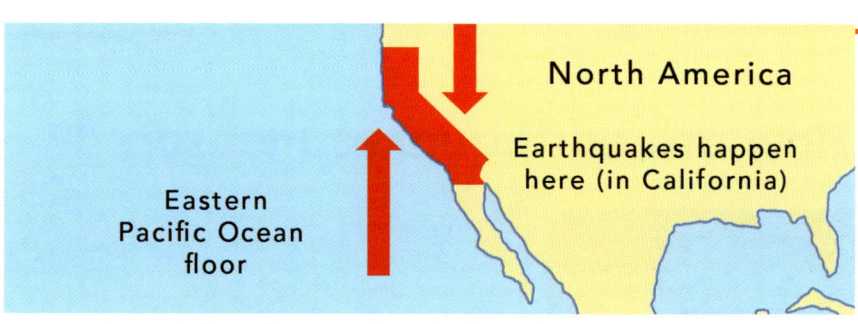

c California is moving Southwards and the Pacific Ocean is moving northwards. Where plates move past each other, earthquakes occur

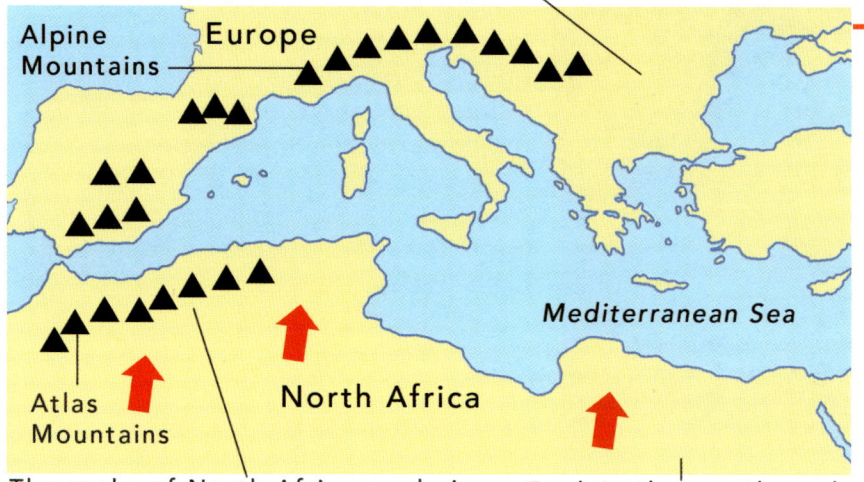

d The solid surface rocks which make up the African continent are moving Northwards and are very slowly crashing into Europe. Softer (molten) rock layers in-between, on the edge of the Mediterranean Sea, have been folded and crushed up to become the Alps and the Atlas Mountains. With every jolt, earthquakes happen

Why do earthquakes happen and how do we measure them?

Tsunamis and landslides

e A landslide caused by an earthquake in Santa Tecla, El Salvador

Most earthquakes cause little or no damage, but a large earthquake and the aftershocks which follow it can cause a huge amount of damage, especially if they occur near cities. Earthquakes can also cause damage by creating **tsunamis** (giant waves) and **landslides**.

When the focus of an earthquake is under a seabed it can move the seabed, and therefore also the water in the sea, up and down to create a tsunami wave. Most tsunami waves cause no damage, but large ones can be devastating.

When an earthquake shakes a steep slope, it can cause the slope to break up and landslides of soil and rock to fall down the slope, perhaps onto roads or houses below.

How are earthquakes measured?

f Professor Richter in his lecture room

In 1880, An Italian called Guiseppe Mercalli invented a scale of 12 degrees to show how earthquakes can be measured by their effect on people and buildings.

In 1934 Professor Charles Richter invented a scientific scale to measure the energy released by an earthquake. Each number on the scale releases *32 times* more energy than the one below it.

Newspapers still use the **Richter Scale**, but modern scales for measuring earthquake strength use the ideas from both scales.

Why do earthquakes happen and how do we measure them?

Richter magnitude	Explosivity TNT* equivalent * TNT is a high explosive used in bombs.	Mercalli degree	Effects
< 3.5	Less than 100 tons	I	People hardly notice.
3.5	100 tons	II	People on top floors might notice.
4.2	1 000 tons	III	People indoors notice slight vibration.
4.5	5 000 tons	IV	Doors rattle. People outside notice.
4.8	30 000 tons	V	Everyone feels it. Dishes break. Trees shake.
5.4	75 000 tons	VI	Pictures fall off. Plaster cracks. Walking is difficult.
6.1	1 million tons	VII	Tiles and bricks fall. Old buildings collapse.
6.5	5 million tons	VIII	Houses move. Towers collapse. Drivers cannot steer.
6.9	30 million tons	IX	Ground cracks open. Gas pipes break. Buildings fall.
7.3	150 million tons	X	Bridges, dams, railways damaged. Landslides.
8.1	1 000 million tons	XI	Modern structures fail. Tsunamis likely on coast.
9	32 000 million tons.	XII	Almost everything is destroyed. The earth moves in waves. Violent tsunamis affect coastal areas.

g How the Richter and Mercalli Scales compare

CHALLENGE

4 News is coming in from the British Geological Survey that earthquakes are happening. The details are set out in the table below. You are a geographical TV team (presenter, sound engineer, cameraman and interpreter) and your producer wants a story about one of these earthquakes. Which do you choose?

To help you make your decision, ask yourself:

- Which earthquake will interest viewers in the UK most?
- What damage is likely to have occurred in each place?
- How many people have been affected?
- How easy is the place to get to?
- Will I be able to get my story back while the news is still fresh?

Number	Magnitude	Country	Rich, middle, or poor	Environment	City or Countryside or wilderness	Lots, some or few people	Hours to fly to the scene
1.	7.6	Algeria	middle	desert	wilderness	few	4
2.	6.9	Rome	rich	gentle hills	city	lots	4
3.	5.6	Nepal	poor	mountains	countryside	some	18
4.	4.2	Moscow	rich	plain	city	lots	4
5.	8.9	Tonga	poor	island in the Pacific Ocean	countryside	few	28

What was the biggest earthquake ever recorded?

The largest earthquake ever recorded was in Chile, South America, on 22 May 1960. It had a magnitude of 9.5. It was so strong it released 25% of all the energy released by earthquakes in the twentieth century. The biggest earthquake in the United Kingdom occurred in the North Sea on 7 June 1931, with a magnitude of 6.1. In this lesson, we will study both earthquakes and explore the similarities and differences between them.

a Map showing Queule, Chile. The red dot shows the epicentre of the earthquake

The biggest earthquake

The earthquake at Queule, Chile, was so strong that it caused enormous and widespread damage. More than 2000 people were killed and 3000 were injured. Two million were left homeless. There was £200 million damage caused in southern Chile. The quake created a tsunami, which caused 61 deaths and £50 million damage in Hawaii, 138 deaths and £30 million damage in Japan, and 32 deaths in the Philippines.

The **epicentre** of the earthquake (the point on the Earth's surface directly above the focus of the earthquake) was 60m down below the ocean floor about 160km off the coast of Chile out in the Pacific Ocean. Many buildings collapsed, killing people in the nearby towns of Valdivia and Puerto Montt. The loss of human life could have been worse, but large **foreshocks** (smaller shocks before the main one) sent people into the streets talking. About 30 minutes after the foreshocks, when the main jolt came, many people were still outside, which meant that many of the buildings and homes that fell were empty.

Much of the coast near Queule sank by up to 2m after the earthquake and it has stayed that way ever since.

b The fishing village of Queule before the earthquake

c Queule after the earthquake

What was the biggest earthquake ever recorded?

The biggest earthquake in the British Isles

The biggest earthquake in the British Isles occurred in the North Sea on 7 June 1931, with an epicentre offshore in the Dogger Bank area (120km North-East of Great Yarmouth) and a magnitude of 6.1. Map d below shows where it happened.

The earthquake happened 23km below the surface but there were no tsunamis reported. Although damage to buildings was reported from 71 different places in Britain and rocks fell from cliffs, no one was hurt by falling buildings. The aftershock was felt in Britain, Ireland, the Netherlands, Belgium, France, Germany, Denmark and Norway.

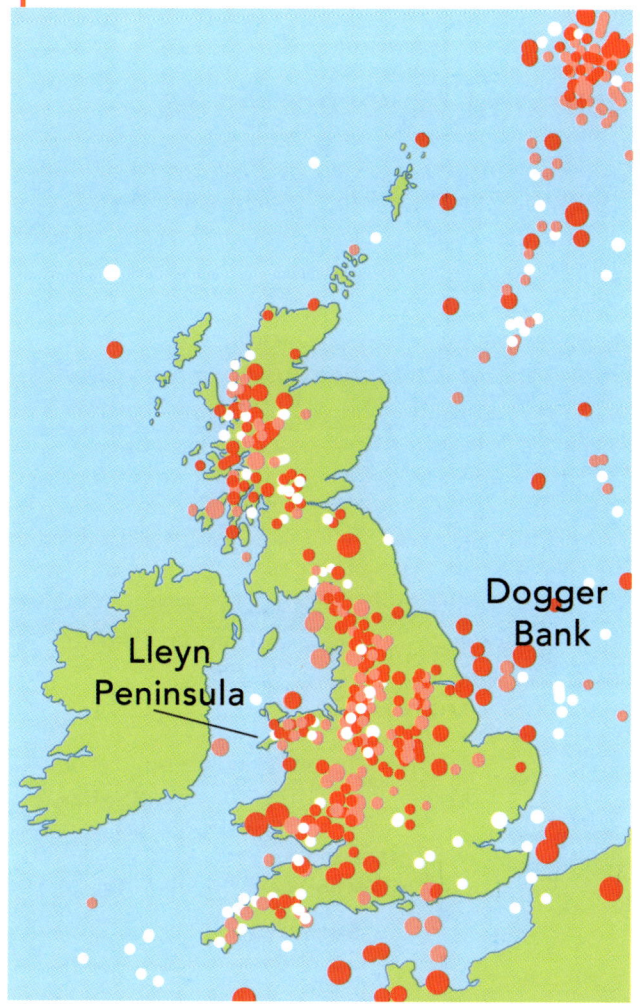

d Where earthquakes happen in the British Isles

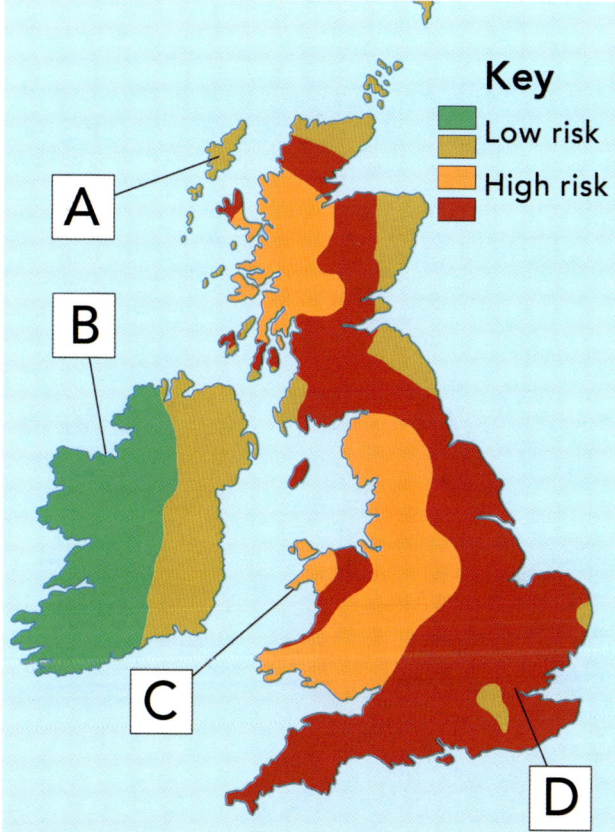

e Map showing the risk of earthquakes in the British Isles. The biggest recorded earthquake on land in the UK was in 1984, in the Lleyn Peninsular, North-West Wales

CHALLENGE

1 Study photographs a and b.
   a) Write down two differences and two similarities between them.
   b) Sum up the change in the environment caused by the earthquake in two sentences.

2 a) Study maps d and e. What is the risk of an earthquake where your school is?
   b) Put these four places in order with (1) being at the highest risk of an earthquake and (4) being at the lowest risk of an earthquake.
      A: The Outer Hebrides of Scotland
      B: Western Ireland
      C: The north-west tip of Wales
      D: London.

3 List two similarities and two differences between the earthquake in the British Isles and the earthquake in Chile.

How do earthquakes cause tsunamis?

If tsunamis remain at sea they may go unnoticed, but they can build into terrifying walls of water travelling at great speed towards the land. In this lesson we will learn more about tsunamis and the devastation they can cause. We will also find out whether people can protect themselves against these giant waves.

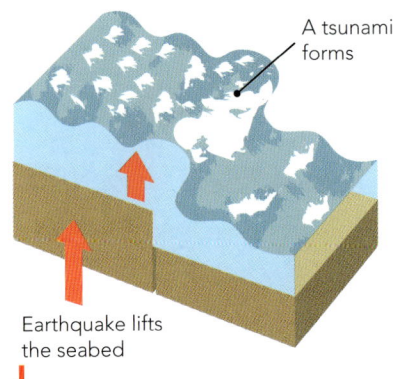

a This diagram shows how an earthquake causes a tsunami

How is a tsunami formed?

A tsunami is a large ocean wave caused by violent earth movements or eruptions out at sea. If the focus of an earthquake is under the seabed, it can move the seabed and the water in the sea up and down to create a tsunami wave. Most tsunami waves cause no damage, but large ones can be devastating. We think of a tsunami as a 'giant wave' or even a 'wave train', as it often consists of several giant waves following each other. The first one is not always the biggest!

The biggest tsunami of recent times

At 1am, UK time, on 26 December 2004 an earthquake of 9.0 mag suddenly lifted up the ocean floor by 13m, 160km west of the island of Sumatra. The Indian Ocean above that part of the ocean floor lifted up as well, causing a tsunami that rushed outwards at up to 800km per hour.

In the ocean, the wave was less than 1m high and was hardly noticed, but when it hit shallow water, the series of waves piled up into a front of water up to 10m high. The giant tsunami rushed 8km inland in some places, killing more than 220 000 people around the shores of the Indian Ocean.

b People running from the first wave in the seaside resort of Koh Raya in the Andaman Islands

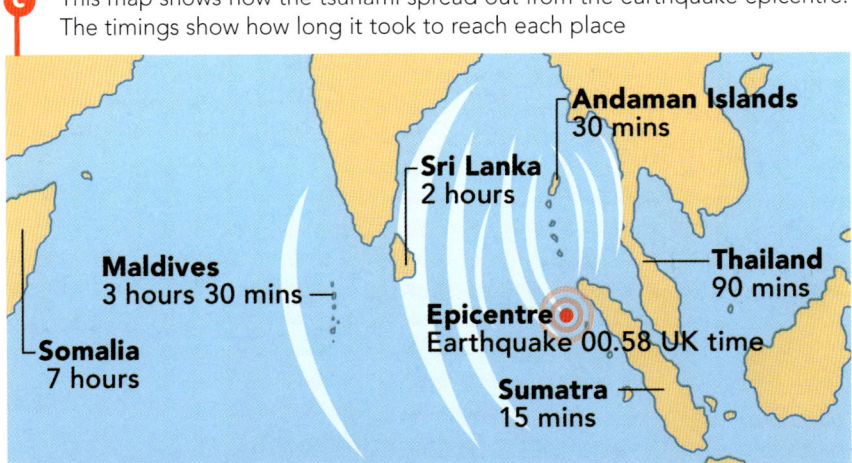

c This map shows how the tsunami spread out from the earthquake epicentre. The timings show how long it took to reach each place

How do earthquakes cause tsunamis?

Can we protect people against tsunamis?

The answer is 'Yes'. The key is to learn what to look, listen and feel for, and to know what to do next.

What happens in a Tsunami?		
An earthquake causes a tsunami.	The seawater along the shore line is drawn back into a huge wave.	The approaching wave creates a lot of noise.
What do you feel?	**What do you see?**	**What do you hear?**
You feel the ground shaking.	You see sea water drain back from the shore.	You hear a loud roaring sound like a train or jet plane.
How you should react?		
Walk to high ground or a third floor in a concrete building.	Run to high ground or the third floor in a concrete building.	Sprint to high ground or up to a third floor in a concrete building. Now!

d Sensing a tsunami: the warning signs

Having as much advance warning as possible about an approaching tsunami could save many lives. Electronic sensors on floating buoys, like the one in photo d, can be placed in the oceans. They beam signals to satellites when an earthquake happens. The satellite then sends messages to warning sirens in low-lying coastal areas nearby. This is an almost instant warning. Radio and TV stations can also break into programmes to warn people that a tsunami is approaching.

Are tsunamis only caused by earthquakes?

Tsunamis are not only caused by earthquakes.

In 1999, scientists at University College London published a paper about a volcano on the island of La Palma in the Canary Islands. They predicted that, if it erupted, the volcano could cause a landslide during which a massive chunk of land would fall into the ocean. A wall of seawater maybe 50m high might then sweep across the shores of Africa and Western Europe, and wash up to the shores of Britain.

Other research has said that this is very unlikely. It has said that if the tsunami moved at 500km/per hour it would take three hours to reach the British Isles and it might only be 30m high.

CHALLENGE

1. In groups, discuss how it might be possible to get an automatic satellite tsunami warning to teenagers on a beach far away from a resort. Think about:
   - What warning is relevant to young people?
   - What sort of equipment could be used?
   - What equipment might need to be invented in the future?

2. a) If La Palma did erupt, would the tsunami affect your school?
   HINT: How high is your school above sea level?
   b) What instructions would you give to students in schools in the path of the tsunami?

e An electronic sensor on a floating buoy could save lives if a tsunami strikes

What types of volcanoes and eruptions are there?

Volcanoes cause some of the Earth's most spectacular events when an eruption pushes an explosion of hot gas, molten rock and solid rock into the atmosphere or ocean. In this lesson, we will study how and why volcanoes erupt and learn how to write about them and view them with 'geographical eyesight'.

Why do volcanoes happen?

Volcanoes happen where the Earth's crust is thin and where there are weak points between the tectonic plates (solid slabs of rock that float on molten rock below them) that make up the crust. Molten rock inside the Earth is called magma. Pressure inside the Earth pushes the magma up through the weak points and cracks.

The hole out of which the lava erupts is called the crater of the volcano and when the magma is forced out to the surface it is known as lava. When the lava flows or explodes out, this is a volcanic eruption. The lava fountain falls back down as ash to build up the sides of the volcano's cone.

a This photo-diagram shows the spectacular eruption of Mount Nyiragongo and why it happened

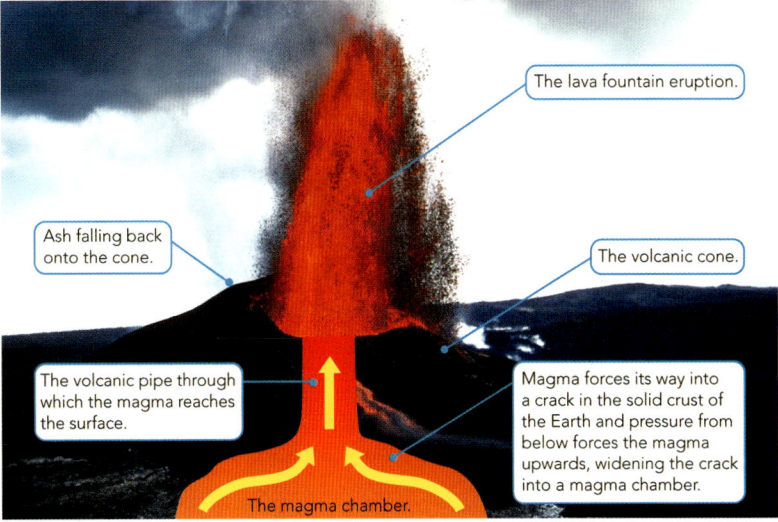

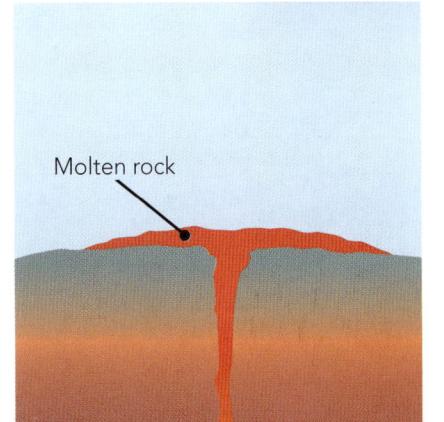
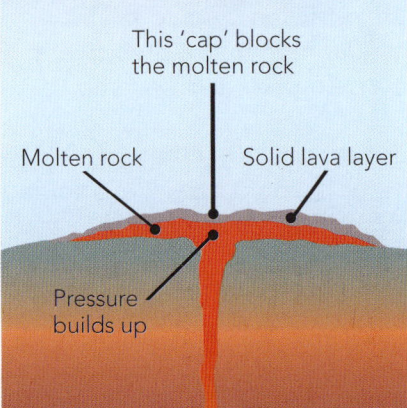
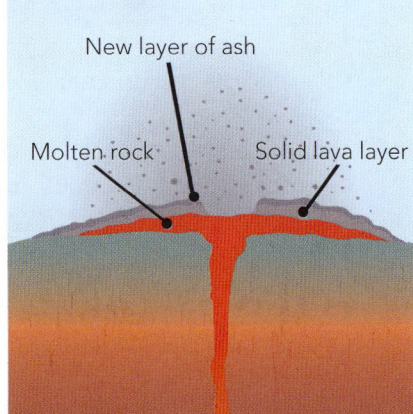

What types of volcanoes and eruptions are there?

b The spectacular eruption of La Réunion volcano in the Indian Ocean, 4 July 2007. This was taken looking down from an aircraft directly over the eruption. You can see the eruption at the bottom of the photo and a stream of lava flowing to the top of the photo

What types of volcanoes and eruptions are there?

CHALLENGE

1 Write your own captions for the photo of La Réunion erupting (photo b on the previous page). You could use the following words:

> lava fountain   lava flow   crater   cloud of gas and steam
> old lava flow

Remember, for a caption to be really useful it should explain what is happening.

Do volcanoes stay active?

Volcanoes like the Icelandic volcano Krafla and La Réunion are obviously **active**, meaning that they have erupted in recent years. Volcanoes like Mount Kilimanjaro, the highest in Africa, which have gone cold and stopped erupting are said to be **extinct**. Volcanoes like Mount Hood in the USA are just 'sleeping' and could erupt again. They are said to be **dormant**.

① Krafla, Iceland, is a fissure volcano

② Mount Fujiyama, Japan, is a stratovolcano; it is not active but still hot

What types of volcanoes and eruptions are there?

3 Paricutin, Mexico, is an ash cone volcano that last erupted in 1977

4 Mount Kilimanjaro, Tanzania, is a stratovolcano which has ceased to erupt

5 In the foreground is Mauna Kea, Hawaii, the biggest volcano in the world. It is 4 169m from ocean floor to summit. It is called a shield volcano because its sides are gently sloping and so it looks like a warrior's shield thrown down on the ground

6 This is Arenal Volcano in Costa Rica, Central America. It is made of layers (strata) of ash and lava, so it is called a stratovolcano. As you can see, it is still active

CHALLENGE

2 Read the captions and look at photos 1–6. Decide whether volcanoes 1–6 are active, dormant or extinct.
3 Which three of the volcanoes shown in this lesson would you most like to visit and why?

Where do we find volcanoes in the world?

Volcanoes happen where the Earth's crust is weak and lets through molten rock from deep in its core. This occurs in different locations around the world. In this lesson, we will learn where these places are and whether they form a pattern.

CHALLENGE

1. a) Which continent does not have any active volcanoes at present?
   b) Which two continents have volcanoes down their western coastlines?
   c) Which ocean has arcs of island volcanoes all down its western side?

Where do we find volcanoes in the world?

There are five types of location where volcanoes are found:

1. The coastal mountains of some continents.
2. The middle of some oceans.
3. From north to south in East Africa.
4. Island arcs near where oceans meet continents.
5. In isolated 'hot spots'.

a A map showing where the five types of volcanoes are found in the world

Key
- ▲ Edge of continent lines of volcanoes (found in mountains of western North and South America).
- ▲ Mid-ocean ridge lines of volcanoes (found on the ridges in the centre of oceans).
- ▲ Africa-splitting volcanoes (where Eastern Africa is splitting away from the rest of Africa).
- ▲ Island arc lines of volcanoes (forming islands on the edges of the Pacific Ocean, the Mediterranean Sea and the Caribbean).
- ▲ 'Hot spot' volcanoes (in small clusters in oceans, for example Hawaii H and the Cameroon Line C).

Where do we find volcanoes in the world?

CHALLENGE

2 Copy and complete the True or False activity below, using map a to help you.

Descriptions of the patterns of the world's volcanoes	True	False
1. The volcanoes seem to form both lines and individual mountains.		
2. The lines on land are on the east coasts of continents.		
3. There are a few volcanoes in the centre of the oceans.		
4. The pattern of volcanoes is evenly spread out.		
5. There are lots of volcanoes in Asia and Australia.		
6. There are lines of volcanoes down the western coasts of North, Central and South America.		
7. Between the Pacific Ocean and the Indian Ocean there are lines of island arc volcanoes.		
8. There is an island arc of volcanoes between the Caribbean Sea and the Atlantic Ocean.		
9. There are no 'hot spot' volcanoes on land.		
10. There are no volcanoes in Africa		

3 Refine your skills in how to describe a pattern: use the ideas in the table opposite to write a paragraph of no more than 50 words to answer the question 'Where do we find volcanoes in the world?'

4 Choose one of the volcanoes shown in map b and find out more about it.

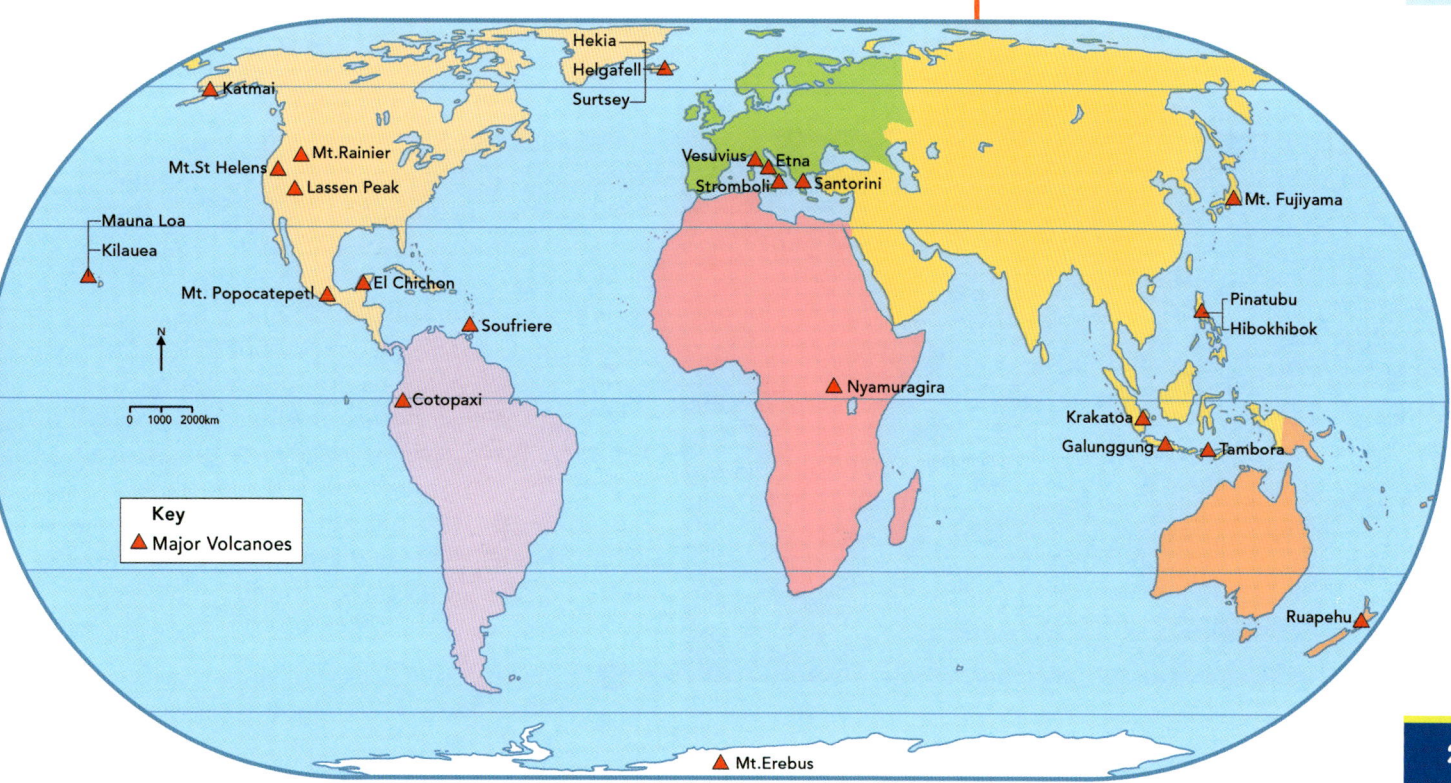

b The major volcanoes of the world

Do South America and Africa fit together like two jigsaw pieces?

In the 16th century, one man created the first reasonably accurate map of the world. He also spotted how South America and Africa looked like they once fitted together. Several hundred years later, other men set about proving that this was true. In this lesson, we will learn about the work of these men and see how the continents did once all fit together.

Mapping the world

In 1570 a cartographer (map maker) called Abraham Ortelius lived and worked in Antwerp, which is in modern-day Belgium. He listened to many sailors and explorers and plotted their information to draw a map of the world. It looks wrong to us, but in 1570 it was a magnificent achievement. No one had drawn as useful a world map before from so many sources of information. Business people and sea captains paid him high prices for his maps to help them with their trading voyages. As a result of following Ortelius' maps, ships carried out faster and safer journeys and so traders in Antwerp made a lot of money. Ortelius became famous and rich.

a Abraham Ortelius

Ortelius' map is called *Typus Orbis Terrarum*, which means *Map of the World*. It shows the coastlines of the world's continents as they were known in 1570.

By 1590 Ortelius had put his maps together to form the world's first atlas, the *Theatrum Orbis Terrarum* or *Theatre of the World*. As he was drawing it, he became interested in the shapes of Africa and South America. Even with his inaccurate map he felt that the West coast of Africa fitted neatly into the east coast of South America, like two jigsaw pieces. He was the first person in the history of the world to notice this.

b Ortelius' map: *Typus Orbis Terrarum*, meaning *Map of the World*

Do South America and Africa fit together like two jigsaw pieces?

CHALLENGE

1 Study Ortelius' map of the world (map b) with a partner. Can you recognise the continents?
   a) Would you have agreed with Ortelius that South America and Africa fit together like two jigsaw pieces?
   b) Compare Ortelius' map with an accurate world map in your atlas. Can you spot where Ortelius did not quite get things right? Why do you think he got them wrong?
2 Trace this simplified world map and cut out the shapes. Work out how the shapes of the continents might fit together like jigsaw pieces.

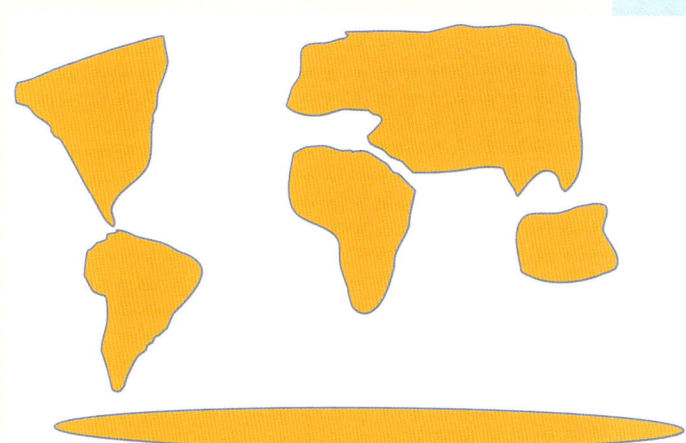

The first theories on the movement of continents

In 1858 a French geographer, Professor Antonio Snider-Pellegrini, published a book called *La Création et ses mystères dévoilés Creation and its Mysteries Unveiled*. He wrote that all of the continents as we now know them were once connected together into one great continent. He believed that it was the Great Flood in the Bible (from the story of Noah's Ark) that had caused the fragmentation of the supercontinent. Figure c shows how he thought that South America and Africa had once fitted together.

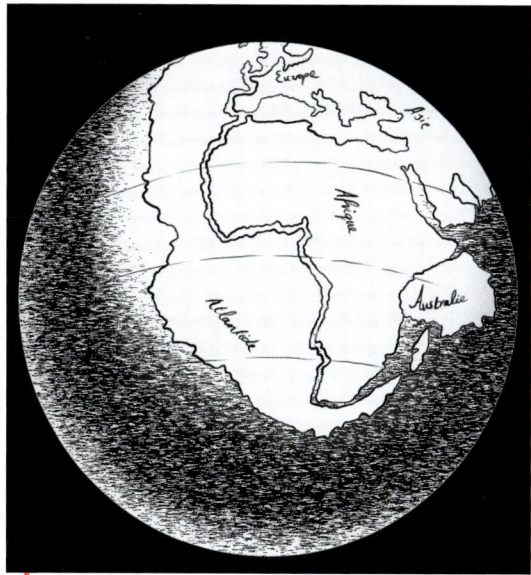

c Avant le separation (Before the separation)

d Après le separation (After the separation)

Do South America and Africa fit together like two jigsaw pieces?

In 1908 Frank B. Taylor's work for the Geological Society of America made him think that continents move. He suggested there was fossil evidence that the same plants and animals used to live in South America, Africa, India and Australia. The map below shows his theories.

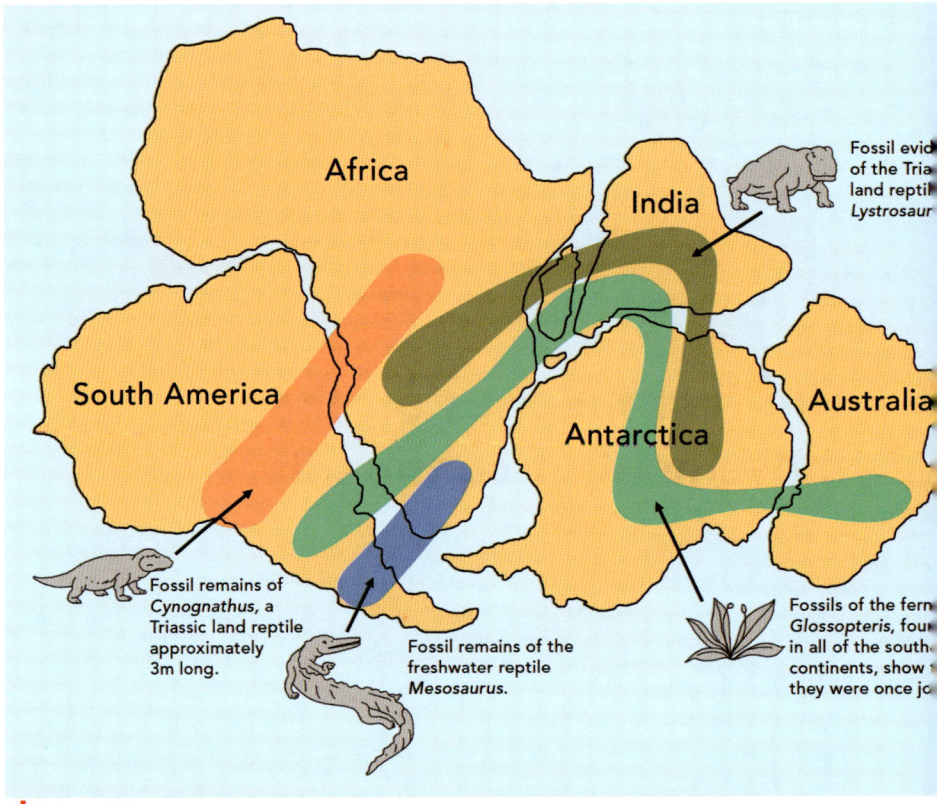

e This map shows Frank B. Taylor's theories on the movement of continents

Professor Alfred Wegener came from Berlin in Germany. He earned his PhD (Doctor of Philosophy) in astronomy, which is the study of stars. He was also a meteorologist (a student of the weather), a geologist (a student of the earth), a soldier, balloonist and explorer.

Wegener believed there was no doubt that the continents were once one land mass. He called this, Pangaea, which means 'all of the Earth'. Professor Wegener's idea was that Pangaea was torn apart into two separate continents, which then drifted away from each other. He called his idea 'continental drift'. The series of maps in figure c show how he saw Pangaea breaking up to form the present world.

At the time people thought Professor Wegener was wrong. But he was right!

CHALLENGE

3 Which continents shared:
   a) the reptile *Lystrosaurus*?
   b) the fern *Glossopteris*?
   c) the reptile *Cynognathus*?
   d) the freshwater reptile *Mesosaurus*?
   e) Why do you think this was a breakthrough for the study of the continents?

Do South America and Africa fit together like two jigsaw pieces?

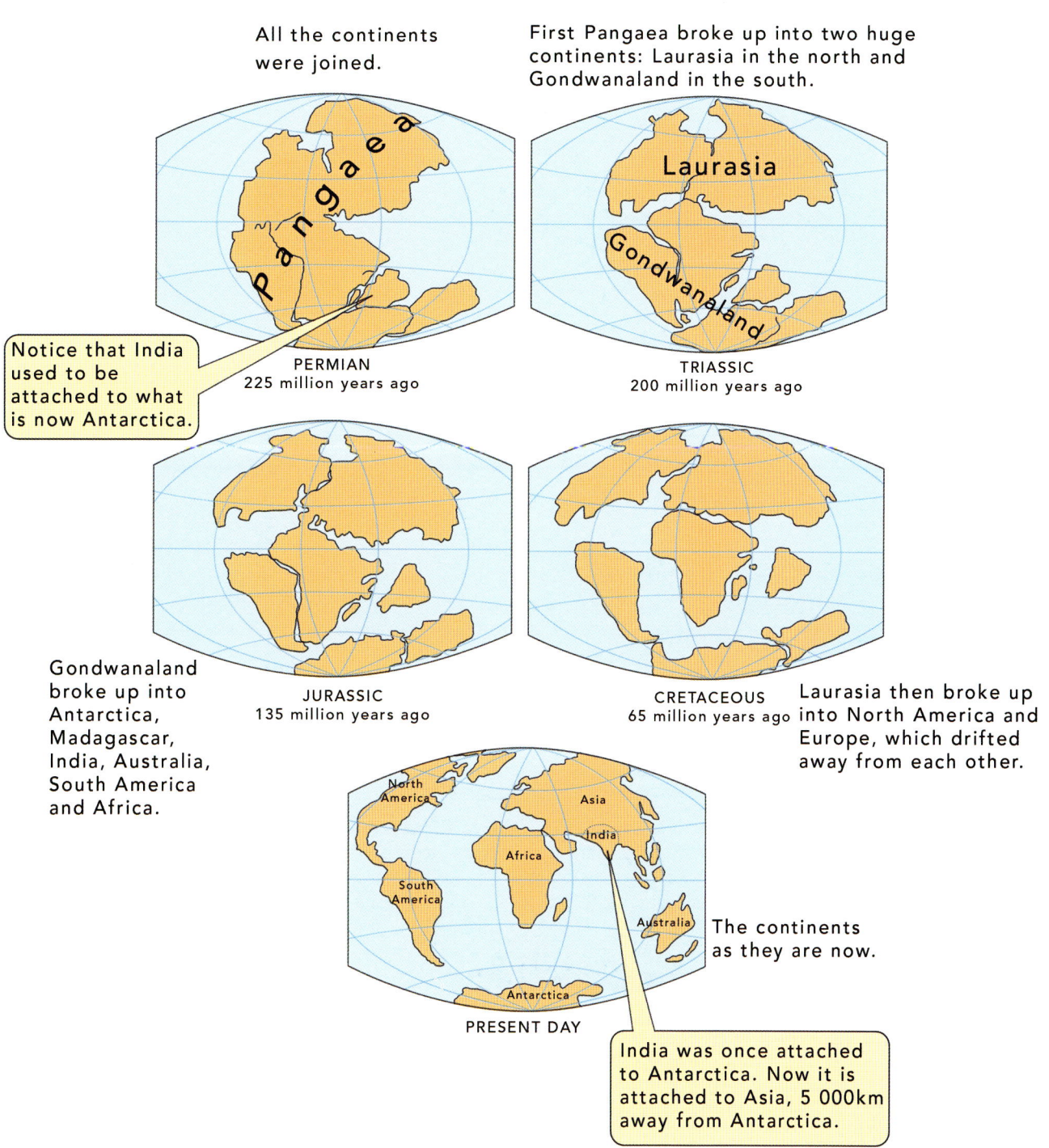

How Professor Wegener thought that Pangaea broke up to form today's continents

Why are there earthquakes and volcanoes in the middle of oceans?

From 1872–74 a British expedition led by Sir Wyville Thomson sailed around the world surveying the depths of the oceans in a ship called *HMS Challenger*. The crew were surprised to discover that, in the middle of some oceans, there are underwater mountain chains. In this lesson, we will learn more about these underwater mountain chains and what has caused them.

Where are the underwater mountain chains?

In the North and South Atlantic Oceans there is a line of underwater mountains stretching from north of Iceland to south of Cape Horn. The scientists who first surveyed this mountain chain called it the Mid-Atlantic Ocean Ridge. Between Australia and Antarctica there is a similar mountain range, which those who discovered it called the Mid-Indian Ocean Ridge. Because in later years nuclear submariners needed to know about underwater places to hide, we now know a lot about the ocean floor and we know there are many more mid-ocean ridges.

Geologists who studied the islands of the Mid-Atlantic Ocean Ridge, which rise out above the ocean surface to form Iceland and Tristan De Cunha, found that they were all made of volcanic rock. Seismologists (scientists who study earthquakes) also noticed that along all of the mid-ocean ridges there are earthquakes. Some of the biggest mid-ocean ridges are shown on map a.

CHALLENGE

1 Name the mid-ocean ridges between:
   a) South America and Africa
   b) Australia and Antarctica
   c) Africa and India
   d) South America and Australia
   e) Africa and Antarctica.

Why are there earthquakes and volcanoes in the middle of oceans?

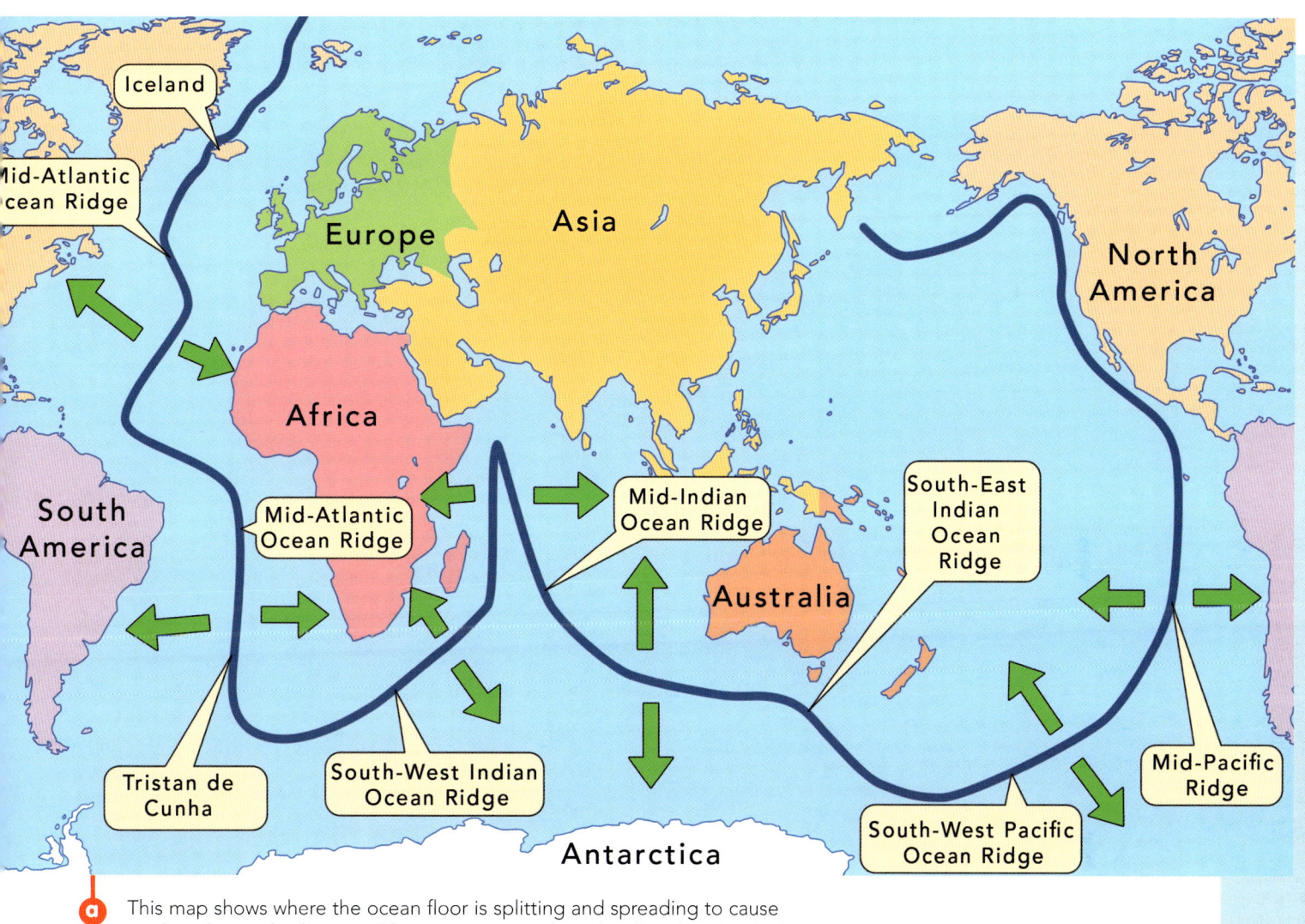

a This map shows where the ocean floor is splitting and spreading to cause earthquakes and volcanoes. The green arrows show the directions in which the ocean floors are stretching and jerkily moving

What is happening under the oceans?

Lots of earthquakes occur along the lines of ocean ridges and there are also some volcanoes along them. Why? What is happening under the oceans? The person who answered these questions was Professor and Admiral Harry Hess.

In the 1930s Professor Hess was a geologist at Princeton University in eastern USA. He joined the US Navy during the Second World War and spent time as a Naval Captain in the Pacific. His crew surveyed the floor of the Pacific Ocean, with its trenches and undersea mountains, and he thought about how they might have formed.

After the war, Hess became an Admiral and was given the task of surveying the whole of the Pacific Ocean so that nuclear submarines could navigate through it safely underwater. He also dived down to the dark depths of the ocean to see for himself what was there.

Why are there earthquakes and volcanoes in the middle of oceans?

Admiral Hess decided that the ocean floor must be splitting apart down the centre of the ocean ridges, like paper tearing along a fold. And, every time a bit of the ocean floor tears, an earthquake takes place. If the tear goes deep enough, molten rock from the mantle finds a way through to the floor of the ocean and then cools to build that part of the ocean floor a bit higher. Over millions of years, more and more lava has flowed out along the tear, to form the mid-ocean ridges.

Other scientists have shown that Admiral Hess' ideas were correct, even though we know there is much more to find out about the Pacific Ocean floor.

b How the Mid-Pacific Ocean Ridge was formed

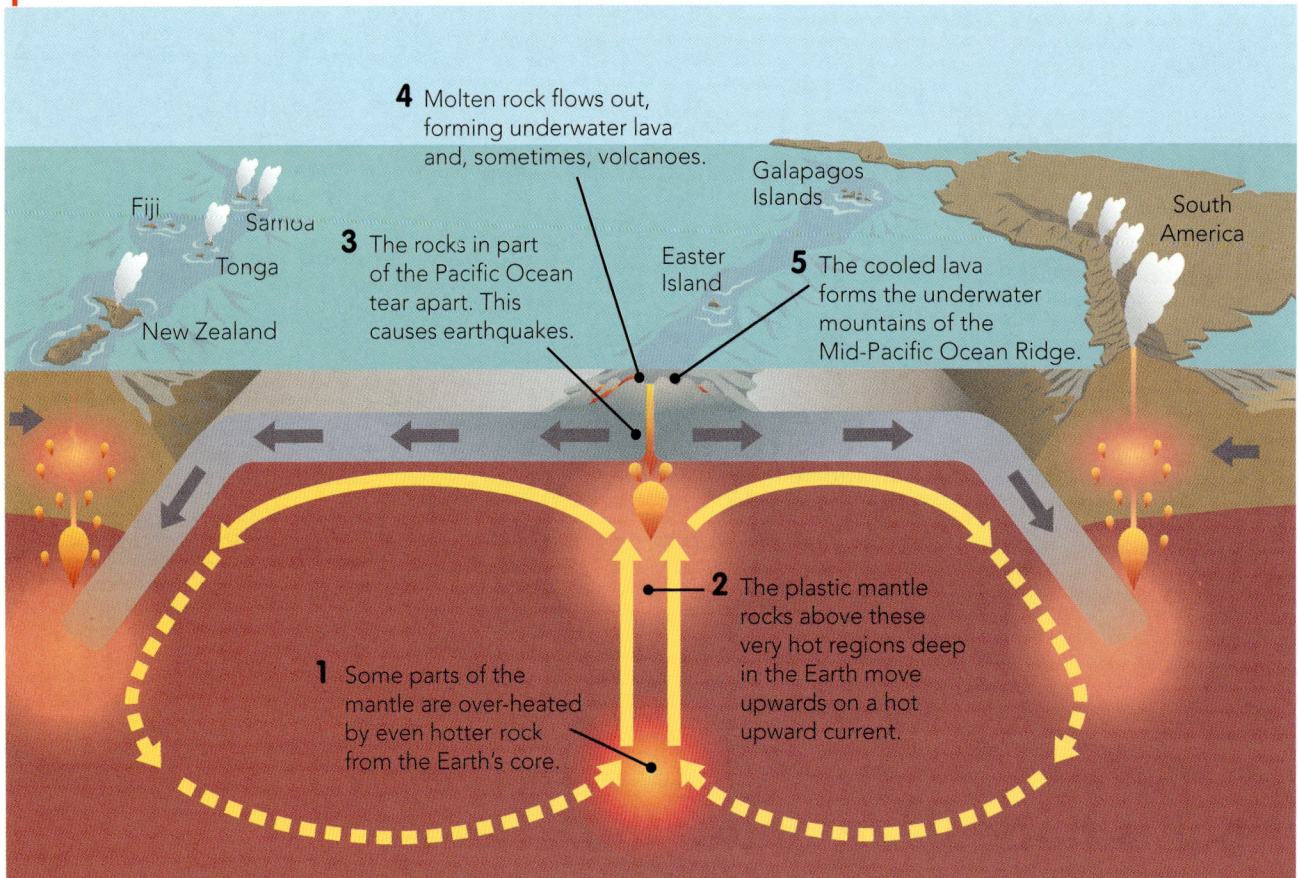

CHALLENGE

2 With your partner, use your hands to illustrate the process of molten rock rising, the ocean floor splitting and spreading outwards and volcanoes forming a mid-ocean ridge. Your actions should be accompanied by a commentary explaining what is happening.

Why are there earthquakes and volcanoes in the middle of oceans?

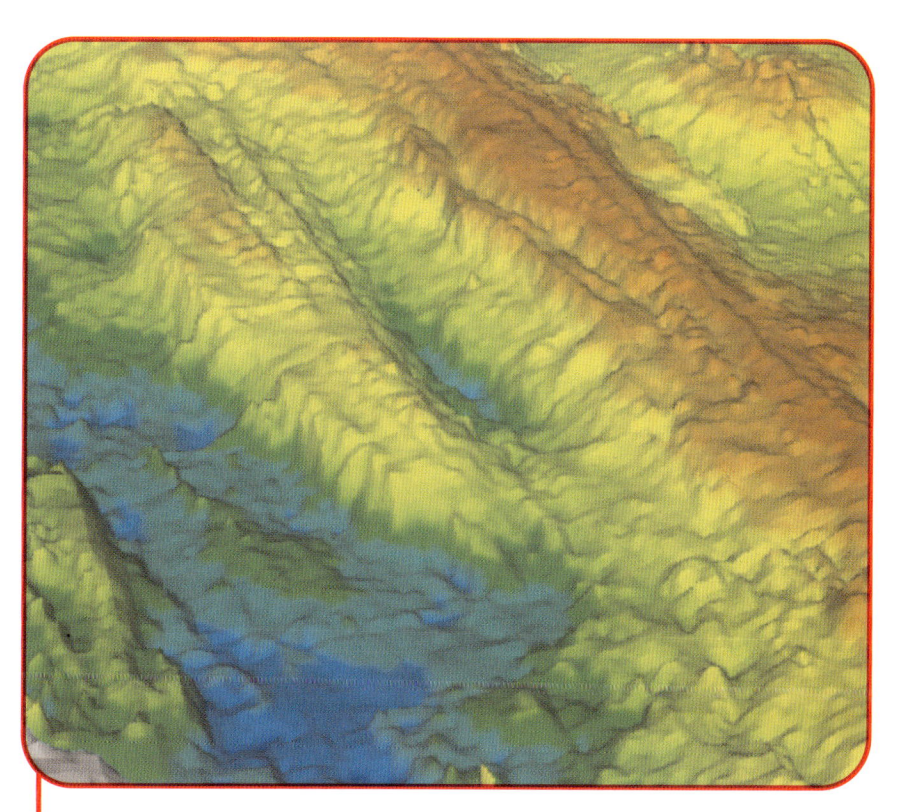

c Part of the Mid-Pacific Ocean Ridge. The image was created by echo-soundings taken from French and American ships. It has been electronically coloured to show the high parts of the ridge in red and the lower parts in green

d Taken from the submersible (underwater scientific ship), *Alvin*, this image shows hot gases coming out of part of the Mid-Pacific Ocean Ridge at 400°C. This 'hot smoker' vent shows that there is molten rock not far below

CHALLENGE

3 Copy the following statements about the Mid-Atlantic Ocean Ridge, placing them in the right order. Start with **Underneath**....

- Underneath the middle of the Atlantic Ocean,
- If the tear is deep enough,
- deep in the Earth,
- there is an area of very hot rock in the Earth's mantle, under great pressure.
- each time causing an earthquake.
- reaching the floor of the ocean as an underwater lava flow, or even a volcano.
- then it spreads out underneath the ocean floor, pulling the ocean floor with it.
- The ocean floor stretches and then tears open, a bit at a time,
- some of the molten rock might find a way through the tear,
- It forces its way upwards on a hot upwards current of 'plastic' rock,
- An example is the island of Iceland, which is made from many volcanoes.
- Some very large volcanoes might break the surface of the ocean.

What are tectonic plates and where do they start and end?

It took the work of several scientists to discover and prove that the Earth's crust is made up of tectonic plates that are slowly moving. In this lesson, we will learn how these difficult facts were established and where tectonic plates are to be found in the world. We will also learn about subduction and island arc volcanoes.

What are tectonic plates?

In the 1930s, scientists understood parts of the story of earthquakes and volcanoes but could not yet explain them. Professor Arthur Holmes from the University of Durham, in England, suggested that:

- Ocean floors are slowly being carried along by convection currents of molten rock below the Earth's crust.
- These currents are powered by very hot areas of the Earth's mantle.
- The rocks of the crust are stretched and then jolt forwards, causing earthquakes.

Scientists at the time were not sure he was right, but we now know that all these ideas are true.

In 1960, Professor Hess of Princeton University in the USA suggested that the ocean floor is actually formed by molten rock coming up from deep in the Earth, spreading out and cooling to make solid rock. We now know that this is also true.

In 1965, Professor J.T. Wilson of Toronto University in Canada invented the phrase '**tectonic plate**'. He said that the Earth's crust is made up of a patchwork of these plates. A plate forms when the ocean floor splits and lava flows build up the new plate.

In 1973, Professor Xavier Le Pichon, of the Oceanology Centre of Brest in France, created a map of tectonic plates and how they are moving. Map a shows that the Mid-Atlantic Ocean Ridge is where the South American plate and the African plate are slowly being created. The two continents used to fit together. Now they are being pushed further apart.

CHALLENGE

1 Knowledge is built up by people thinking hard about evidence and making sense of it, even though they may live in different countries, in different parts of the world and at different times. List the different countries mentioned in this lesson from where scientists have added knowledge about this topic.
2 Study map a.
   a) Name each tectonic plate
   b) How many tectonic plates are there?

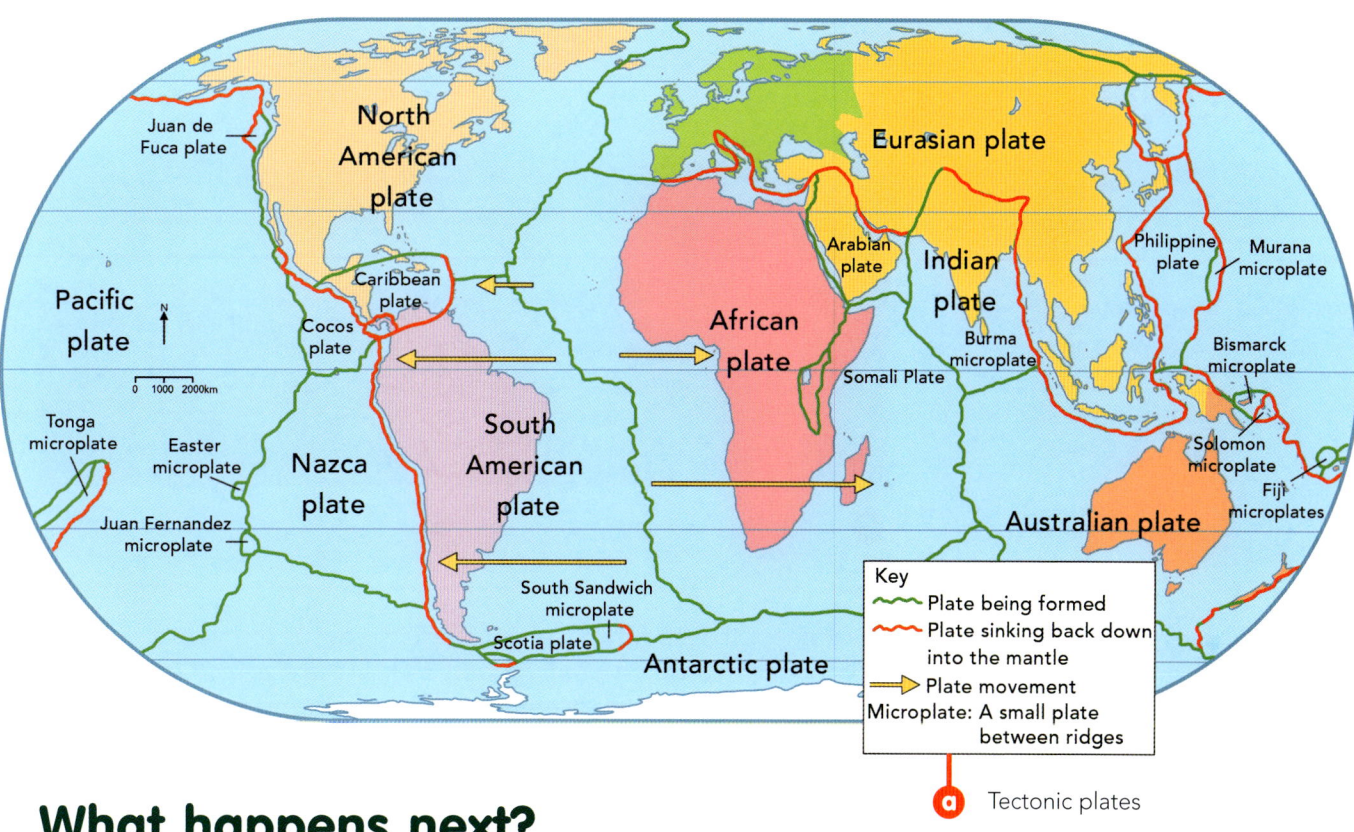

What are tectonic plates and where do they start and end?

a Tectonic plates

What happens next?

We now all know that we live on tectonic plates. In the UK, for instance, we live on the Eurasian plate. And we know that tectonic plates are formed in the middle of oceans, by a process involving earthquakes, hot smokers and lava flows. But what happens to the tectonic plates next?

The South American plate, for example, does two things. Diagram b shows that, north of the equator, the plate moves Westwards until it meets another plate with ocean on it, the Caribbean plate. The South American plate is heavier than the Caribbbean plate and sinks underneath it, back down into the mantle. As it sinks, it pulls down the ocean floor to form a deep trench. As it sinks further, the rocks of the plate melt and force their way back up into the floor of the Caribbean Sea, collecting lots of broken rock and water along the way to become very explosive volcanoes.

Some volcanoes reach above the sea surface, to form volcanic islands such as the 'island arc' of the Windward and Leeward Islands of the West Indies.

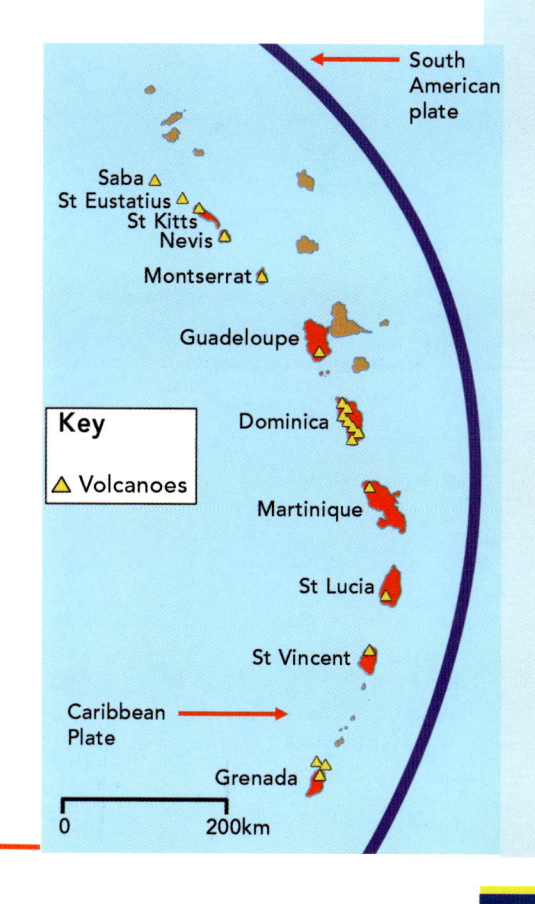

b The island arc of the Windward and Leeward Islands. The 19 live volcanoes mark where the South American plate is sinking beneath the Caribbean plate

What are tectonic plates and where do they start and end?

CHALLENGE

3 Scientists think there is a pattern linking island arcs, lines of land volcanoes and where tectonic plates meet.

Study maps a and e and see if you can work out what the pattern is. Copy and complete the following sentences.

a) Where ocean plates meet, _____ form.

b) Where an ocean plate meets a plate with a continent on it _____ form.

4 Explain how 'subduction' causes earthquakes, deep ocean trenches and volcanoes.

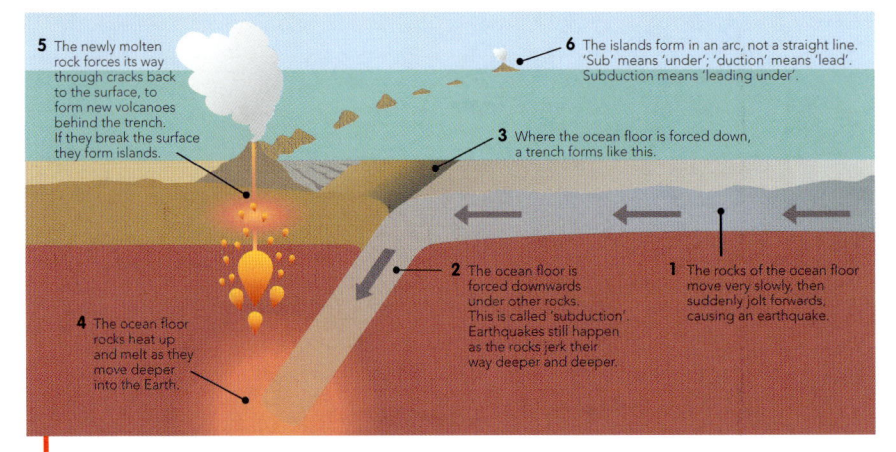

5 The newly molten rock forces its way through cracks back to the surface, to form new volcanoes behind the trench. If they break the surface they form islands.

6 The islands form in an arc, not a straight line. 'Sub' means 'under'; 'duction' means 'lead'. Subduction means 'leading under'.

3 Where the ocean floor is forced down, a trench forms like this.

4 The ocean floor rocks heat up and melt as they move deeper into the Earth.

2 The ocean floor is forced downwards under other rocks. This is called 'subduction'. Earthquakes still happen as the rocks jerk their way deeper and deeper.

1 The rocks of the ocean floor move very slowly, then suddenly jolt forwards, causing an earthquake.

c An ocean plate sinks under another ocean plate to form an arc of volcanic islands

Further south, the South American plate carries the continent of South America with it until it meets the Nazca (Pacific Ocean) plate. Here the Pacific Ocean plate is heavier and subducts (sinks below) the South American continent. At the same time, just as in the Caribbean, the sinking rock melts and the molten rock forces its way through to form a line of volcanoes all along the west coast of South America. Geologists call this 'subduction' meaning 'carried under', as one plate is carried under another.

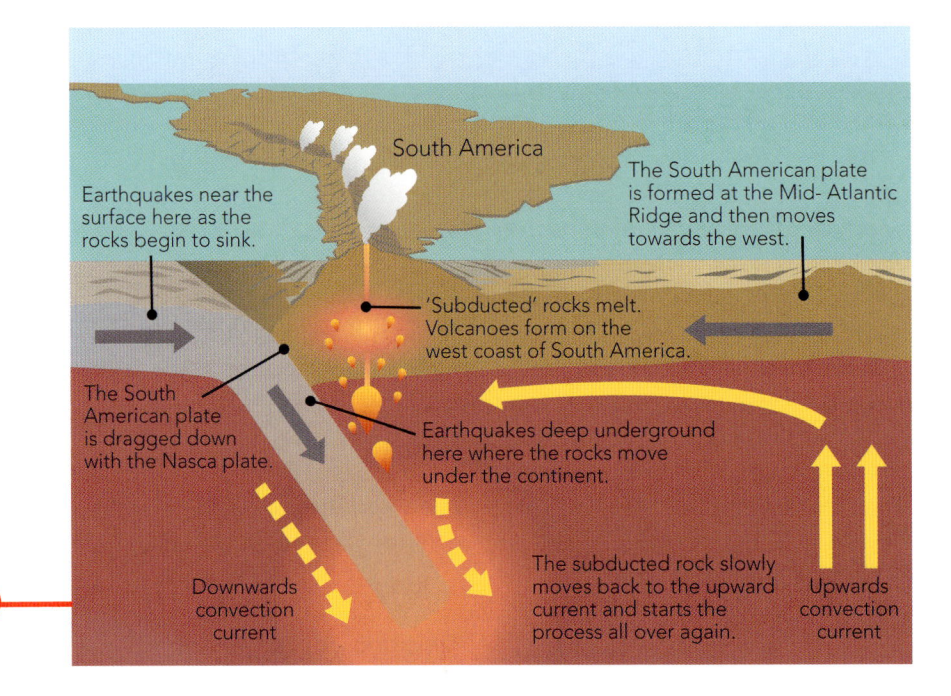

South America

Earthquakes near the surface here as the rocks begin to sink.

The South American plate is formed at the Mid-Atlantic Ridge and then moves towards the west.

'Subducted' rocks melt. Volcanoes form on the west coast of South America.

The South American plate is dragged down with the Nasca plate.

Earthquakes deep underground here where the rocks move under the continent.

Downwards convection current

The subducted rock slowly moves back to the upward current and starts the process all over again.

Upwards convection current

d An ocean plate sinks under a continental plate to form a line of volcanic mountains on land

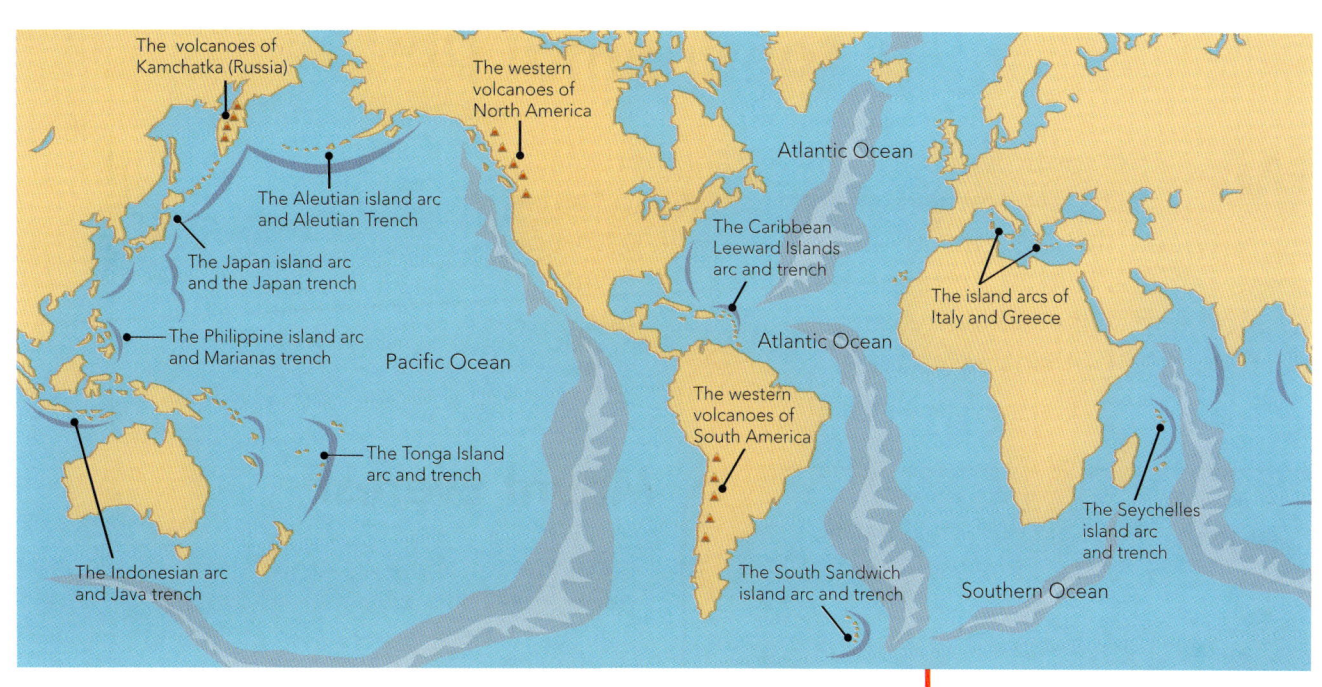

What are tectonic plates and where do they start and end?

e World map showing where island arcs and lines of land volcanoes are found

The satellite photograph below (f) shows an eruption on Chuginadak volcano in the Aleutian island arc. It shows how this island is made from a single volcano. It is a result of the Pacific plate subducting (sinking below) the Arctic Ocean section of the North American plate.

f A satellite photograph of Chuginadak Island volcano in the Aleutian island arc erupting. It was taken at 3:00pm. (Alaska Daylight Time) on 23 May 2006 by Flight Engineer Jeff Williams from International Space Station (ISS) Expedition 13

CHALLENGE

5 Using one sheet of A4 paper, your hands and a pen or pencil, make a model of Chuginadak volcano with all the labels in place. Write a paragraph to accompany your model explaining how the volcano is being formed.

What happens when one continental plate meets another continental plate?

When one continental plate meets another one, mountains are formed, then crushed and folded up between the two. In this lesson, we will learn how some famous fold mountains, the Himalayas, were formed and will study why continental collisions cause earthquakes but not volcanoes.

a A young Tibetan monk in front of Mount Everest

b Chinese scientists on Mount Everest. The white balaclava protects the skin from being burned by the strong ultra-violet light found at this height. It also reflects the sun's heat to keep the wearer cooler

Mount Everest

Photos a and b show people standing on Mount Everest, in the Himalayan mountains, which have been crushed and folded up between the Indian tectonic plate, which is moving North-Eastwards, and the Eurasian tectonic plate, which is hardly moving at all.

Mount Everest is the highest mountain in the world. It is known in Nepal, Tibet and China as Mount Qomolangma. Tibetan monks, like the trainee monk in photograph a, believe that these high peaks are the spiritual home of the gods they worship.

In 2005, Chinese scientists were interested in taking accurate measurements on Mount Qomolangma. They used the latest technology, including GPS (Global Positioning System) satellite equipment, to carry out their survey. They found that the exact height of the mountain is 8844.43m above sea level and that the summit (highest peak) is moving North-Eastwards.

This result confirmed what geologists have suspected. India, to the south of the Himalayas is crashing into China, to the north of the Himalayas. The scientists measure the movement at approximately 6cm per year. This seems slow, but the Earth must have tremendous power to move the billions and billions of tons of rock making up India, even at this slow speed.

What happens when one continental plate meets another continental plate?

How were the Himalayan mountains formed?

Diagram d shows how India has, over many millennia, gradually moved North-Eastwards into Eurasia.

Diagram e shows that in the past there was an ocean, the Tethys Ocean, between India and Eurasia, which were two separate continents on their own plates. Sand and mud from both continents were washed by rivers into the ocean. Rocks, containing seashells, were formed on the seabed. As the Indian plate moved towards Eurasia, the rocks on the seabed in between India and China were crushed and folded to form the Himalayas. The water of the ocean flowed away into what is now the Indian Ocean.

There used to be volcanoes in the Himalayas, but the folded rocks are now so thick that magma cannot find a way through. However, every time a part of the plate moves forwards it does so with a jolt, creating an earthquake.

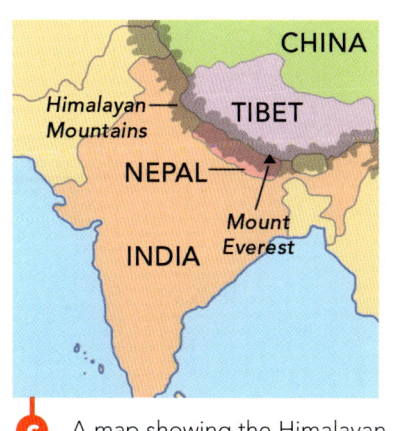

c A map showing the Himalayan mountains and the countries surrounding them today

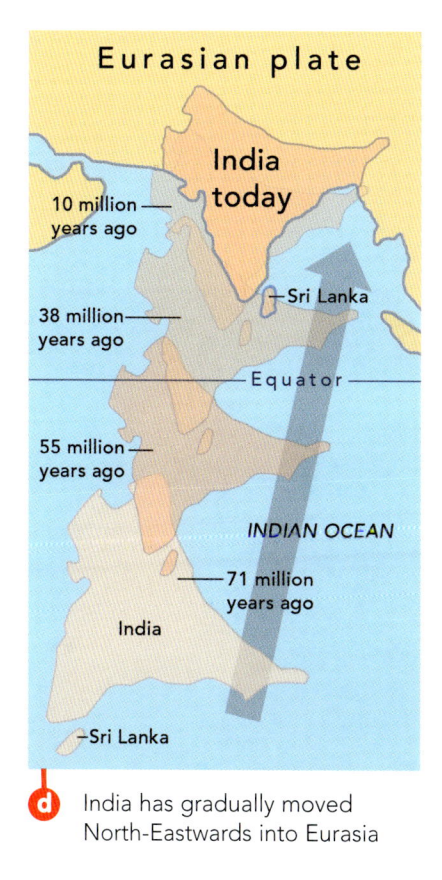

d India has gradually moved North-Eastwards into Eurasia

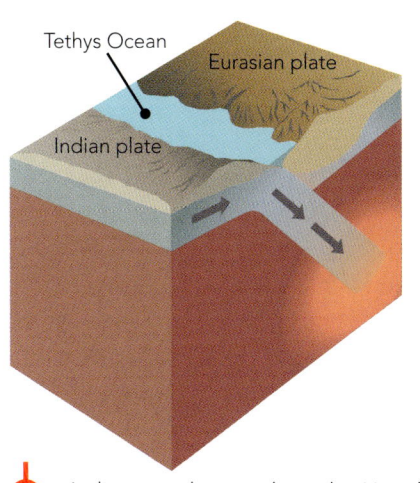

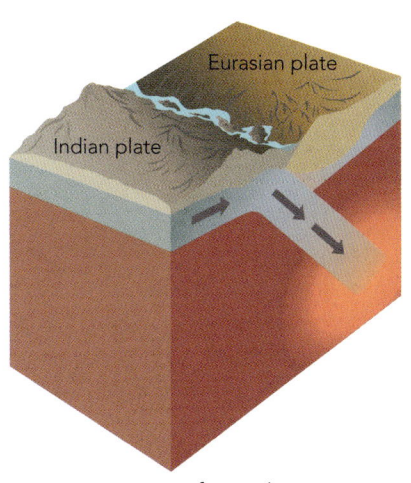

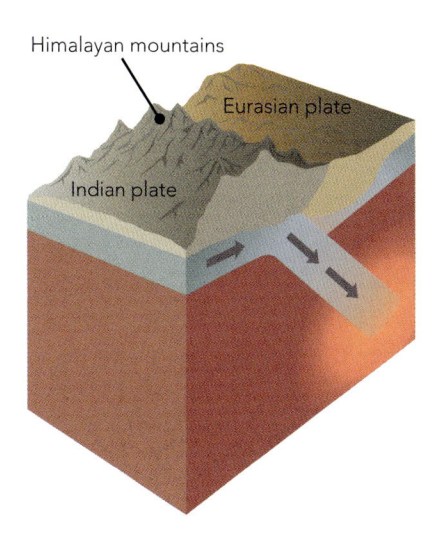

e A diagram showing how the Himalayan mountains were formed

What happens when one continental plate meets another continental plate?

How did we get the evidence?

In 1933 Professor Laurence Wager from Oxford University climbed almost to the summit of Mount Everest and collected 200 rock specimens. When he studied them he found that the rocks had been formed under a sea and that there were fossils of sea creatures in them. Fossils are ancient creatures whose hard parts, like skeletons and shells, have been replaced with stone. This evidence, with more evidence from other scientists, supports the idea that the Himalayas, the world's greatest mountain chain, were once layers of rock below the sea.

f The north face of Mount Everest

CHALLENGE

1. Use one sheet of A4 paper to simulate the creation of the Himalayan mountains. Explain how your model shows that earthquakes are part of this process and demonstrate why Mount Everest has fossils in it.
2. Choose a fold mountain range from Map g. Then, using Map h, work out which tectonic plates have caused your chosen fold mountain range to form.
3. Why are there earthquakes but no volcanoes in the Himalayas, but earthquakes and volcanoes in the Andes Mountains?

What happens when one continental plate meets another continental plate?

Are there other fold mountains?

The Himalayas are not the only fold mountains to be created by a continental plate colliding with another plate. Map g shows how the movement of plates has created long mountain ranges called fold mountains around the world.

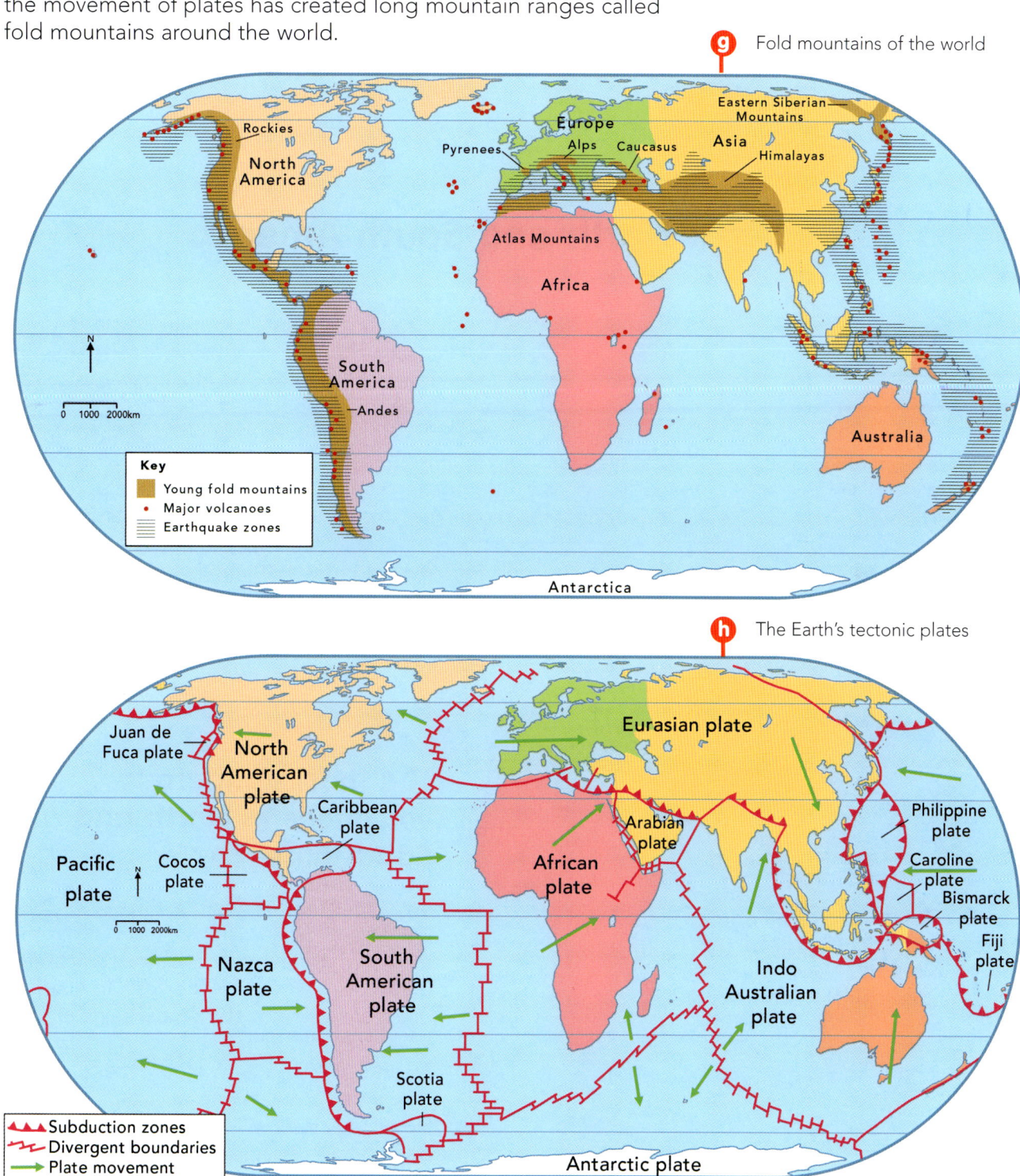

g Fold mountains of the world

Key
- Young fold mountains
- Major volcanoes
- Earthquake zones

h The Earth's tectonic plates

- Subduction zones
- Divergent boundaries
- Plate movement

45

How is the power of the Earth showing through in North and South America and Africa?

As we know, North and South America were once joined together with Africa. Now they are moving apart and earthquakes and volcanoes are taking place. In this lesson, we will learn where the most dangerous volcanoes are in North and South America and which major cities are threatened by them. We will also study volcanoes and rift valleys in Africa.

North and South America

The North American and South American plates are both slowly crashing into the Pacific Ocean plate. Every time the rocks jerk forwards or down, an earthquake, which is often very powerful, happens. It is no coincidence that the world's most powerful earthquake since records began happened in Chile in 1962.

The collision process has folded rocks on the old seabed up so that the tallest mountains in both continents are found along their western coasts. Magma forces its way up through the cracks in the rocks of the mountains to create volcanoes. A lot of rock and water is collected by the magma as it passes through the rock, making the volcanoes in North and South America very explosive – they are some of the most dangerous in the world. Canada has 18 active volcanoes, the USA has 169 and Mexico has 42.

a The ten most dangerous volcanoes in the USA, in order of danger

Key
1. Kilauea, Hawaii
2. Mount St Helens, Washington State
3. Mount Rainier, Washington State
4. Mount Hood, Oregon
5. Mount Shasta, California
6. South Sister, Oregon
7. Lassen Volcanic Center, California
8. Mauna Loa, Hawaii
9. Redoubt Volcano, Alaska
10. Crater Lake area, Oregon

The most dangerous volcanoes in North and South America

John Ewert, a volcanologist with the US Geological Survey (USGS), has drawn up a list of the ten most dangerous volcanoes in the USA. These can be seen in map a. Eight are in the western mountains of the USA, while the other two are in Hawaii. Ewert calls these 'Very High Threat Volcanoes'. Which one will erupt next? How many lives will it take and how much damage will it cause?

How is the power of the Earth showing through in North and South America and Africa?

b Mount Popocatepetl, near Mexico City

These active and dangerous volcanoes have devastated large areas with volcanic blasts, invaded their surroundings with lava flows and produced huge mudflows that have swept over hundreds of square miles. They have given off poisonous gases that have caused lung ailments, as well as producing tephra plumes (bits of debris thrown out by the volcano) that have brought down passenger jets and covered thousands of square miles.

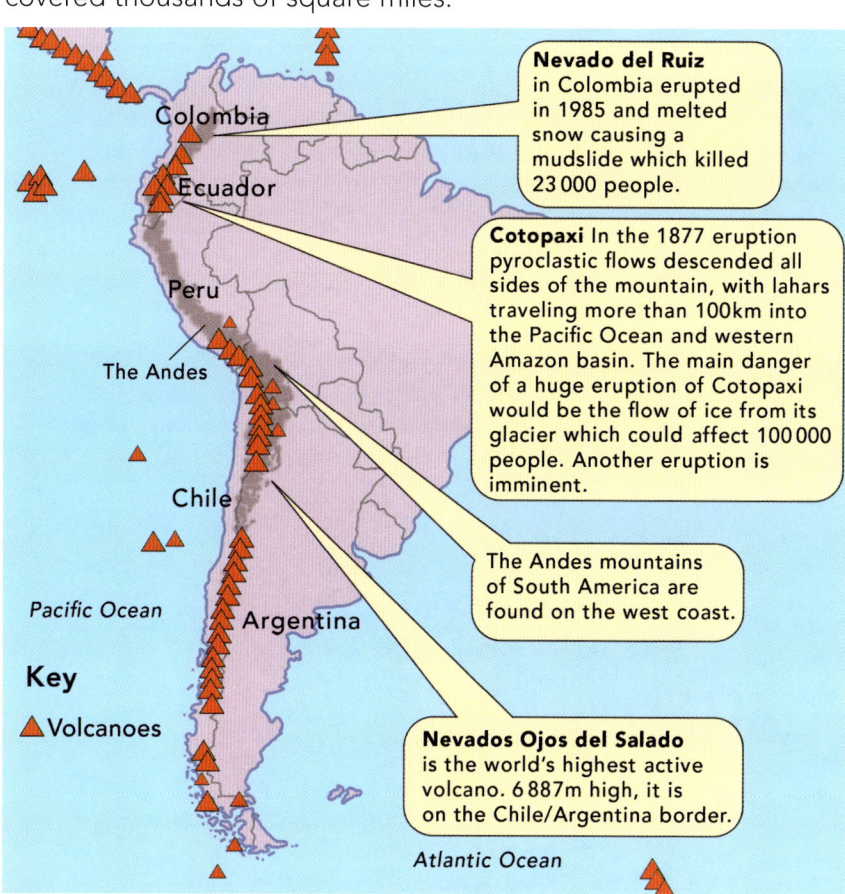

Nevado del Ruiz in Colombia erupted in 1985 and melted snow causing a mudslide which killed 23 000 people.

Cotopaxi In the 1877 eruption pyroclastic flows descended all sides of the mountain, with lahars traveling more than 100km into the Pacific Ocean and western Amazon basin. The main danger of a huge eruption of Cotopaxi would be the flow of ice from its glacier which could affect 100 000 people. Another eruption is imminent.

The Andes mountains of South America are found on the west coast.

Nevados Ojos del Salado is the world's highest active volcano. 6 887m high, it is on the Chile/Argentina border.

Key
▲ Volcanoes

c The most dangerous volcanoes in South America

CHALLENGE

1 Study maps a and c and photo b, then read the sentence starters and endings below. Which starter matches which sentence ending?

SENTENCE STARTERS:
1 A lava flow
2 A volcanic blast
3 A tephra plume
4 Poisonous gases
5 A mudflow
6 Mount St Helens
7 Cotopaxi
8 Popocatapetl
9 Nevados Ojos del Salado
10 Mount Redoubt

SENTENCE ENDINGS:

a is a flow of mud down a volcano. It is caused by hot gas and rock melting the snow.

b such as sulphur dioxide and carbon dioxide can be given off by volcanoes.

c is molten rock flowing down the volcano from a crater.

d is the force of the eruption in a shock wave which can flatten trees and homes.

e can reach up to where jet planes fly and cause their engines to stop.

f is a volcano in Ecuador which vulcanologists think is due to erupt soon.

g is the second most dangerous volcano in the USA.

h is a volcano in Alaska, USA.

i threatens 15 million people.

j is the highest active volcano in the world.

How is the power of the Earth showing through in North and South America and Africa?

a) Mount St Helens before the eruption

b) Mount St Helens during the eruption in 1980

c) After the eruption of Mount St Helens

Mount St Helens erupts

Mount St Helens is a volcano in Washington on the West coast of the USA. It was thought to be dormant (sleeping), but in 1980, it woke up! Here are some facts about what happened next.

- The 1980 eruption of Mount St Helens was the most destructive volcanic eruption in the history of the USA. 57 people were killed by the eruption, including USGS scientist Dr David Johnston who was at a monitoring site five miles from the volcano on the morning of the eruption. An estimated £1 billion damage was caused by the eruption.

- Mount St Helens was 2950m before the eruption and 2549m after. 401m were removed by the 18 May eruption.

- The largest landslide in recorded history swept down the mountain at speeds of 112–241kms per hour and buried the North Fork of the Toutle River under an average of 46m of debris. Some areas are covered by as much as 183m. In all, approximately 37km^2 of material was removed from the mountain.

- The sideways blast swept out of the north side of Mount St Helens at 482kms per hour, creating a 370km^2 fan-shaped area of devastation reaching a distance of 27kms from the crater. With temperatures as high as 348°C and the power of 24 megatons of thermal energy, it snapped 100 year-old-trees like toothpicks and stripped them of their bark.

- The snow on Mount St Helens that was not instantly flashed to steam by the heat melted and formed large mudflows that destroyed 27 bridges, 200 homes, 298kms of roadway and 24kms of railway.

- 'On 18 May 1980 the eruption of Mount St Helens in South-West Washington state disrupted the lives of thousands and changed more than 200 square miles of rich forest into a grey, lifeless landscape.' Valerie Smith, geologist and local resident.

CHALLENGE

2 Study the facts about Mount St Helens. Then, either:
   a) Write 50 words to describe the differences between the photos taken before and after Mount St Helens erupted (photos a and c).
   b) Draw a simple sketch of the after photo of Mount St Helens (photo c), then pick out five facts from the information on this page and add them to your sketch as captions.

How is the power of the Earth showing through in North and South America and Africa?

Africa

Photo e shows the Great Rift Valley of Africa. A rift valley is a valley formed when the Earth is pulled away on each side. This land is so high and is cracking apart partly because of the African superswell, a mass of warm volcanic rock which is rising under much of South-Eastern Africa, producing a buoyancy effect which is helping to pull the crust apart. In some places, like Nyiragongo and Oldoinyo Lengai, the Earth is cracking so much that the hot rock is reaching the surface as volcanoes. Every time part of the land breaks further apart, there is an earthquake.

The superswell is a problem to building projects in Africa. If you dig a big enough reservoir, you're going to get earthquakes.

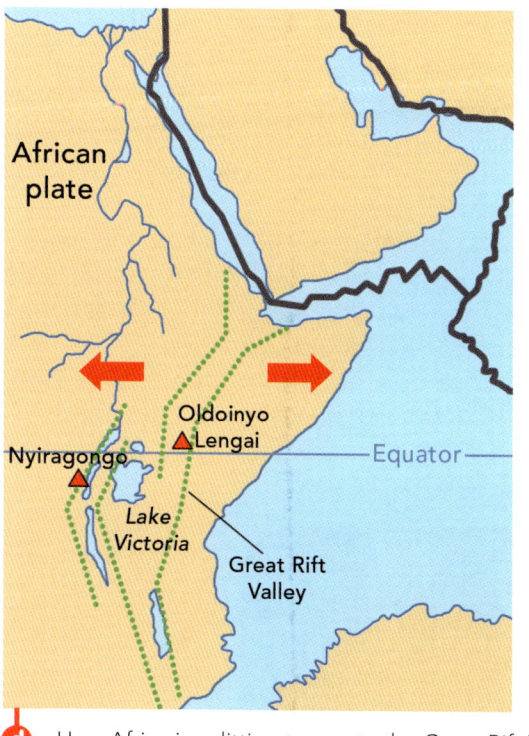

e The mountains in the background are being pulled Westwards (left) and the mountains in the foreground are being pulled Eastwards (right) because of the 'superswell' underneath. The lower ground in the middle is called the Great Rift Valley

f Nyiragongo, Democratic Republic of Congo

d How Africa is splitting to create the Great Rift Valley

g Oldoinyo Lengai, North Kenya.

CHALLENGE

3   How is the power of the Earth showing through in East Africa? Draft a 60-second talk to answer this question.

Why do people continue to live in earthquake zones and near volcanoes?

All over the world, people continue to live where earthquakes might happen and volcanoes might erupt. They could be in considerable danger. In this lesson, we learn which countries and cities are most at risk and look at the reasons why people continue to take such chances with their lives.

CHALLENGE

1 Study the views that people have about why they continue to live in Tokyo despite the risk of a major earthquake. List the views in order of how sensible you think they are.

Tokyo, Japan, where people have a 1 in 2000 chance of dying in an earthquake

1. It is a geographical fact that most people stay near where they are born.

2. Many people have a fatalistic attitude to natural events. If they are going to happen, so be it; there is nothing they can do.

3. Tokyo is a rich city with an attractive lifestyle.

Why do people continue to live in earthquake zones?

There are two famous cities where the people live with the knowledge that a major earthquake will cause massive destruction, knocking down buildings, tearing up roads, starting fires and killing people.

One city is San Francisco, USA, where a massive earthquake in 1906 officially killed 700 people (but probably a lot more). There have been subsequent smaller earthquakes.

The other major city that is prone to earthquakes is Tokyo, Japan, which is home to 20 million people.

The Japanese government predicts that there is a one in three chance that a big earthquake will hit Japan within the next 20 years. If it was a magnitude 7 earthquake, they estimate that over 10 000 people would die and 200 000 would be injured. There would be nearly 100 million tons of wreckage and the total cost to Japan would be $1 000 000 000 000. People living in Tokyo have a 1 in 2000 chance of dying in an earthquake. So why do 20 million people continue to live in Tokyo?

4. In rich countries such as Japan, people hope that the scientists, politicians and engineers will solve the earthquake problem.

5. People feel that a 1 in 2000 chance of dying in an earthquake is too small to worry about.

Why do people continue to live in earthquake zones and near volcanoes?

Why do people continue to live near volcanoes?

In 2004, Professor Franco Barberi of the University of Rome said that Mount Vesuvius in southern Italy is the world's most dangerous volcano, because it is a constant threat to hundreds of thousands of people who live in its shadow. Mount Vesuvius is the nearest volcano to the UK, although we are not at risk from it and many British tourists go to see it and climb to the crater rim every year.

The main risk is from an explosive eruption, with red-hot clouds of steam and other gases hurling molten rock onto 1 700 000 people living in nearby local villages, towns and the city of Naples. They might only have a few hours warning that an eruption is likely.

CHALLENGE

2 a) If you had to, would you prefer to live in an earthquake zone or near a volcano?

b) Would you live on the side of a volcano (if you were born there) or would you move away?

1. Many volcanoes are safe for long periods between eruptions. Local people feel that if their volcano does erupt, its eruptions can be predicted by scientists. Scientists are not so sure.

2. When volcanic rocks weather into soil, it is the best in the world. Some of the world's best coffee comes from volcanic soils in Kenya and Colombia.

3. Most farmers need the land just to survive. When the Philippine volcano of Mayon erupted in 1993 it killed 75 people – all of them tomato farmers in the Bonga Valley, which is declared off-limits by the government.

b The Philippine volcano of Mayon erupted in 1993

4. Today nearly 20 000 locals live and farm within Mayon's Permanent Danger Zone. Half of these farmers refused to move out during the most recent eruption. Others returned to tend their fields and animals – without their crops, they risked starvation.

5. Volcanoes are beautiful. Tourists want to go and visit them. People build hotels to look after the tourists.

6. Once a town or city grows, with the money from farming and tourism, its development is often unstoppable. People buy up land on the slopes of the volcano because it is cheap.

7. Volcanic tephra can be quarried for use as building stone and for use in cleaning liquids. The sulphur produced by volcanoes is used to make sulphuric acid and many other useful chemicals.

Can we protect ourselves against earthquakes?

Is it possible to prevent earthquakes? Is it possible to predict when they will happen? The answer to both of these question is, unfortunately, no. However, precautions can be taken against earthquakes and in this lesson we will learn how it is possible to minimise the damage caused by them.

What precautions can we take against earthquakes?

Scientists cannot see how it would be possible to prevent even the smallest earthquake. The focus (point of origin) of earthquakes is usually hundreds of miles underground.

No scientist has ever predicted an earthquake successfully. However, people who live in an earthquake zone can take the following precautions.

A Before an earthquake
- Know what can happen to outside walls and windows.
- Know what to do. A torch, a whistle and first-aid kits should be in every room, where people can find them.
- Know where safe places are, such as, under a sturdy table or against an inside wall away from windows. Practise drills.
- Know that the shorter the distance to move to safety, the less likely you are to be injured.

B During an earthquake
- Be aware of the injury statistics: persons moving more than 3m during an earthquake are most likely to be injured.
- If you are indoors during an earthquake, follow 'Drop, cover and hold on'. Drop under furniture. Hold on to it. Cover your eyes.
- Keep away from windows, bookcases or heavy furniture.
- Don't run outside because roofs and walls may fall.
- Wait in your safe place until the shaking stops, then check to see if you are hurt. You will be better able to help others if you take care of yourself first. Then check the people around you.

a Survivors of an earthquake

Can we protect ourselves against earthquakes?

b Smoke shows where fires have been caused by broken gas pipes after the earthquake in Kobe, Japan

C After the earthquake
- After you have taken care of yourself, help injured or trapped people. Ring emergency services or friends to let them know where you are. Give first aid when you can. Don't try to move seriously injured people unless they are in immediate danger of further injury.
- Look for and put out small fires to prevent them from spreading. Fire is the most common hazard following earthquakes. Fires can cause more damage than the earthquake.
- Leave and go to the earthquake assembly point.

CHALLENGE

1. Study photo a and captions A and B. Imagine your present classroom is in an earthquake zone. What precautions could you take against an earthquake within your classroom:
   a) before the earthquake?
   b) during the earthquake?

2. Where buildings are constructed can be very important to how well they will survive an earthquake. If a building has already been built there is little that can be done, but people can choose where to put new buildings. Do you think it would be best to construct a new building on:
   a) A fault line (where the Earth is cracked already and no one else wants to build, so it is cheap)?
   b) Bedrock (this has solid rock underneath, so it is expensive)?
   c) A landfill site (where rubbish has been tipped to fill in low or soft ground, so it is cheap to build on)?
   Make your choice and explain your decision.

Can we predict hazards from volcanoes?

Volcanoes can cause a huge amount of damage and can result in a devastating loss of life. Is there any way that scientists can predict when volcanoes will erupt and perhaps minimise the damage they cause? In this lesson, we will study volcano hazards.

a Pyroclastic flow

b The mudflow from Nevado del Ruiz volcano

c The landslide caused by the Unzen volcano

What are the main dangers from volcanoes?

The United States Geological Survey (USGS) Hazards Program says, 'Volcanic activity since 1700 AD has killed more than 260 000 people, destroyed entire cities and forests and severely disrupted local economies for months to years. Now over half a million people are at risk from volcanoes worldwide.' The hazards below are in order of how dangerous they are:

1 **Pyroclastic flows** (pyroclastic means 'broken by fire') of gas, steam and flying bits of molten rock can rush down volcanoes at over 100km an hour with temperatures over 500°C. These flows burn everything in their path and can kill even very experienced volcanologists. They can travel for tens of kilometres.
2 **Mudflows** (also called lahars) happen when a snowy volcano erupts or heavy rain falls on recently erupted tephra (see below). Water rushes down the volcano's valleys, picking up rocks until it looks like wet concrete flowing at up to 50km an hour. When it meets low ground it buries any farms or villages in its path, killing everything there. A single mudflow from Nevado del Ruiz volcano in Colombia in 1985 travelled 10km and killed over 20 000 people.
3 **Landslides** caused by eruptions are also killers. In 1792 a landslide on Unzen Volcano in Japan slid into the sea and caused a tsunami, which killed people living in a city on the opposite shore. 13 000 people were killed by the landslide and the tsunami.
4 **Poisonous gases** may be given off by some volcanoes. On the night of 21 August 1986 gas escaped from a volcanic crater lake, Lake Nyos, Cameroon. It gently flowed down over a local village, suffocating 1 800 local people in their sleep.
5 **Lava Flows** Even though lava can flow at up to 50kms per hour, most flows are slow enough to walk away from, so they are not usually a great threat to life. They can, however, flow over property, burning and burying everything in their path.

Can we predict hazards from volcanoes?

6 **Volcanic tephra** (ash and dust) is rarely a killer, though it does cause these problems:

d Daylight turns into darkness

e Roofs may collapse from added weight

f Vehicles will be scarred

g Farmland will be covered

h Roads will be slippery or blocked

i Power systems may shut down

j Waste-water systems may clog

k Gutters may fill and collapse

CHALLENGE

1. Draw a geographical sketch of Mount St Helens (photo l) and add five captions.
   HINT: Remember, a geographical sketch doesn't have to show everything, just what is important to this topic. This topic is about volcano hazards.

l Mount St Helens in the USA

55

Can we predict hazards from volcanoes?

Can we predict when volcanic eruptions are likely to happen?

The simple answer is 'Yes – but not precisely'. Nearby earthquakes can be a warning sign. Tilt-meters can measure if a volcano is swelling as another warning sign. Global Positioning Systems (GPS) can also measure swelling. Scientists place sensors around the volcano, that send signals to satellites in orbit, which measure where the sensors are with great accuracy.

GPS sensors are already in position on the slopes of Arenal Volcano in Costa Rica. The volcanologists download the satellite data. They can then work out whether the volcano is swelling and is ready to erupt, or if it is staying the same and so not likely to erupt.

In future, GIS maps could tie in with GPS data to give automatic real-time warnings to local radio stations and set off sirens to warn people that a pyroclastic flow is likely.

A satellite image of another volcano with a city nearby, showing the extent of a P1 (small), P2 (large) and P3 (very large) pyroclastic flow

Key to pyroclastic flows

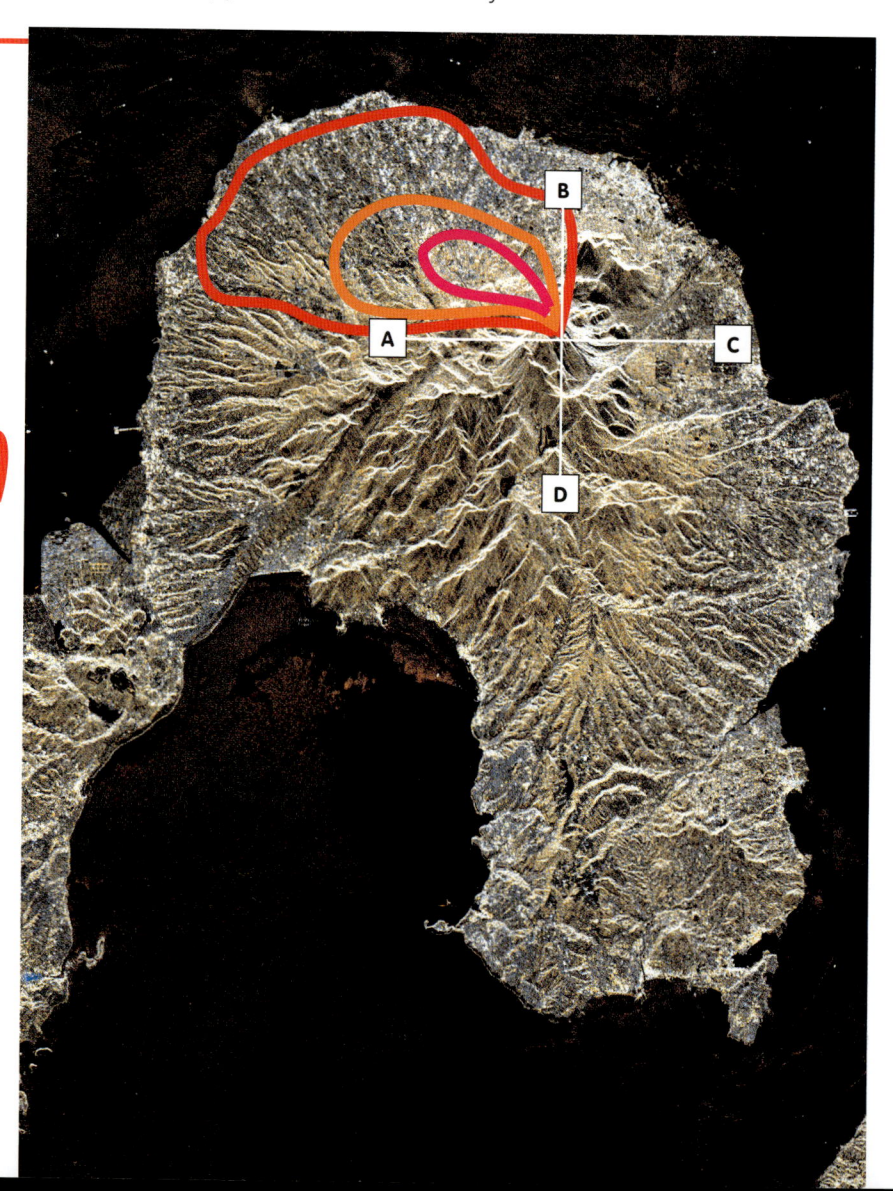

P1   P2   P3

Can we predict hazards from volcanoes?

CHALLENGE

2. Study map m and table n. Look at each of the situations below. For each situation, decide if you will advise the mayor of the nearby city:
   a) To do nothing.
   b) That there is likely to be a P1 pyroclastic flow but no one needs to be evacuated.
   c) That there is likely to be a P2 pyroclastic flow and people on the volcano side of the city must be evacuated.
   d) That there is likely to be a P3 pyroclastic flow and the whole town must be evacuated.

   You could save lives – or cost the city millions.

Situation 1
A–C	Last 24 hours' swelling	= + 8.6 mm
B–D	Last 24 hours' swelling	= + 12.2mm
E	Number of earthquakes in last 24 hours	= 13

Situation 2
A–C	Last 24 hours' swelling	= + 33mm
B–D	Last 24 hours' swelling	= + 47mm
E	Number of earthquakes in last 24 hours	= 83

Situation 3
A–C	Last 24 hours' swelling	= + 23mm
B–D	Last 24 hours' swelling	= + 16mm
E	Number of earthquakes in last 24 hours	= 22

Situation 4
A–C	Last 24 hours' swelling	= + 3mm
B–D	Last 24 hours' swelling	= + 6mm
E	Number of earthquakes in last 24 hours	= 2

Sensor	Now	Increase shows that there is enough swelling for a P1 pyroclastic flow	Increase shows that there is enough swelling for a possible P2 pyroclastic flow	This range of increase shows greater swelling and indicates a possible P3 pyroclastic flow.
A–C	2000m	0–+9mm	+10–19mm	Over 20mm
B–D	2000m	0–+9mm	+10–19mm	Over 20mm
Earthquakes in the last 24 hours	-	0–9	10–19	Over 20

n This table shows how the volcano is swelling and the number of earthquakes under the volcano in the last 24 hours. The data can be used to predict pyroclastic flows

o Arenal Volcano

CHALLENGE

3. You are a Geography teacher living near Arenal Volcano. You have been asked to write an information leaflet to inform people about the hazards the volcano presents to local people and explain what scientists are doing to predict when hazards might occur.

What are 'hot spots' and 'supervolcanoes' and should we worry?

Our world and way of life could be threatened any time now by a 'supervolcano'. Supervolcanoes are caused at a 'hot spot', where magma rises up from deep in the Earth to the surface. In this lesson, we will learn more about both of these and why they could be so disastrous for the world.

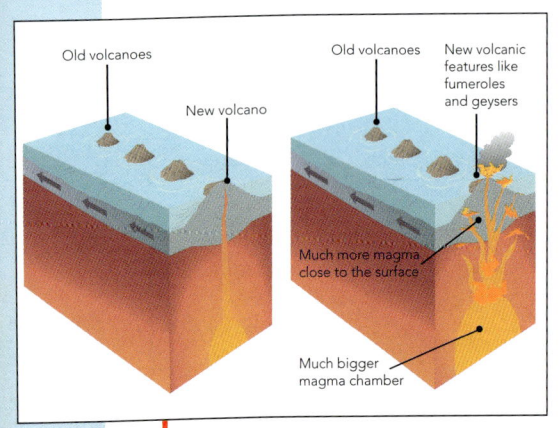

What are hot spots and supervolcanoes?

Underneath one of the USA's areas of outstanding natural beauty, Yellowstone National Park, lies one of the largest supervolcanoes in the world. Scientists have revealed that it has been on a regular eruption cycle of 600 000 years. The last eruption was 640 000 years ago – so its next eruption is overdue! Luckily, the scientists who are monitoring it say the signs are that it is not likely to erupt in our lifetimes.

Formation of hot spot volcanoes

Diagrams a and b show how hot spot volcanoes form. A part of a tectonic plate is burned through by magma welling up underneath it. If the magma burns right through and molten rock comes out onto the surface, a volcano forms. Scientists have noticed that when the plate moves the magma stays in the same place – forming a hot spot – and another volcano is created. This can happen several times so you get a row of volcanoes.

A thin stream of magma creates a hot spot. If the magma builds up to form a huge chamber close to the surface a supervolcano is formed. There are no actual volcanoes in a supervolcano. Instead hot lakes and mudpools, fumaroles (steaming holes) and geysers (jets of boiling water which burst out of the Earth from time to time) are spread over a large area.

If a supervolcano erupts all at once it would be far more explosive than a normal volcano. The last one to erupt was Toba, 74 000 years ago, in Sumatra. Its explosion was 5 000 times bigger than any volcano that has exploded in the last 100 years. It buried huge areas of what is now Indonesia with ash, created a worldwide darkness and cooling and killed many species of wildlife. The human race almost became extinct.

a Volcanoes being created at a hot spot

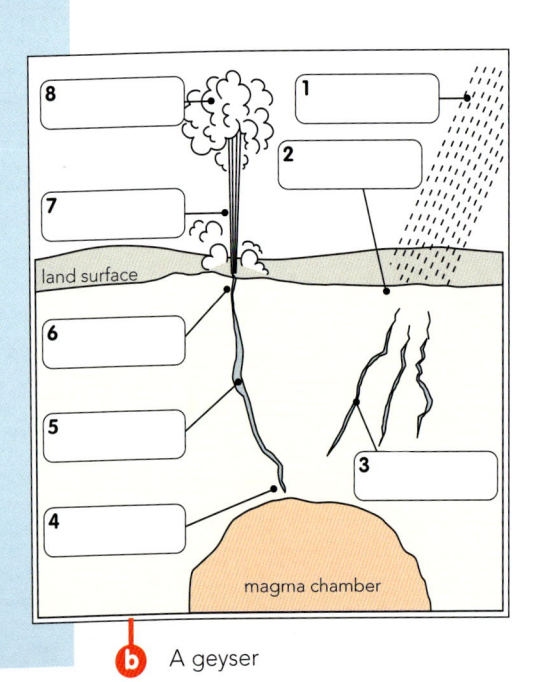

b A geyser

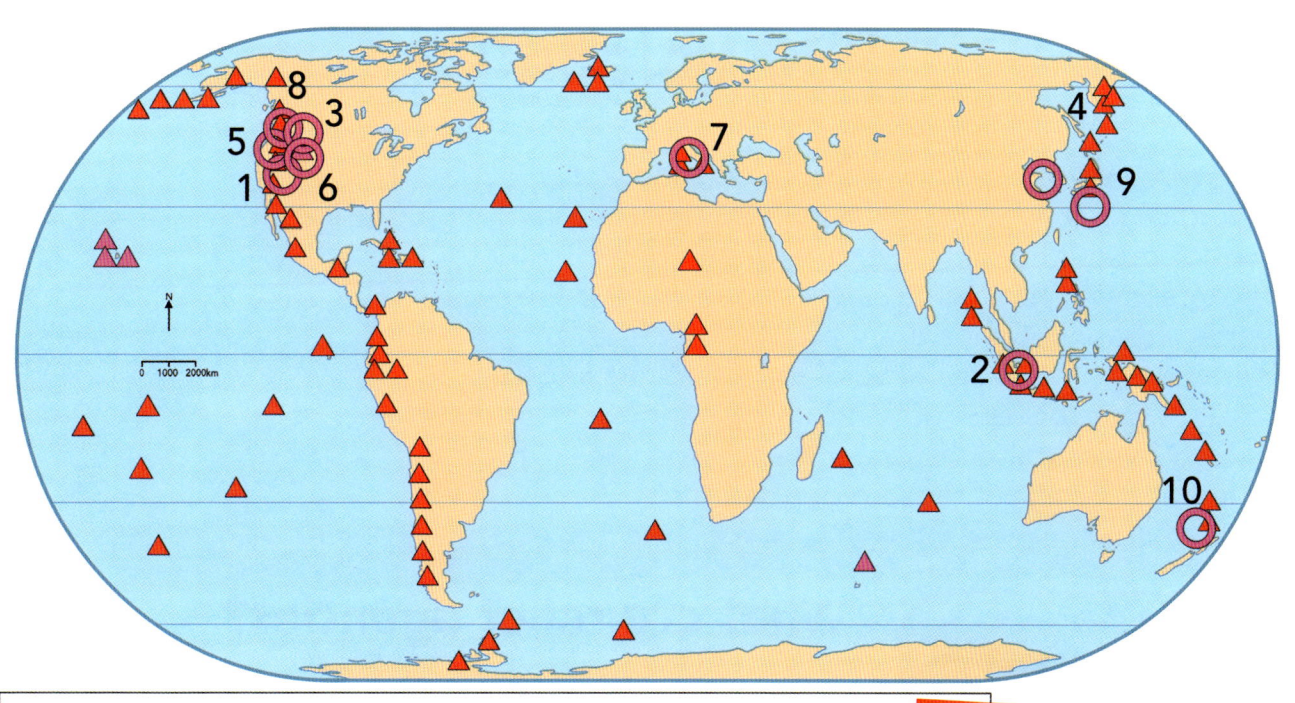

What are 'hot spots' and 'supervolcanoes' and should we worry?

Key
- ▲ Volcanoes active now
- ▲ Active 'hot spot' volcanoes
- ◯ Supervolcanoes

1. **La Garita Caldera**, Colorado, United States: 27.8 million years ago.
2. **Lake Toba**, Sumatra, Indonesia: 75 000 years ago.
3. **Yellowstone Caldera**, Wyoming, United States: 640 000 years ago.
4. **Aso**, Kyushu, Japan: four eruptions between 300 000 to 800 000 years ago.
5. **Long Valley Caldera**, California, United States: 760 000 years ago.
6. **Valley Grande**, New Mexico, United States: 1.12 million years ago.
7. **Campi Flegrei**, Naples, Italy: 12 000 years ago.
8. **Bruneau–Jarbridge**, Idaho, United States: 10–12 million years ago.
9. **Kikai Caldera**, Ryukyu Islands, Japan: 6 300 years ago.
10. **Lake Taupo**, North Island, New Zealand: 181 AD.

c World pattern of supervolcanoes and when they last erupted

CHALLENGE

1. Study diagrams a and b and photo d, then label diagram b to explain what happens when a geyser goes off.
2. With a sheet of blank A4 paper and any other equipment you have (for example, a pencil, pen, pencil case or ruler), make two simple 3D models: one showing a normal volcano and one showing a supervolcano and the areas affected by them.
3. Look at map c.
   a) Where is the nearest supervolcano to the UK?
   b) What should we do if geologists say that it is about to erupt? (We don't think this will happen, but just in case.) Think up at least three sensible responses.

d 'Old Faithful' is the most famous geyser in Yellowstone National Park, Wyoming, USA. It erupts every 35 to 120 minutes for between one and a half to five minutes. Its height ranges from 27m to 56m

How do emergency services work after earthquake and volcano disasters?

Movements of the earth causing earthquakes and volcanoes are forces of nature. When they kill, injure or make people homeless they are called natural disasters. Every natural disaster is different but the people who experience them have similar problems. Over the last 150 years, several organisations known as relief agencies have grown to help people affected by natural disasters. In this lesson, we will learn more about these organisations.

What are relief agencies?

A major relief agency is the International Red Cross and Red Crescent Movement, which has its headquarters in Geneva, Switzerland. It combines the work of the Red Cross, which mainly works in Europe, Australia, Japan and America, and the Red Crescent, which works in Islamic countries. The cross and the crescent are joined together in the Movement's emblem.

a The emblem of the International Red Cross and Red Crescent Movement

How did relief agencies help after the 2005 earthquake in Pakistan?

On 8 October 2005 a powerful 7.6 magnitude earthquake struck northern Pakistan, killing over 73 000 people and leaving 3.5 million homeless. Vast numbers of homes, schools, health clinics and shops were damaged or destroyed.

The BBC News on 8 October 2005 gave this report:

'The earthquake in Pakistan is the result of India's long-term, gradual geological movement north into Asia at a speed of 6cm a year – only a millimetre per week. The latest earthquake fits in with the scientists' expectations, but, at 7.6 on the Richter scale, it is relatively weak compared to what they feared. Earthquakes tens of times more powerful must be expected, the experts warn. One could kill as many as a million people on the Ganges Plain where millions of [poor] people live.'

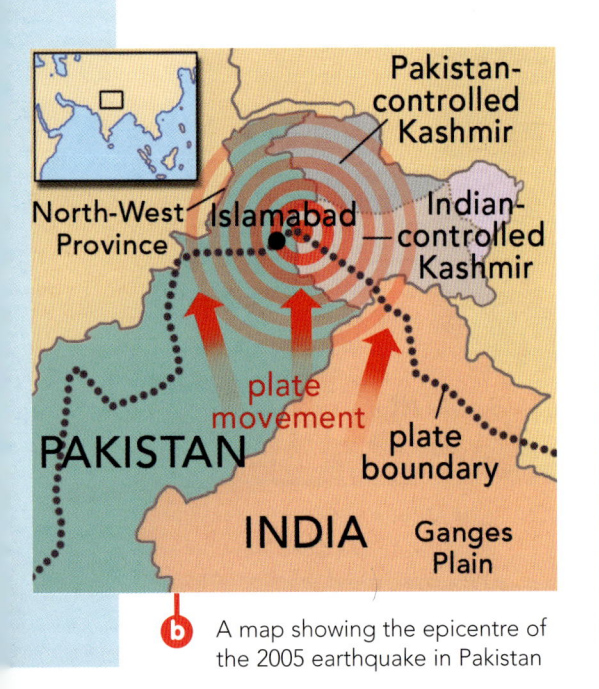

b A map showing the epicentre of the 2005 earthquake in Pakistan

How do emergency services work after earthquake and volcano disasters?

Since the tragic day that the earthquake struck, the International Federation of Red Cross and Red Crescent Societies (IFRC) and the Pakistan Red Crescent Society (PRCS) have been working side by side with survivors in Pakistan's North-West Frontier Province to rebuild their shattered lives. Similarly, the International Committee of the Red Cross (ICRC) has been assisting quake-affected people in Pakistan-administered Kashmir.

e The Red Crescent at work after the October 2005 earthquake in Pakistan

Clean water, food, clothing and shelter were the first things desperately needed by the survivors, who had few possessions or stores of food in their homes anyway. The PRCS, with support from the IFRC, distributed nearly 133 000 metal sheets for making shelters, 25 000 tents, 28 000 tarpaulins, nearly 171 000 blankets and 20 000 quilts to about 200 000 people in the affected areas soon after the disaster.

c Survivors use metal sheets to make shelters to help them survive the harsh winter conditions

d Tents are set up for survivors

CHALLENGE

1 Which items of relief would you not have expected to see used to help the people of Pakistan after the earthquake? Why?
2 If you were a Red Cross or Red Crescent planner, how many tents would you plan to have in store in case an earthquake happens on the Ganges Plain?

How do emergency services work after earthquake and volcano disasters?

How does the IFRC plan for emergencies?

The IFRC divides up its emergency work by: *preparing* for disasters and by *responding* to disasters. It does this by:

1 Organising local Red Cross/Red Crescent volunteers to carry out a search and rescue. This is more effective than rescue teams who are flown in from abroad as these teams often arrive too late.
2 Predicting natural hazards and mapping where they are likely to take place.
3 Planning how to transport emergency workers and supplies into an area at threat.
4 Providing emergency surgery units for high numbers of seriously injured people who require surgery within 48–72 hours; after that, little lifesaving surgery can be done.
5 Mapping the places where people live and might be at threat from natural disasters.
6 Providing first aid for people with minor injuries.
7 Assessing how well the people potentially at threat could cope and to decide if emergency supplies should be put in place, just in case.
8 Providing shelter, blankets and clothing for people whose homes have been destroyed.
9 Providing emergency safe water supplies, places to wash and toilets.
10 Persuading people to take precautions and to know what to do if a natural hazard strikes.
11 Setting up field hospitals to deal with the injured and clinics for basic health care and jabs.
12 Setting up a tracing organisation, so that people can find out what has happened to relatives and friends.
13 Planning with governments and other relief agencies, such as OXFAM, to agree who should do what to help people affected.
14 Quickly building new communities – roads, flat-pack homes, water supplies, sewage systems and so on.
15 Offering psychological support, as people are shocked and grieving and need help to think clearly.

CHALLENGE

3 a) The list to the right has been jumbled up. In your exercise books, sort the points into two lists:
- Preparing for a disaster
- Responding to a disaster.
b) Which of the points were most difficult to sort? Why?
c) Which points were you surprised about? Why?

How do emergency services work after earthquake and volcano disasters?

The response to the 2003 earthquake in Iran

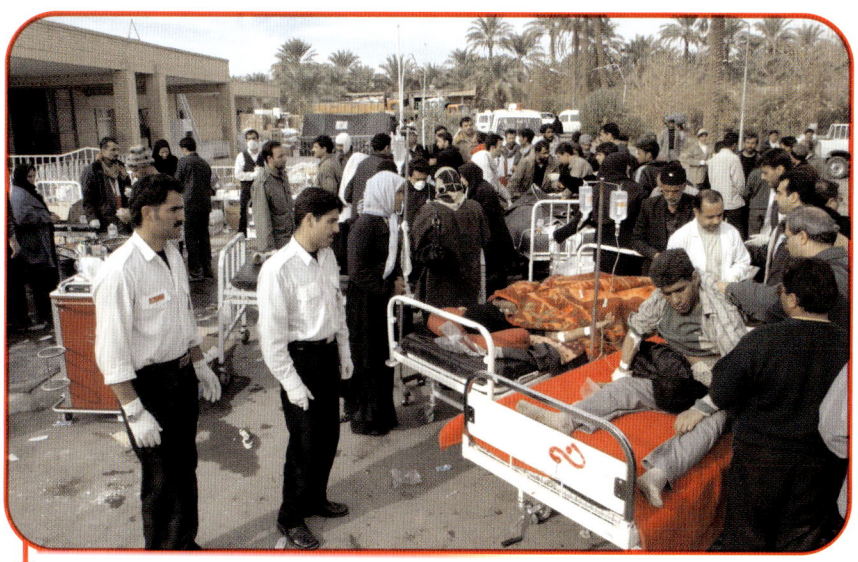

f The relief effort after the earthquake in Bam, Iran

g Map of Iran showing Bam

On 26 December 2003, a major earthquake, registering 6.5 on the Richter scale, hit the South-Eastern province of Kerman in Iran at 05:28 local time. The area most affected was the ancient city of Bam (shown on map g). More than 43 000 people were killed, an estimated 30 000 were injured and up to 75 000 left homeless.

In response to the disaster, the Iranian Red Cross Society (IRCS) mobilised more than 8 500 relief workers, volunteers and vehicles and launched large-scale rescue, evacuation and relief operations.

The first response was to send eight well-trained Iranian Red Cross relief teams with two helicopters to the city. Some teams helped local people to search for trapped survivors and transported serious cases to nearby hospitals in the helicopters. Other teams distributed water (because the water pipes were broken), food (because homes and shops had been shaken down so no food was available) and tents and blankets for survivors to shelter from the icy winter conditions.

Later, more and more relief teams poured into the area from Iran and overseas to cope with the huge disaster.

h A mother and child, homeless after an earthquake

CHALLENGE

4 Try to put yourself in the position of the Iranian rescue team shown in photo f. Think about the difficult decisions they have to make. Now look at the photograph of the mother and child (photo h) and think about which of the decisions listed below would best help the mother and child:
  a) To give the mother a mobile/satellite phone so she can phone relatives or friends to let them know where she is.
  b) To lead them to a tented village and give them a blanket, food and drink.
  c) To ask them where best the relief services should dig to find their loved ones.

Can you think of any other things that might help this mother and child?

DO YOU REALLY KNOW WHERE YOU LIVE?

Contents

Peter Humphries and Simon Howe

1	Why do we find settlements in different places?	66–69
2	Why do settlements change?	70–71
3	How can we make sure settlements change positively?	72–75
4	Where in the city is…?	76–77
5	Here today, gone tomorrow: is the city changing?	78–79
6	Why do we need more houses?	80–81
7	Are urban settlements the same all over the world?	82–85
8	Does everyone in post-apartheid Windhoek now live together?	86–89
9	How can we reduce inequalities in Windhoek and Namibia?	90–91
10	Does where you live symbolise your identity?	92–97
11	What is happening to our rural settlements?	98–101
12	How can we help our rural services to survive?	102–103
13	Can rural services be sustainable?	104–107
14	Is it a waste?	108–109
15	Are you doing your bit?	110–111
16	Is it easy to move within settlements?	112–113
17	Is it easy to move between settlements?	114–117
18	How can we use our industrial heritage?	118–123

Why do we find settlements in different places?

Different types of settlements are found in different places. In this lesson we identify and explore the reasons why towns first appeared where they did. By studying towns today, we will be able to see how the landscape affected their growth

What is a settlement?

A settlement is a place where people live. Settlements can be different shapes and sizes, and they can change over time. Have you ever wondered how the settlement you live in developed and why?

There are many factors that influence the **site** of a settlement, the land a settlement is built on. The **situation** is the description of a settlement in relation to other settlements and the physical factors, or the landscape, surrounding it.

Site and situation

Brigg, a market town in North Lincolnshire, is a good example of how a settlement is affected by location factors.

Brigg was established in the eleventh century as a very small settlement near a crossing point of the River Ancholme. The area was flat, and fertile because it flooded regularly, making it ideal for farming.

In 1205, a Thursday market was started to make the most of the people who passed through Brigg to use the river crossing point. The residents of Brigg also used the river to trade with other settlements, because the River Ancholme is connected to the River Humber which flows out to sea.

Brigg has continued to develop and it is still involved with trade and providing services today.

CHALLENGE

1. Using map a, describe the site of Brigg.
2. Using picture b, describe the situation of Brigg.
3. There are many reasons why Brigg is located where it is.
   a) Make a list of the top four reasons why Brigg is located where it is.
   b) Explain why you have chosen your top four reasons.
4. Do you think there are any disadvantages with:
   a) the site of Brigg?
   b) the situation of Brigg?

Why do we find settlements in different places?

a This map shows the site of Brigg. The scale is 1:25 000.

b This aerial photograph shows the situation of Brigg and its relationship to other settlements and the physical factors around it

Labels on aerial photograph:
- Humber Bridge crossing to Hull
- Bridging point of the River Ancholme
- River Ancholme
- Immingham Docks
- M180
- Barnetby Railway Station
- Humberside International Airport
- Fertile land
- Brigg

Why do we find settlements in different places?

Settlement detectives

CHALLENGE

Are you the next Sherlock Holmes or Miss Marple? Have you got the skills to find out why the settlements of Epworth, Bonby and Durham are located where they are and to decide which has the best location? Follow the clues to help you piece together the evidence.

Clue 1

A photographer has been out in an aeroplane and taken photographs of the settlements shown on the map extracts. Working in pairs:

a match the map extracts to the aerial photographs and
b explain why you made the decisions you did.

HINT: Make sure you and your partner look at the buildings carefully.

Clue 2

The words scattered around the photographs have been left behind by the people who established the three settlements. Use them to help you explain why the three settlements are located where they are.

HINT: Think about the site of the settlements and the situation of the settlements.

Discuss your findings with the other detectives to see if they have collected information that you have missed. Then review your evidence and decide which of the three settlements has the best location.

Building materials

Aerial photograph 1

Fertile soils

Dry point site, a site that is above flood level

Bridging points

Fuel supply

Map a: Epworth at a scale of 1:25 000

Why do we find settlements in different places?

Aerial photograph 2

Defensive site

Relief (how flat or steep the land is)

Food supply

Map c: Durham at a scale of 1:25 000

Map b: Bonby at a scale of 1:25 000

Spring-line settlement

Wet point site, a site with an accessible source of fresh water

Aerial photograph 3

Why do settlements change?

Settlements are dynamic – they are changing all the time: buildings go up, buildings come down; inhabitants come and go. In this lesson, we will look at how and why settlements change, and how settlements are sometimes forced to change in order to survive.

A village is born

In the nineteenth century, growing cities such as Liverpool and Manchester needed solid roads that could cope with an increasing amount of traffic. The answer was to build the roads with sets. Sets are bricks shaped from granite.

In 1861, Port Nant Quarry was opened by the Kneeshaw and Lupton Company from Liverpool. Quarrymen extracted the granite from the quarry and then it was shipped to where it was needed to build roads.

In the early days, the quarrymen lived in barracks near the quarry during the week and returned to their families at the weekend. But as the number of workers grew the quarry owners decided to build houses for the quarrymen and their families nearby. In 1878, the village of Nant Gwrtheyrn was built. There were 26 houses, a mansion for the quarry's manager, a shop, a bakery and a chapel.

a Map showing the location of Nant Gwrtheyrn

b Nant Gwrtheyrn during the 'boom' period

Why do settlements change?

Ghost town

As asphalt (tarmac) started to become the main surfacing material for roads, the demand for stone lessened. The quarry closed and Nant Gwrtheyrn was abandoned: the village no longer had a function, a purpose. In 1959, the village was like a ghost town. Its cottages and chapel were deserted.

c Nant Gwrtheyrn in the 1960s/1970s

A new beginning

When, in 1978, local doctor Dr Carl Clowes heard that the owners of Nant Gwrtheyrn were planning to sell the village, he realised that it was a golden opportunity to develop the area. It would bring jobs for local people and stop them leaving.

The deserted village of Nant Gwrtheyrn was turned into the Welsh Language and Heritage Centre. Since 1982, over 25 000 people have benefited from attending courses at the centre.

d Nant Gwrtheyrn today

CHALLENGE

1. Using map a, describe the location of Nant Gwrtheyrn.
2. Using the information you have gathered about Nant Gwrtheyrn's location, why do you think the settlement was built? What do you think its function, or purpose, was?
3. Why was Nant Gwrtheyrn abandoned?
4. Now answer these questions about your own settlement:

    a) Has your settlement changed over time?
    HINT: Have the reasons why people live there, or visit, changed? Has the sort of jobs people do changed?

    b) Do you think your settlement will survive? If so, why? Or do you think your settlement needs a new function to keep it alive?

    c) List the sources where you found the information to answer questions a and b.

How can we make sure settlements change positively?

Some settlements grow because they have a geographical advantage – they are in the right place at the right time. In this lesson, we see how a town grew because of such an advantage, how and why the settlement changed, and whether such changes can be positive.

Rapid growth

The growth of Scunthorpe took place in the late nineteenth century. The nearby settlements of Brumby, Frodingham, Ashby and Crosby became part of the town as it grew because people moved in to work for the new industry – iron and steel production.

Raw materials

The area surrounding Scunthorpe had the basic **raw materials** needed to produce iron and steel: iron ore was found in the Lincolnshire Heights, limestone came from the nearby Lincolnshire Wolds quarries; and coal from the nearby Yorkshire and Nottinghamshire coalfields. Between 1864 and 1876 several ironworks opened in the area:

- Frodingham Ironworks in 1864
- North Lincoln Ironworks in 1866
- Redbourn Hill Iron and Coal Company in 1872
- Appleby Ironworks in 1876.

Steel production

Steel was first produced in 1890 at the Frodingham Ironworks. Photo b shows a steam-powered digger excavating iron ore, a raw material used to make steel and iron, from the Lincolnshire Heights 4km north of Scunthorpe. Steel is still made in Scunthorpe today by Corus, a company owned by the Indian firm Tata Steel.

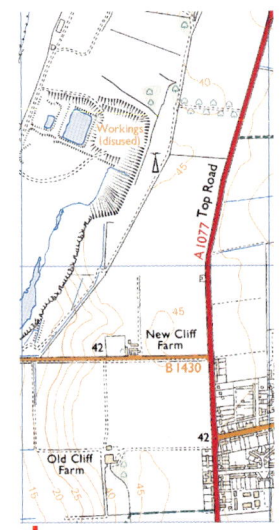

a Section of an Ordnance Survey (OS) map showing part of the Lincolnshire Heights, north of Scunthorpe. The scale is 1:25 000

How can we make sure settlements change positively?

b A large, steam-driven digger at work in the area shown in map a. Note how a layer of the land is being extracted

c Inside Scunthorpe steelworks in the 1960s when making steel was labour intensive (required lots of manual workers). These men are putting iron ore in the furnace

CHALLENGE

1. Look at map a. What has happened to the pattern of the contour lines?
2. Look at photo b:
   a) What is happening? How has this activity changed the shape of the land?
   b) What is the train for and where could it be going? Why were trains used?
   c) When do you think the picture was taken?
3. What was the main function of Scunthorpe? Look at picture c for another clue.
4. a) Use the data in the table below to draw a bar graph showing numbers of workers employed by the Scunthorpe steelworks.

The number of workers employed by the Scunthorpe steelworks	
1960	22 000
1970	20 000
1980	27 000
2007	4500

   b) Using your graph, describe what has happened to the number of workers at the Scunthorpe steelworks.
   HINT: Describe the overall pattern of change and use numbers in your answer.
   c) When was there a dramatic reduction in the number of steelworkers?

73

How can we make sure settlements change positively?

CHALLENGE

5 Look at the three scenarios open to the management of the steelworks.
   a) What are the positive and negatives aspects of each option for:
      - the social environment (the people)?
      - the physical environment (the land)?
      - the economic environment (money)?
   b) What option would you choose? Why?

All change for the steel town

At the beginning of the 1980s the UK steel industry was losing money. The steel industry in Europe and the USA had old, inefficient steelworks compared with the new steelworks in Asia. The wages for people working in Europe and the USA were much higher than for people working in Asia. Lower wages and better equipment in Asia resulted in better quality, cheaper steel. This was not good news for the settlement of Scunthorpe, which depended on the steel industry for a lot of its jobs. It was time for the management of the steelworks to make some tough decisions.

Scenario 1: Close the steelworks

The closure of the steelworks would create 27 000 unemployed people. Most of those who would lose their jobs would be the men who provided the main income for the families of Scunthorpe. House prices in the region would decline and closing the steelworks would generate a lot of derelict land.

Scenario 2: Make steel more cheaply

This could be done by:
- finding cheaper raw materials.
- increasing productivity, making more steel without spending any more money.
- reducing workers' wages.

Re-structuring the steel-making process would lead to job losses.

Scenario 3: Increase the price of the steel

Continue to make the steel in the same way, but increase the price of the finished product by improving the quality of steel by using the latest technology.

Scunthorpe's future

In 1980, the government invested in new technology for the UK steel industry, so that it could compete with the rest of the world. Because the new technology required fewer manual workers to operate it, lots of jobs in Scunthorpe's steelworks were lost.

Today, Scunthorpe has a viable steelworks employing 4 500 people, and a number of other industries that depend on the steelworks.

From table d, we can see that there is an optimistic future for the steel industry in Europe. Current production should remain more or less constant until 2015. But what will happen then?

	2005	2015	Projected change in output 2005–2015
	Tonnes (millions)		% per annum
European Union (EU)	195	216	1
Commonwealth of Independent States (CIS)	117	157	3
North America	134	141	0.5
Asia	538	1 157	8
Rest of World	1 107	1 804	5

d This table shows the crude steel output projections for 2005–2015. This is what is expected to be produced in the different areas of the world

How can we make sure settlements change positively?

Changing the economic base of Scunthorpe

> My name is Christine Edwards. I am the Principal Town Centre Management & Tourism Officer for Scunthorpe. It is my job to make Scunthorpe a better place to live and relax, and to bring more visitors and new businesses into the area. This will help Scunthorpe widen its economic base (the companies that provide jobs in a given settlement, community or geographic location) and create more jobs for the local people. Scunthorpe must make sure it is not reliant on just one major industry for its jobs in the future.

d An aerial photograph of Scunthorpe today

Number of tourists in Scunthorpe 2000–2006	
2000	790 000
2001	800 000
2002	890 000
2003	1.5 million
2004	1.4 million
2005	1.73 million
2006	1.83 million

e A shopping Centre, Scunthorpe

CHALLENGE

6 Imagine you want to open a new business in the high street. Why would Scunthorpe be a good place to open your business? Make a list of the pros and cons.

Where in the city is . . . ?

In this lesson, you will discover how to spot and name the different parts of a town or city. You will be able to predict what sort of housing, transport, shops and services might be found in each key area.

CHALLENGE

1. Look at the transect.
   a) Where do you think the least expensive housing is? Why?
   b) Where do you think the most expensive housing is? Why?

   HINT: Think about the services AND the amount of space nearby.

2. Study Scenarios 1–4.
   a) Where would you suggest the people in each scenario live? Give reasons for your answers.
   b) How and why would the lives of the people in Scenarios 1 and 4 change over time? How would this affect their choice of housing?

Urban development

Urban areas – towns and cities – develop over time. This means that as you move around a town or city, you will see different types of homes and services in different areas. Shops, banks and bus routes are all examples of services.

For example, as transport improved during the latter half of the twentieth century, people were able to live further away from where they worked, so towns and cities expanded outwards.

Below is a transect showing how housing and services change as you move from the centre of Kingston upon Hull, on the left, to its outskirts, on the right. It also shows the zones that areas of towns and cities have been grouped into in the UK.

Inner city: homes
Terraced houses, developed in the nineteenth century for workers in nearby factories. The houses have small backyards and no garages. This is high density housing which means that lots of houses are built in a relatively small area.

Inner suburbs: homes
Housing built in the 1920s and 1930s, largely located near main roads leading into the CBD. Houses often have bay windows, three bedrooms and small gardens at the front and back.

CBD (Central Business District): services
This is the city or town centre, where transport links meet. Major land users are offices and shops, including department stores, which are willing to pay the high rents because a lot of people travel to the CBD. The CBD is often called the '24 hour city' because it is home to bars and clubs.

Inner city: services
Inner city roads are narrow and usually laid out in a grid-like pattern. Corner shops sell frequently-used goods such as milk, bread and newspapers.

Inner suburbs: services
Regular bus services on main roads. Convenience stores, banks, public houses, petrol stations and takeaways are located at some intersections (where two main roads meet).

Where in the city is...?

Scenario 1:
Richard and Alison, a young couple, have just bought their first home together and started new jobs. Richard is a self-employed builder and Alison is a secretary at a primary school.

Scenario 2:
Dave is a middle-aged single parent with two children who are too young to go to school. He works in the CBD as a solicitor and pays for child care which is located in the inner suburbs.

Scenario 3:
Jim and Margaret are an elderly retired couple who are dependant on their state pensions. They have a lot of spare time but neither of them can drive so they rely on bus services to get about.

Scenario 4:
Peter and Julie are a middle-aged couple with two children, both of whom go to secondary school. The couple have full-time jobs; Peter is a pilot and Julie is an estate agent.

Outer city council estate: homes
Built by the council in the 1960s and 1970s. High-rise and low-rise flats, often with no gardens.

Outer suburbs: homes
Developed mainly by private building companies from the 1990s to the present day. Detached houses with three or four bedrooms, a garage and a large garden.

Commuter settlement
These are relatively recent developments outside the main urban area, but connected to it via a number of roads. They contain a mixture of housing, including many large detached houses with double garages, large gardens front and back and private driveways. Becoming increasingly popular as transport improves.

Green belt
An area of undeveloped land which is protected to try and reduce the spread of the urban area.

Outer city council estate: services
Communal park areas lie between the blocks of flats. A parade of shops, which can include a post office, a newsagents, a butchers, a chemist and a hairdresser, plus a health centre and a youth centre. There is usually a regular bus service to the CBD.

Outer suburbs: services
Out-of-town retail parks containing many well known clothing and electrical stores, and the main supermarkets. Also an entertainment complex, with cinemas, restaurants, bowling alleys and so on. Retail parks, with large, free car parks and easy road access, develop as more people have cars. They also have a regular bus service so they can be accessed by people without cars.

Here today, gone tomorrow: is the city changing?

In this lesson, we focus on the changing face of the inner city. We look at how changes link with the city's industry and the needs of the people who live there.

CHALLENGE

1 Look at pictures a–b. What changes have taken place at the docks in Hull over the last hundred years? Why do you think this is?
2 What improvements have been made to:

- the economic environment (the number and type of jobs that are available)
- the physical environment (the way the area looks)
- the social environment (the houses, entertainment and transport services)?

Declining industries

In many urban areas, the inner city was once the home of industry. Many people used to work in the factories or – if the settlement was near the sea – at the docks. In Kingston upon Hull, often called Hull, the docks thrived throughout the 1800s. Hull was the centre of a large fishing and whaling industry, and fish brought to the docks by fishermen was processed in factories on the quayside. But the fishing industry declined in the 1960s due to rising fuel costs and disputes over fishing grounds. Also, a number of the docks were unable to accommodate the larger modern ships.

Brownfield sites

Areas that become derelict, like the closed docks in Hull, are called **brownfield sites**. Many brownfield sites have been redeveloped and new uses found for them. For example, in Hull:

- Prince's Dock is now home to a modern shopping complex.
- A marina has been created out of the Humber and Railway Docks.
- St Andrew's Dock is being transformed into a leisure and retail development.
- Victoria Dock has become Victoria Dock Village.

a Prince's Dock, Hull, 1905

b The changing image of Hull docks. This is how it looks today

Here today, gone tomorrow: is the city changing?

Victoria Dock Village

Victoria Dock was redeveloped in 1988 and a range of homes were built for private ownership, from apartments to three and four bedroom houses. The village also acquired a primary school, a community centre and a neighbourhood shopping centre with a supermarket, a hairdresser, a takeaway and a public house.

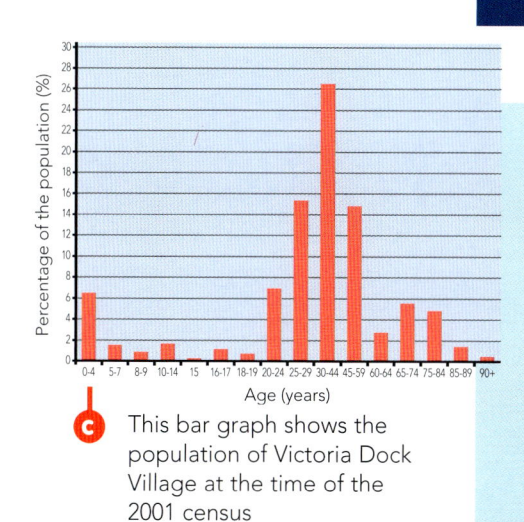

c This bar graph shows the population of Victoria Dock Village at the time of the 2001 census

Key
- Higher and intermediate managerial/administrative/professional
- Supervisory, clerical, junior managerial/administrative/professional
- Skilled manual workers
- Semi-skilled and unskilled manual workers
- On state benefit, unemployed, lowest grade workers

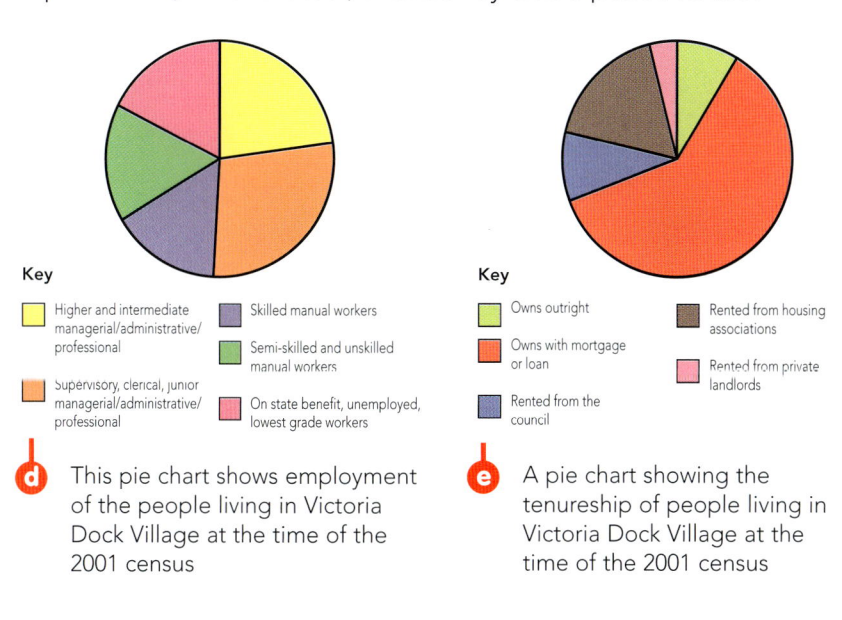

d This pie chart shows employment of the people living in Victoria Dock Village at the time of the 2001 census

Key
- Owns outright
- Owns with mortgage or loan
- Rented from the council
- Rented from housing associations
- Rented from private landlords

e A pie chart showing the tenureship of people living in Victoria Dock Village at the time of the 2001 census

Key
- Detached houses
- Semi-detached houses
- Terraced houses
- Flats/maisonettes

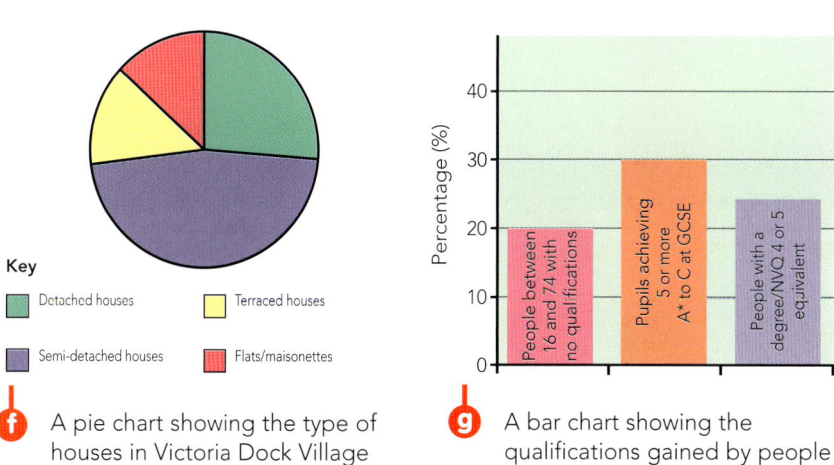

f A pie chart showing the type of houses in Victoria Dock Village at the time of the 2001 census

g A bar chart showing the qualifications gained by people living in Victoria Dock Village at the time of the 2001 census

CHALLENGE

3 a) Write a profile of the average person who lives in Victoria Dock Village. Include the following in your answer:
- the person's age
- the type of job the person does
- the type of house the person lives in
- the person's qualifications.

b) Why do you think the person in your profile was attracted to Victoria Dock Village?

4 This page contains some statements about Victoria Dock Village from local people. Which do you agree with and why?

5 What do you think the successes and failures of the redevelopment of Victoria Dock Village have been?

1. The redevelopment has been a great success and has attracted lots of people from a range of backgrounds to live in an area that was once derelict and unused.

2. It might be a good area for housing, but there isn't anything else. No jobs or entertainment has been provided for people.

3. I work in the city centre and with the improved transport links I can easily get a bus to work. I'm really happy about living here.

Why do we need more houses?

In recent years there has been an increasing amount of news about the housing problem. Have you ever thought about why we need more housing? Have you thought about where new houses should be built?

Housing shortages

The first housing shortage was after the Second World War when many homes had been damaged or destroyed. The New Towns Act 1946 was an attempt to find a solution by creating 11 New Towns between 1946 and 1955. But, in 1955, the government also asked local authorities of new and existing towns to establish green belts – strips of green that can't be built on around towns and cities – to stop too much urban sprawl (expansion of urban areas).

In the 1960s, a sudden rise in births led to nine more New Towns. The New Towns were built on **greenfield** sites so that people were housed outside the already overcrowded cities on sites that had never been built on before.

Today, English Partnerships is the government agency that seeks to create housing and services to meet the changing needs and wishes of the UK population, including:

- more low-cost housing for an increasing number of single parent families
- more houses that first-time buyers can afford
- more homes near the countryside for people who want to escape from crowded cities and can use improved transport to commute to work.

a New Towns built since 1961 with date of designation, location and population in 2001

October 1961: Skelmersdale
Population: 39 279
13 miles north east of Liverpool

10 April 1964: Redditch
Population: 78 807
15 miles south of Birmingham

10 April 1964: Runcorn
Population: 61 252
12 miles south east of Liverpool and 22 miles south west of Manchester

26 July 1964: Washington
Population: 55 454
6 miles south east of Newcastle

23 January 1967: Milton Keynes
Population: 207 057
42 miles north west of London and 58 miles south east of Birmingham

1967: Peterborough
Population: 156 061
80 miles north of London

14 February 1968: Northampton
Population: 156 061
59 miles north west of London and 45 miles south east of Birmingham

26 April 1968: Warrington
Population: 191 080
14 miles south west of Manchester and 16 miles east of Liverpool

12 December 1968: Telford
Population: 158 325
26 miles north west of Birmingham

26 March 1970: Central Lancashire
Covers the towns of Chorley, Leyland and Preston and the immediate area.
Population: no data
Close to Liverpool and Manchester

CHALLENGE

1. a) On a map of the UK, mark the locations of the cities of London, Liverpool, Manchester, Birmingham, Leeds and Newcastle, and the New Towns from the timeline.
   b) Describe any patterns you notice between the location of the main cities and the New Towns. Can you explain the patterns?
   c) Think about the differences between New Towns and large cities. Why do you think some people would prefer to live in New Towns?

Why do we need more houses?

Cambourne: A new community

Like the New Towns, Cambourne was created because of a housing shortage. Its construction began in 1998 on a greenfield site which had been used for farming. It has become a self-contained community for around 10 000 people. As well as houses there are also services, which are shown on map c. A business park also provides employment for over 5000 people.

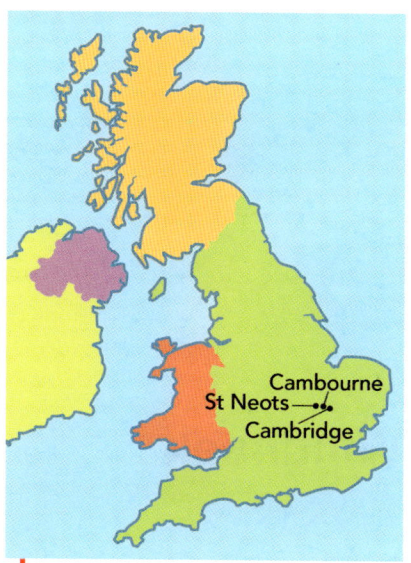

b Cambourne is located in the South East of England, 9 miles west of Cambridge and on a main road between Cambridge and St Neots

c Services in Cambourne

1. Business Park
2. Eco Park
3. The Monkfield Arms Public House
4. Monkfield Park Primary School
5. Country Park
6. Hotel
7. Allotments
8. Multi-use Sports Area
9. Supermarket
10. Church
11. The Vine Inter-State Primary School
12. Medical Centre and Library
13. Community Centre
14. High Street
15. Dentist
16. Day Nursery
17. Veterinary Surgery
18. Planned Golf Course
- Multi-purpose Sports Centre
- Skateboard Park
- Care Home
- Fire Station
- Police Station
- Garden Centre/DIY Store

d Cambourne's high street

CHALLENGE

2. a) Cambourne is a self-contained community. Use map c to describe what has been provided for the people in terms of:
   - housing
   - employment
   - entertainment.
   b) What would you like about this new community?
3. Develop a plan for a New Town in the South East of England on a greenfield area. It must house 10 000 people.
   Create an outline map showing the layout of your community, similar to map c. Annotate it with the reasons why you have put housing and facilities where you have.

Are urban settlements the same all over the world?

In this lesson we are going to compare two cities in different parts of the world: Windhoek in Namibia, an LEDC (less economically developed country), and Hull in the UK, an MEDC (more economically developed country).

Windhoek

Windhoek, which is pronounced 'Vind hook', is the capital city of Namibia. The city has a population of 230 000 people.

a) A political map of Africa, showing all the country borders. Can you locate Namibia?

b) A map of Namibia, showing the main physical features and cities

CHALLENGE

1. Using the maps above, or an atlas, describe:
   a) the location of Namibia within the continent of Africa.
   b) the location of Windhoek within the country of Namibia.

Are urban settlements the same all over the world?

Parts of the city

Like Hull, Windhoek is made up of identifiable areas, as shown in the map below.

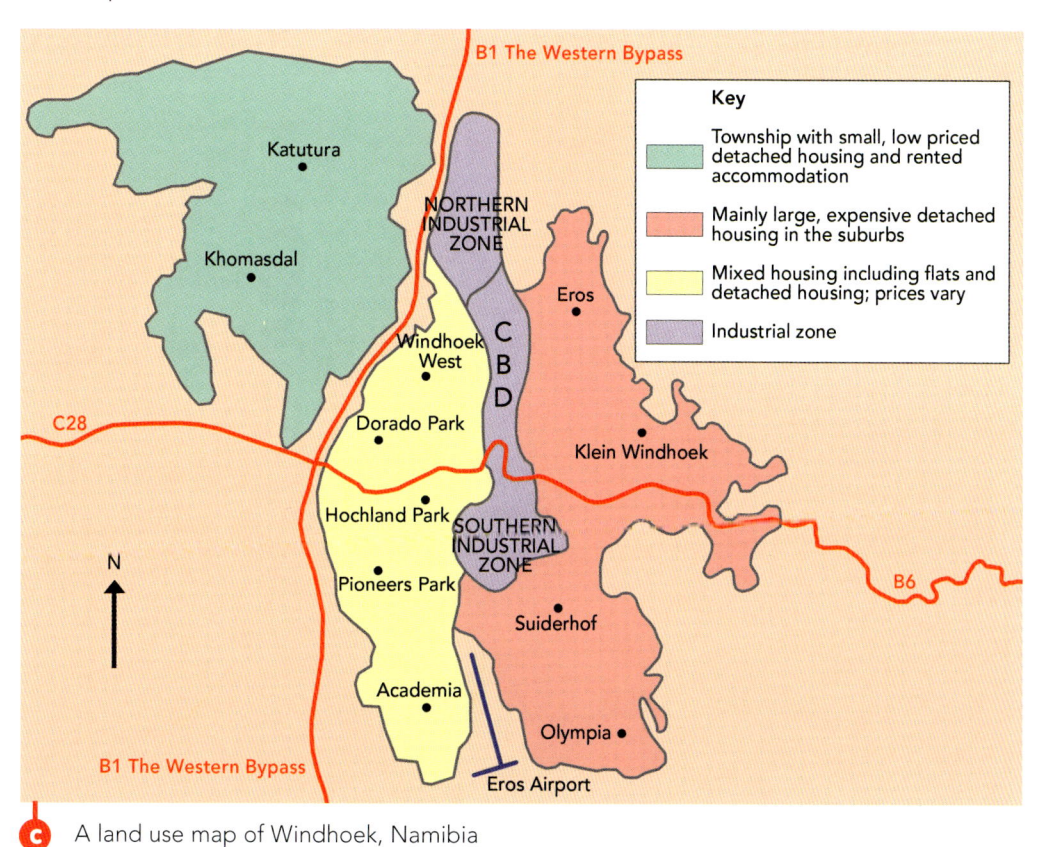

c A land use map of Windhoek, Namibia

Key:
- Township with small, low priced detached housing and rented accommodation
- Mainly large, expensive detached housing in the suburbs
- Mixed housing including flats and detached housing; prices vary
- Industrial zone

d The township of Katutura

e There are a lot of German-style buildings in the Central Business District of Windhoek. They are a reminder that Namibia was once a German colony

83

Are urban settlements the same all over the world?

Comparing services in Windhoek and Hull

By exploring where services are found, the layout of Windhoek and Hull can be compared.

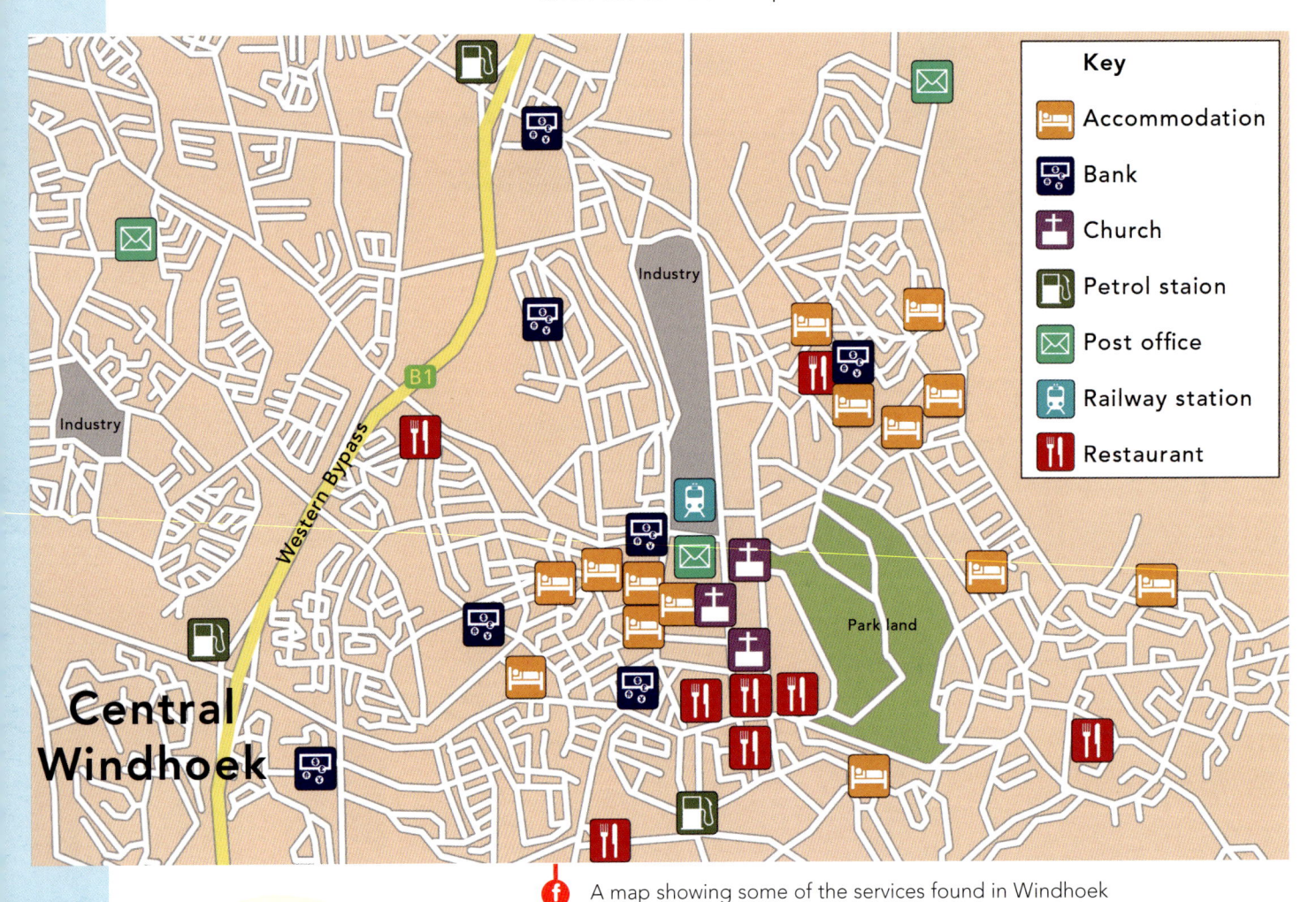

Key
- Accommodation
- Bank
- Church
- Petrol staion
- Post office
- Railway station
- Restaurant

Central Windhoek

A map showing some of the services found in Windhoek

CHALLENGE

Use the maps and information about Windhoek on pages 82–84 and the photographs and information about Hull on pages 76–79 and 85 to answer the following questions:
2. Compare the CBDs of Hull and Windhoek. Is the CBD at the centre of both cities?
3. Compare the services and retailers – the petrol stations car dealers and so on – in Hull and Windhoek, and identify any patterns in their location. For example:
- Are certain services grouped together in each city? Why?
- Is the location of petrol stations similar in both cities?

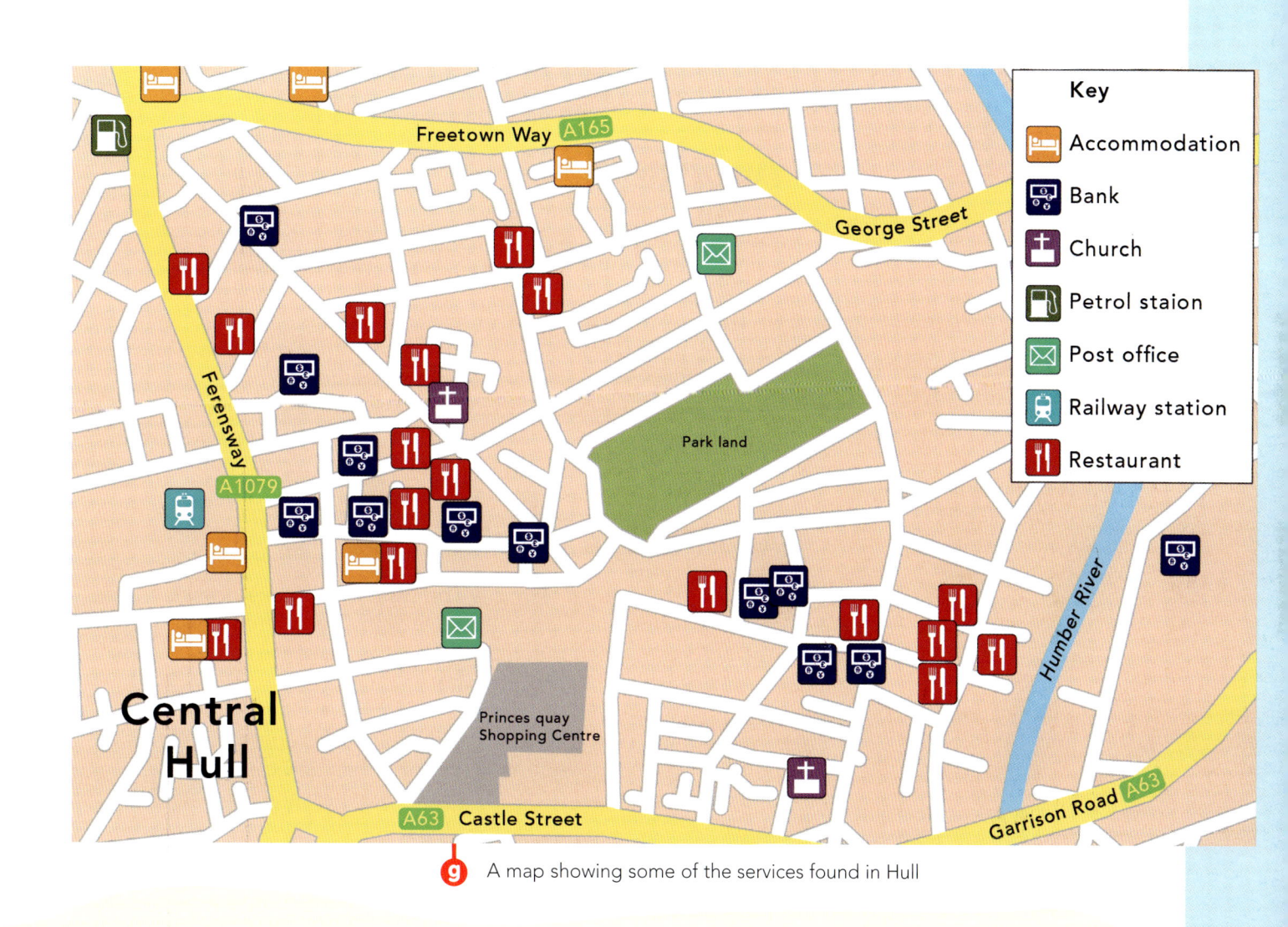

Are urban settlements the same all over the world?

Key
- Accommodation
- Bank
- Church
- Petrol staion
- Post office
- Railway station
- Restaurant

g A map showing some of the services found in Hull

4 a) Identify the main industrial areas in Windhoek. Where are they and what are they called?
   b) Are there similarly large industrial zones in Hull? Why?

5 a) What type of housing is in Windhoek, and where?
   b) Compare the houses in suburban areas of Windhoek with those in suburban areas of Hull. How they are similar and how are they different? Remember to be specific. Are the homes detached or semi-detached, or are they flats?
   c) Is there a variation in the wealth of housing in Windhoek, as in Hull? Which suburban areas in Windhoek are the richest and which are the poorest?
   d) There is high-density housing in Hull. Is there high-density housing in Windhoek?

Does everyone in post-apartheid Windhoek now live together?

Many people were segregated (forced to live apart) in Windhoek because of Namibia's policy of apartheid. But after apartheid ended, did things change in Windhoek? In this lesson, we explore what happened and how segregation lingers on, but for a different reason.

Apartheid

Apartheid means 'separateness' in Afrikaans, one of the official languages of South Africa. A policy of apartheid was introduced into South Africa in 1948 to keep different races apart.

The apartheid laws meant that white people were not allowed to marry non-white people. A sanction authorised 'white-only jobs', so that non-white people were excluded from numerous professions. By 1950, all South Africans were categorised into four groups: white, black, coloured or Indian. Coloured people were of mixed descent – neither black nor white.

Apartheid in Namibia

Apartheid spread to Namibia and was used to keep black, mixed race and white Namibians apart. In Namibia, a strict 7pm curfew was enforced which meant that black and people of mixed race could not leave their homes after that time.

Ethnic groups were also segregated. The Damara, Nama, Ovambo and Herero groups were limited to separate areas of the country by local government organisations. Dividing the black people of Namibia made sure they were powerless to fight against apartheid.

As Windhoek grew, black Namibians were forced to move into the north-west of the city, to Katutura. Katutura means 'the place where we do not want to settle' in Herero. These settlements became known as 'townships'.

CHALLENGE

1 Imagine you are a black Namibian living in Windhoek in the 1950s and that you have been forced to move to Katutura. Describe your feelings in a few sentences.
2 Write a mnemonic for 'apartheid'.

a The township of Katutura, during the years of apartheid

	Blacks	Whites
Population	19 million	4.5 million
Share of land	13%	87%
Share of national income	Below 20%	75%
Percentage of people on an average wage	1%	14%
Maximum taxable income	360 rands	750 rands
Number of people looked after by one doctor	44 000	400
Infant death rate	20% urban 40% rural	2.7%
Annual expenditure on education per student	$45	$696
Number of students taught by one teacher	60	22

Does everyone in post-apartheid Windhoek now live together?

b Residents of Windhoek, during the period of apartheid

c The township of Katutura, during apartheid

Does everyone in post-apartheid Windhoek now live together?

Independence for Namibia

Namibia gained independence from South Africa in 1990. Today, Windhoek is the capital of the Republic of Namibia. Since independence, Windhoek has changed little. The enforced racial segregation of apartheid has now been replaced with a socio-economic segregation. This means that different income groups are located in different parts of the city. The racial split is still evident, with the regions of Katutura and Khomasdal still occupied by black and mixed race people.

Integration has been slow but is beginning to take place. Small businesses have developed in Katutura and the community now has most of the services it requires. Successful black and mixed race groups with good jobs have moved into the eastern and south-eastern areas of the city (mainly Dorado Park, Hockland Park and Pioneers Park).

However, the east and south-eastern areas of the city are still dominated by white families. The housing has a suburban layout and is very similar to what you find in Germany because of Windhoek's colonial past. The dwellings are large, detached houses with big gardens. Only those with good jobs and money can afford to live in these locations. The communities in the east tend to use the services found in the CBD.

C There are a lot of German-style buildings in the CBD of Windhoek, a reminder of the city's colonial past

Does everyone in post-apartheid Windhoek now live together?

d Everybody with money to spare can take advantage of the shopping malls in Windhoek

> The biggest change we have had since independence is that we can now go out after 7pm. During apartheid we had to be inside by 7pm. We have lots of new businesses starting in Katutura. In the local market we can get all our requirements. We have seen a lot more housing being built which reflects the wealth that some people have.

e New businesses and retail developments in Katutura mean that residents do not have to travel into the city centre so much

CHALLENGE

3 Look at map e of Windhoek on page 83:
   a) Where do the majority of the city's black and mixed race people live today?
   b) Where do the majority of the city's white people live today?
4 Write down a list of possible reasons why there is still segregation in Windhoek today.
5 Imagine you are a journalist interviewing a person who lives in a specific part of Windhoek today. What five questions would you ask about how life has changed where they live and what responses would you expect to get?

How can we reduce inequalities in Windhoek and Namibia?

We have seen how the people in a city can be segregated by economic and social differences. In this lesson we will explore ways in which the Namibian government is trying to bring about integration through greater equality between its people.

Key objectives

Namibia's future will depend upon the forward thinking of its government and its people. The Namibian government's strategy is to improve the built, social and economic environment. How can they do this? How long will it take? Will it be successful?

Here are some of the key objectives of the Namibian government:

- speeding up the process of job creating by increasing support for small and medium-scale enterprises, including the creation of 50 000 jobs over the next five years
- expanding the rural electrification programme, bringing electricity to rural homes
- speeding up the building of low cost housing
- working towards social and behavioural changes to counter diseases such as HIV/Aids.

Micro-loans

Bank Windhoek is providing micro-loans to the people of Namibia to help small-scale enterprises flourish. A micro-loan is a small amount of money, perhaps just £25, to get a business started. The interest rates are low so that the companies can thrive and prosper. The aims of the micro-loans are to:

- create employment opportunities for large numbers of people
- stimulate the vast potential for entrepreneurship
- support a wide economic base and create wealth
- increase Namibia's wealth through the use of its indigenous people.

a Bank Windhoek, in Namibia

CHALLENGE

1 Think about what you have already learned about the people of Windhoek, then consider how micro-loans could help them. Think about:
- How will micro-loans affect the wealth of people living in Katutura?
- How will micro-loans help the process of integration?

How can we reduce inequalities in Windhoek and Namibia?

Rural electrification in Namibia

b Many pylons are needed to carry electricity to remote, rural areas of Namibia

In Namibia, there is electricity in 75% of urban areas and 9% of rural areas. By 2010, the government hopes that 90% of all urban areas and 25% of rural areas will have electricity.

In some remote, rural areas of Namibia, the government has helped install diesel-powered generators to supply electricity. These will be replaced when there is a full national grid covering most of the country. A national grid is a network of cables that takes electricity from power stations to the places where it is used. The Namibian government is also funding off-grid solar power systems to provide many homes in rural places with electricity. These systems work by changing energy from the sun into electricity.

HIV, AIDS and poverty

HIV is a virus that infects people and can sometimes develop into AIDS. AIDS is thought to have killed about 12 million people worldwide, mostly in developing countries like Namibia.

The international charity, Oxfam says:

"HIV and AIDS have a huge impact on poverty because they affect millions of adult women and men whose work drives their countries' economies and services, and who care for the young and the old. While HIV and AIDS push more and more families into poverty, poverty makes them more vulnerable to infections. For Oxfam's mission to overcome poverty and suffering to succeed, it is vital that this cycle is broken."

CHALLENGE

2 Imagine there was no electricity. How would it affect your daily life? Produce a diary entry describing a typical day without electricity.
3 What essentials is electricity needed for in rural settlements in Namibia?
4 Why do you think it is important for Oxfam and the Namibian government to combat HIV and AIDS?
5 Mr John Pandeni is Minister of Regional and Local Government, Housing and Rural Development in Namibia. Imagine that you have to prepare for a five-minute video conference with him to discuss how new housing plans could encourage integration in Windhoek. Make a list of points you would make or ideas that you have.
HINT: Use your knowledge and understanding of different types of housing in the UK and in Namibia.

Oxfam

Does where you live symbolise your identity?

The world is a diverse place. Settlements can be found in all kinds of extreme physical environments and challenging social environments. In many areas, a wide range of people live together, each with their own special culture. Most people need to feel that they belong to their own community, region or country. They believe that their community represents or symbolises their identity. So any threat to the place where they live may be seen as a threat to their identity as well.

Human rights

On 10 December 1948, the United Nations proclaimed the Universal Declaration of Human Rights. Its aim is to ensure that people can live in peace with each other and respect all cultures. There are thirty articles which make up the Human Rights charter, three of which are as follows:

Article 1
All human beings are born free and equal in dignity and rights. They are endowed with reason and conscience and should act towards one another in a spirit of brotherhood.

Article 15
Everyone has the right to a nationality.

Article 21
1. Everyone has the right to take part in the government of his country, directly or through freely chosen representatives.
2. Everyone has the right of equal access to public services in his country.
3. The will of the people shall be the basis of the authority of government; this will shall be expressed in periodic and genuine elections which shall be by universal and equal suffrage and shall be held by secret vote or by equivalent free voting.

Globalisation and conflict

Many people believe that globalisation can be a threat to people's rights. The world has become a global village in which diverse people who live thousands of miles apart can interact through advanced technology. Remote places have become more accessible and people have become more interconnected. What happens in one place can have a direct impact on people somewhere else and even threaten their way of life, culture or identity.

Does where you live symbolise your identity?

Conflict is also seen as a common threat to people's identities. Different views over who has the right to control or live in an area can lead to conflict. The conflict, and violence that erupts as a result, can in turn threaten not only people's identities, but their lives and homes as well.

Srinagar and the Kashmir crisis

A wide range of people live in, and identify with, the region of Kashmir. Kashmir has suffered from conflict since 1947. Many civilian people have been killed and there have been many attempts to try and resolve the problem. Srinagar, a settlement in Kashmir, is at the heart of the conflict.

a The Kashmir region

b The famous houseboats on the side of Lake Dal, Srinagar

Does where you live symbolise your identity?

The Kashmir crisis is a conflict of ownership over the Kashmir region. The dispute is between India, Pakistan and China. There have been a number of flash points between India and Pakistan (in 1947, 1965 and 1999), and one between India and China (in 1962), over the region.

The Jammu and Kashmir area of the Kashmir region is administered by India. India's claim is contested by Pakistan which controls a third of Kashmir. Since the early 1990s, Islamic insurgents have clashed with the Indian Army in Jammu and Kashmir. This has resulted in thousands of deaths and civilian casualties.

Sunset over the tranquil Lake Dal, Srinagar

People with different religious beliefs live in the Kashmir region.

REGION	Buddhist	Hindu	Muslim	Other
Kashmir Valley	-	4%	95%	-
Jammu	-	66%	30%	4%
Ladakh	50%	-	46%	3%

d) Religious groups in Indian-administered Kashmir. India is a mainly Hindu country

REGION	Buddhist	Hindu	Muslim	Other
Northern Areas	-	-	99%	-
Azad Kashmir	-	-	99%	-

e) Religious groups in Pakistani-administered Kashmir. Pakistan is a mainly Muslim country

CHALLENGE

1. a) Describe the scenes in the photographs of Srinagar (photographs b and c).
   b) If you lived here, what might you like about it?
2. Using an atlas and map a describe the location of the settlement of Srinagar.
3. Which two main countries are in dispute over the ownership of Kashmir?

Does where you live symbolise your identity?

Read the following views of people living in Kashmir.

I don't see why I should be asked to leave Kashmir; it is my home. I was born there.

Khayaal, 63, has lived in a refugee camp close to the Jammu border for over 10 years

f

There is such confusion about Kashmir. I feel like I am losing my identity.

g Manohar, 45, is a maths teacher at the University in Kashmir

I have to leave everything behind as soon as the fighting starts; my belongings, my home, everything.

h Rahul, 38, works in a small grocery shop close to the Pakistani-administered border of Kashmir

CHALLENGE

4. Using tables d and e label and shade a map of the regions of Kashmir with their dominant religious group.
5. Using your completed map answer the following questions.
   a) What region is Srinagar located in?
   b) Who administers the region?
   c) What is the main religious group of India?
   d) What is the percentage of Hindu people living in the Kashmir Valley?
   e) What is the main religious group in the Kashmir Valley?
   f) What is the main religious group in Pakistan?
   g) Why do you think there is conflict in Srinigar?

95

Does where you live symbolise your identity?

The future of Kashmir

Scenario 1: Keep things as they are

Since 1989, there has been a boundary called the Line of Control which divides the region in two. India administers the southern area and Pakistan administers the northern area. India would like to keep this situation but Pakistan and Kashmiri activists do not want to. With Kashmir as a whole being mainly Muslim, Pakistan believes Kashmir should belong to Pakistan.

Scenario 2: Kashmir joins Pakistan

Pakistan favours this solution. If the people were able to vote, the majority Muslim population would be in favour of being with Pakistan. However, if a vote takes place, the Hindus of Jammu and the Buddhists of Ladakh would protest at the outcome.

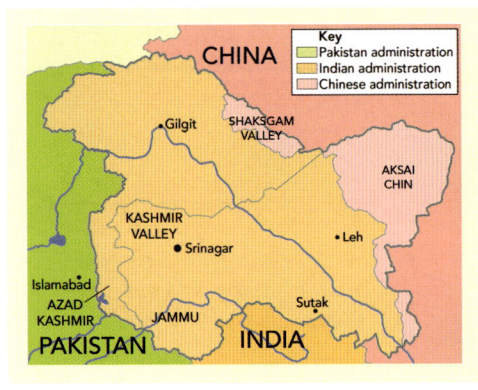

Senario 3: Kashmir joins India

The Muslim inhabitants of Jammu and Kashmir and the Northern Areas do not want to become part of India. They would not be happy with this situation.

Scenario 4: Independent Kashmir

Both India and Pakistan would have to give up territory for this scenario to become a reality. The people who would prefer no change to the current situation would not be happy. It would also not be acceptable to the people who wish to remain Indian or Pakistani.

Does where you live symbolise your identity?

Scenario 5: A smaller independent Kashmir

An independent Kashmir could be created from the Kashmir Valley and Azad Jammu and Kashmir. This would leave Pakistan with the Northern Areas. India would control Ladakh. India and Pakistan would not agree to this.

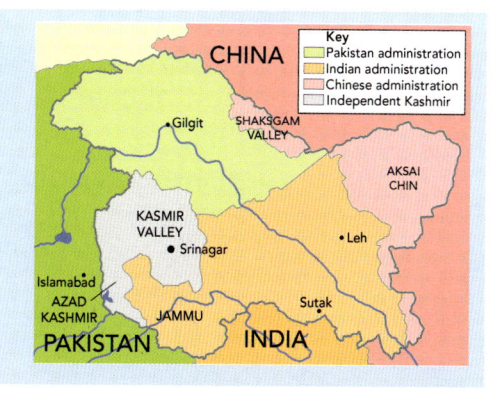

Scenario 6: Independent Kashmir Valley

An independent Kashmir Valley would be supported by those people who have been in conflict with the Indian government. The problem for this small state is how would it generate enough wealth to provide services for its people? What jobs could it create?

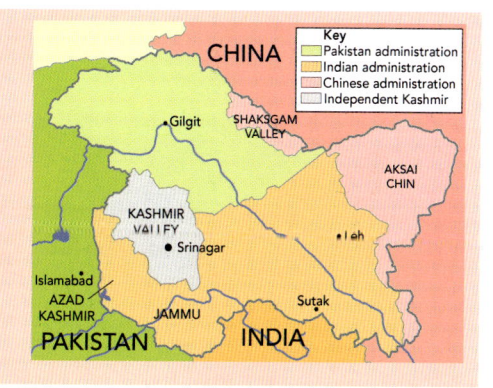

Scenario 7: The Chenab formula

Kashmir could be divided along the line of the River Chenab. Pakistan would get the largest piece of land and the Muslim majority would be part of Pakistan. India would not be happy with this situation as it would lose territory.

CHALLENGE

6 Read through each of the scenarios on the future of Kashmir. For each scenario:
   a) State whether the dominant religious group in the area and India and Pakistan are happy, not happy or neutral over the future possible outcome.
   b) Which solution do you, personally, think would be best? Explain why.
7 Write a letter to one of the people on page 95, explaining what you would like to happen to resolve the conflict.

What is happening in our rural settlements?

During the last 40 years there has been social, economic and environmental change in our rural communities. What are these changes? Why are they taking place? How are the rural areas tackling issues that will affect their future? In this lesson, we will begin to answer these questions and examine the changes that have affected Ickham, a rural settlement in Kent.

What is a rural settlement?

Before exploring rural changes, we need to understand what rural settlements are and how they are classified. In 2004, the government defined a rural settlement as a settlement with a population of less than 10 000 people. Settlements with a population greater than 10 000 are classified as urban.

Rural areas are then subdivided into two categories – sparse settlements and less sparse settlements – according to population density. Sparse settlements have a low density of people living in them. The settlement is in a situation with fields or woods around it, not many households and not many people. A less sparse settlement has a higher density of people and households, and fewer open spaces. Map c shows these two categories in the UK.

Within these two categories there are the following rural settlement types; town and fringe is a settlement that is smaller than a city – the fringe is the edge of the town. Villages are a group of houses and other buildings in a rural area. A very small group of buildings is known as a dispersed hamlet and where a house is on its own it is referred to as an isolated dwelling; this is the smallest size settlement.

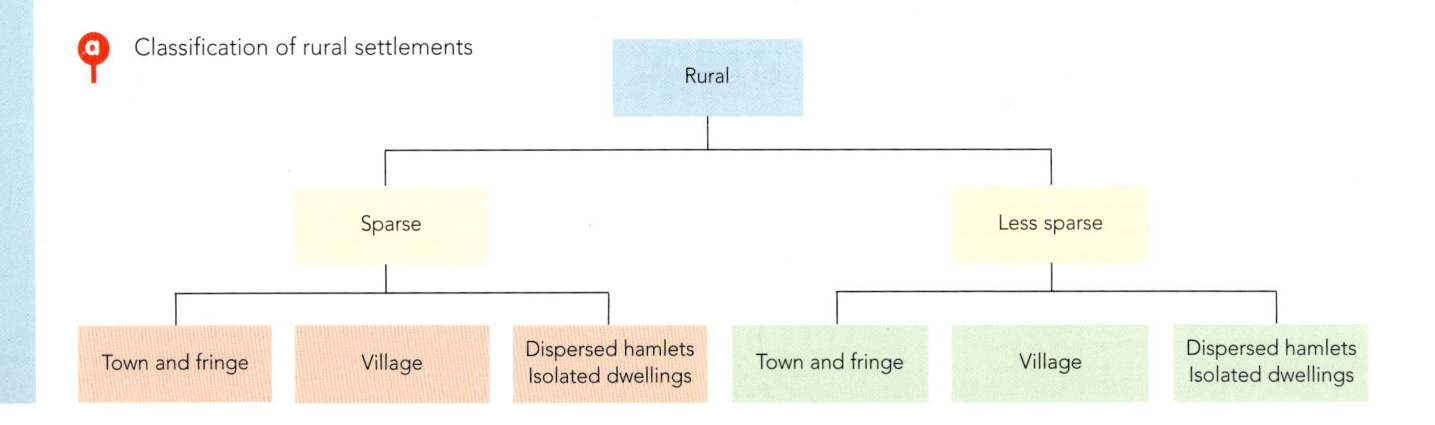

a Classification of rural settlements

What is happening in our rural settlements?

	Area definition	Population	Percentage of UK population in this category
Less sparse	Less sparse hamlets and isolated dwellings	1 380 115	2.8%
	Less sparse villages	3 285 346	6.7%
	Less sparse towns	4 230 458	8.6%
	Urban >10 000	39 527 964	80.5%
Sparse	Sparse hamlets and isolated dwellings	145 234	0.3%
	Sparse villages	246 448	0.5%
	Sparse towns	217 811	0.4%
	Urban >10 000	103 126	0.2%
Total	**Rural population**	9 505 412	19.3%
	Urban population >10 000	39 631 090	80.7%

b Population of rural and urban England, 2001 (Source: Office for National Statistics)

How are rural settlements changing?

The Commission for Rural Communities, which advises the government about the needs of rural England, outlined some changes in the countryside in a report called *State of the Countryside 2007*. The key points it made are:

- There continues to be a movement of people into rural areas from urban areas.
- We are seeing clear and growing differences between the age profiles of rural and urban England with rural areas showing more older people, and a reduction in the proportion of people aged between 20 and 35.
- There is a continuing reduction in the number of physical service outlets – both private (e.g. petrol stations) and public – in rural areas. This in turn has reduced the overall levels of services available and accessible to rural people.

CHALLENGE

1. Using table b, draw a bar chart showing the distribution of people living in rural settlements. Make sure your bar chart shows a distinction between sparse settlements and less sparse settlements.
2. Using your bar chart and map d, describe the distribution of rural settlements in the UK.

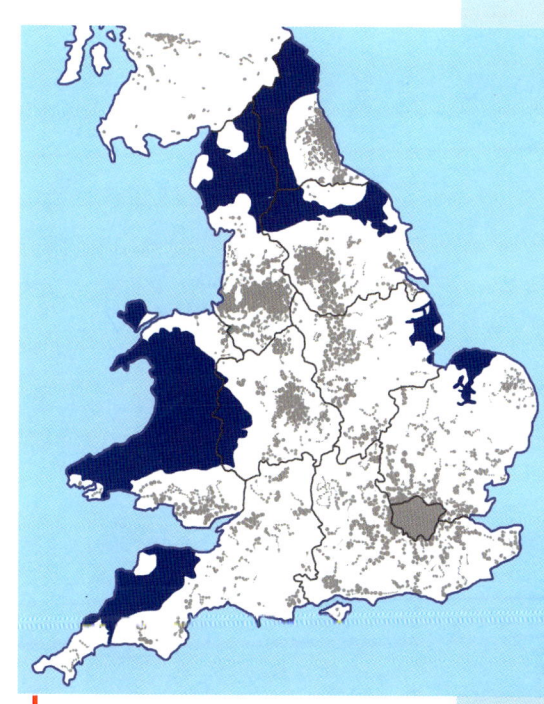

c The dark blue areas of this sparsity map show where rural areas are sparsely populated

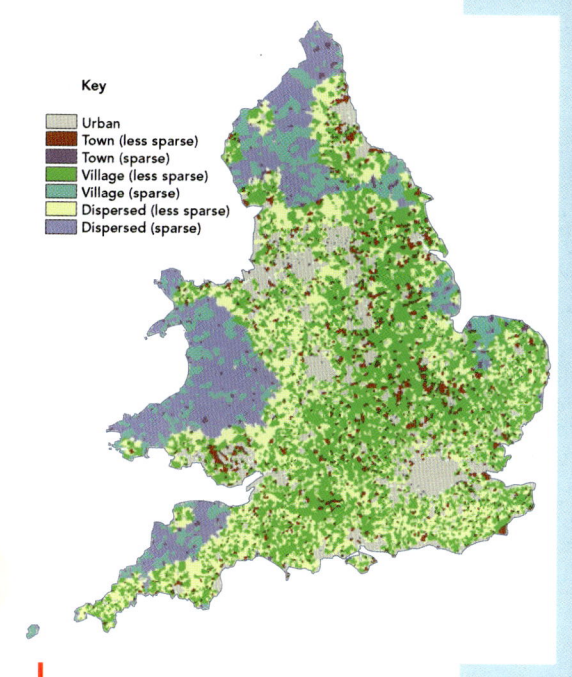

d The distribution of different rural settlements

What is happening in our rural settlements?

How has Ickham, Kent changed since 1959?

Ickham is a village in a less sparse rural area. It is located in the county of Kent in the South East of England. It is approximately 9.5km east of the urban settlement of Canterbury.

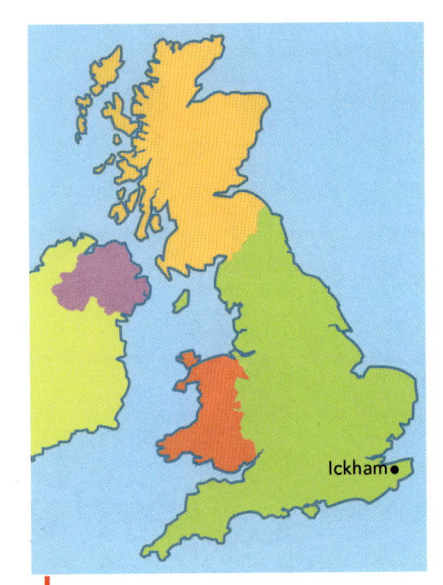

e A map showing the location of Ickham, Kent

	Population	Services
1959	400 people	Blacksmith and forge Local shop Post Office Carpenter/coffin maker Village pub
2007	500 people	Village pub Postbus: Monday to Friday, Duke William, Ickham to Canterbury Mail Centre Departs Ickham 11.10; arrives Canterbury 12.05. Departs Canterbury 14.05; arrives Ickham 14.45.

g A table showing the changes that have taken place in Ickham between 1959 and 2001.

h House prices in Ickham, 2006–2007

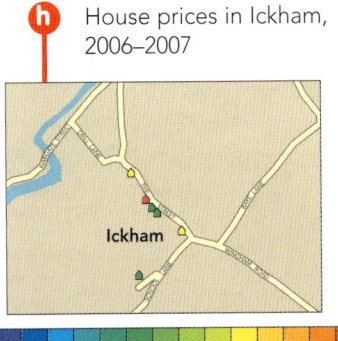

£ 0 50k 75k 100k 125k 150k 175k 200k 225k 250k 275k 300k 350k 400k 450k 500k 600k 700k 800k

f An aerial photograph of Ickham, Kent

Housing

House prices provide clues about the population of Ickham today. As you look at source f, think about what sort of people could afford to buy a house in Ickham in 2007. Are they the same kind of people who lived in Ickham in 1959?

By looking at planning applications which people have to make if they want to change properties, we can see ways in which the use of buildings in Ickham is changing. For example, plans have been drawn up to convert barns at Ickham Court Farm into new homes.

What is happening in our rural settlements?

From town to country

In 2007, the Commission for Rural Communities noted in its *State of the Countryside 2007* report that 'We continue to see net migration of people into rural areas.' This movement of people from urban to rural areas is known as counter-urbanization. It can have a major impact on rural settlements, like Ickham:

- Conflicts can develop between newcomers and local residents. For example newcomers don't get involved with the local community and get annoyed with slow moving vehicles like tractors.
- House prices rise due to the increased demand for the properties.
- New residents purchase their commodities, such as petrol and groceries, from the urban settlements where they work, rather than from the rural settlement where they live.

Ickham, Kent in 1959

CHALLENGE

3 Imagine you are a resident living in Ickham in 1959. Describe what life is like during a typical week, mentioning work, entertainment and shopping.

4 Compare the differences in services between 1959 and 2007. Which services have disappeared and which have survived? Why?

5 Explain the possible reasons why the only public transport from Ickham today is a Postbus, that runs to Canterbury once a day, and only on Mondays to Fridays.

6 a) Using the map h, calculate the average house price in Ickham during 2006–2007.
   b) What type of job will someone need to be able to afford a house in Ickham?
   c) How old do you think someone will be before they are able to afford a house in Ickham?

7 The population of Ickham has increased by a hundred since 1959 but the size of the village has remained the same. Explain how this could happen.

8 If more people moved from urban areas into Ickham, how do you think the settlement would change? Write a short report predicting what would happen to Ickham's:
   a) homes (prices and structures)
   b) population (age and type of people, for example how wealthy they are)
   c) local services.

How can we help our rural services to survive?

Post offices are under threat in rural locations and many have already closed down. In this lesson, we will look at why businesses close down, even if there is a need for them, and what can be done to keep them open for those who use them.

What is a service and how does it survive?

A service is something provided by an individual or organisation that satisfies a need. Public transport, post offices, shops and electricity supply are all services. People like solicitors and doctors also provide services.

Service suppliers need to sell at a price and quality that is appropriate to those who need it in order to operate successfully. This side of the business is called **supply**. There must also be enough customers to buy the service. This is called **demand**. If a service supplier achieves a supply and demand balance their business will be economically sustainable. This means it will be financially successful and so will survive.

| SUPPLY Quality Price | + | DEMAND Adequate number of consumers | = | An economical sustainable service |

Sometimes, a service supplier cannot survive, even if local people rely upon it. For example many post offices are under threat of closure, or have already been closed down, because they are no longer economically sustainable. This is because competing services mean there is a lack of demand.

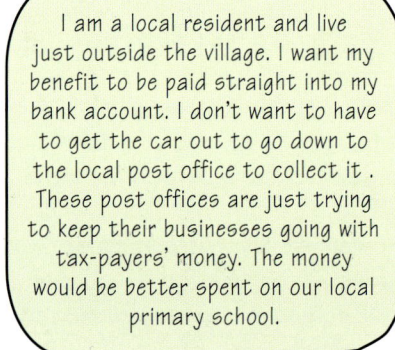

CHALLENGE

1 Consider a service that you use, such as your school canteen. Do you think it is an economically sustainable service? Give reasons for your answer, with reference to supply and demand.

a Some views about the closure of Willoughton post office and shop in Lincolnshire

> I am the local postmaster. The unfortunate thing is that it's the older generation that will suffer. Some of the elderly people in the village will be quite stuck if we have to close. The post office is part of the community like the pub and the local school.

> I am a local resident and live just outside the village. I want my benefit to be paid straight into my bank account. I don't want to have to get the car out to go down to the local post office to collect it. These post offices are just trying to keep their businesses going with tax-payers' money. The money would be better spent on our local primary school.

How can we help our rural services to survive?

Multi Use Centres

Post Office Ltd has made it clear to the government that, without financial support, it would have no choice but to close all but 2000 rural post offices. As a result, the government has agreed to help fund rural post offices until 2008. Government funding is also helping Post Office Ltd to pilot new ways of providing post office services. This includes trials of 'hub and spoke' services.

Multi Use Centres are an initiative from the Lincolnshire County Council, and a possible way of keeping rural services alive. The idea is that the main post office acts like the hub of a wheel setting up Multi Use Centres in the surrounding villages. Each Multi Use Centre is like the spoke of a wheel. They open at different times and on different days, providing post office services, access to computers and adult education classes. Funding for the initiative is coming from two sources:

- the European Union through the European Regional Development Fund (ERDF)
- the UK government.

b The Ruby Hunt Multi Use Centre, Donington

CHALLENGE

2 Write a short article on the plight of a rural post office which is under threat of closure. The article must look at both sides of the argument - why rural post offices should close and why they should stay open - and conclude with your own opinion on what should happen. Use source a to help you.

3 How could a Multi Use Centre help a rural post office? Consider its effect on both supply and demand.

4 Imagine that you are a local bank manager with a client who runs a village post office, and you are discussing their business plan:
   a) Will you advise your client to close the business or stay open?
   b) What can your client do to make the shop economically sustainable if it stays open?
   c) What do you think the long term prospects for the business are and why? Remember to justify your suggestions by referring to evidence.

Can rural services be sustainable?

Competition from local supermarkets makes it hard for village shops to survive. With many people happy to travel by car to places where more choice and lower prices are offered, the only option for many village shop owners is to close their business. In this lesson, we discover how the inhabitants of one village have got together to keep their village shop open.

Maiden Bradley Village Shop

The village shop in Maiden Bradley was threatened with closure in 2001. The shop was under pressure from supermarkets in the nearby towns of Frome, Shepton Mallet and Warminster. However the community came together and formed a co-operative (a business owned and controlled equally by the people who use its services or who work there) called the Maiden Bradley Village Shop Association.

CHALLENGE

1. Where is Maiden Bradley located? Using an atlas and map a, draw a sketch map to show the location of the village.
2. Study your map and the aerial photograph of Maiden Bradley (photo b).
   a) What direction was the photograph taken from?
   b) Describe the site and situation of the village.

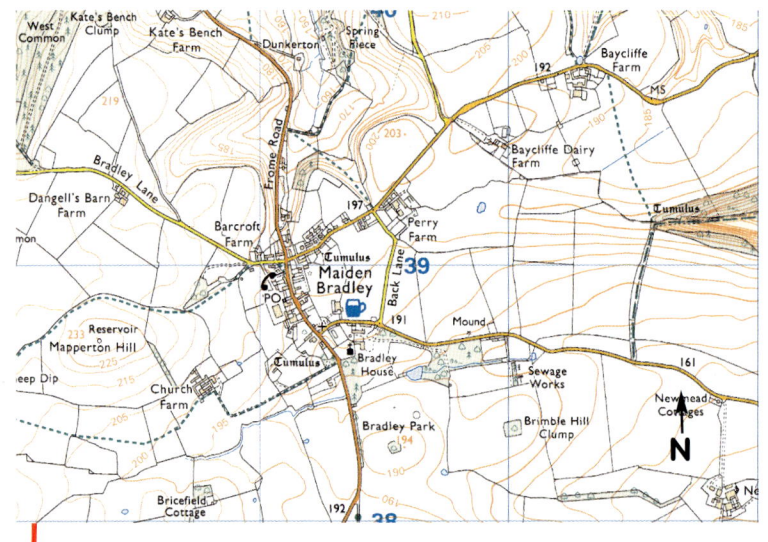

a An extract from a 1:25 000 map showing the location of Maiden Bradley

Can rural services be sustainable?

b An aerial photograph of Maiden Bradley

c Maiden Bradley Village shop before renovation

d Maiden Bradley Village shop after renovation

Community enterprise

Locals began a fund-raising campaign to keep the shop open. The co-operative was organised with the help of ViRSA (Village Retail Services Association), a charity that promotes and supports village shops. With the support of the parish council and a grant of £21 000 from the Countryside Agency, the shop was renovated (made to look like new) and stock was bought.

Read the clues on the next page to find out how Maiden Bradley Village shop became economically sustainable.

Can rural services be sustainable?

SHOP OPENING HOURS

8am – 6.30pm Monday to Friday

8am – 1pm Saturday

10am – 12 noon on Sunday

Clue 1

"The shop is a typical small convenience store, stocking a full range of foods and drink as well as newspapers, cards and stationery. We use several local producers who supply the shop regularly with meat, cheese, dairy products, jams and cider forming approximately 15% of food products in the store."
Mrs Anne Sercombe, Manageress

Clue 2

"My attitude is that a village shop is a community centre that sells food.
We have asked people what they want. If you stick to what people want you don't have to stock nine items they don't want."
Mrs Carol Munt, Parish Councillor

Clue 3

"The shop is the heart of the community, it is a meeting place for people in the village."
Admiral Wid Graham

Clue 4

"When it opened earlier this year, there were some gasps. Instead of a few tins of beans, sliced bread and wilting veg, it boasted wines, choice teas, home-made bread and shelves of local produce, all no more expensive than that sold in the nearest urban supermarkets."
www.guardian.co.uk 10 June 2002

Clue 6

"The shop is open 11 hours a day and turns over £2,600 a week, well over the break-even point and what was expected in the business plan. The home-made bread is sold out every day."

Clue 5

"20% of Maiden Bradley's inhabitants are old or without a car."

Clue 7

CHALLENGE

3 You are a member of the Maiden Bradley Village Shop Association. Prepare a presentation for another village to explain how they could make their shop economically sustainable. You must explain how you have changed the supply side of the business and how you have encouraged the demand side of the business. Don't forget to include information on:

- the products sold in the shop
- the price of the goods sold in the shop
- renovating the shop and where to obtain the finance
- how you keep your customers.

Can rural services be sustainable?

Future threats to rural services: home delivery

More and more people are purchasing goods on the Internet or by telephone. Items, including groceries and clothing, can be bought from all around the world without customers visiting retail outlets. Supermarkets and other shop chains offer a home delivery service, in which the items you order on the Internet are delivered to your door. This means that in many rural locations even those who do not have use of a car can get their groceries without going to a local shop or even a supermarket. This means more competition for village shops like Maiden Bradley Village shop.

e Supermarkets and other national shops deliver items bought online or over the telephone to people's homes

CHALLENGE

4 How will the development of online shopping and home delivery affect village shops?
   a) What are the advantages and disadvantages of virtual shopping?
   b) How does virtual shopping affect the social environment?
   c) How does it affect the natural environment?
   d) How will it affect the demand for the services supplied by village shops?
   e) How will it affect the supply of village shops?
   f) How could a village shop adapt to ensure it remains economically sustainable despite online shopping?

Is it a waste?

In this lesson we look at the big problem of what to do with waste and the reason why it's a good idea to get people to recycle. There is also an opportunity to develop your own plan for how to reduce waste.

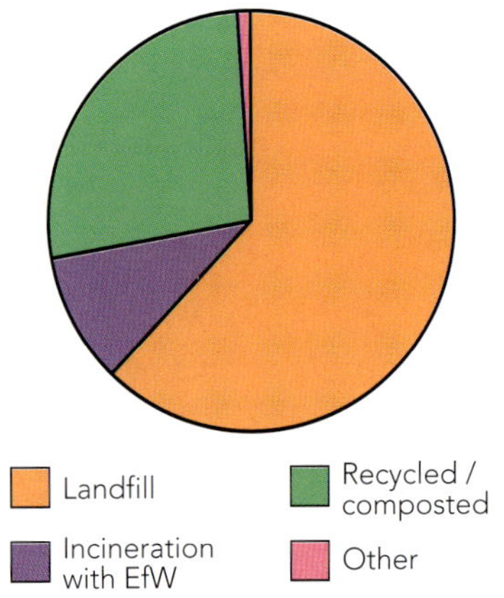

Landfill
Recycled / composted
Incineration with EfW
Other

a This pie chart shows where the waste in England went in 2005 and 2006

What's the problem?

As the population grows so does the amount of waste produced. In the UK, homes and businesses produce about 100 million tonnes of waste per year. This waste needs to be managed in a sustainable way to allow for further development, particularly in urban areas. We need to make sure that valuable resources are not lost in landfill and are recycled.

What is being done nationally?

The government has developed a waste hierarchy (see diagram b) as a guide to help councils make decisions on waste management. It sets out the preferred order for dealing with waste, with the options nearer the top as the most suitable. At present, a large majority of waste is dealt with at the bottom end of the hierarchy, although measures are being made to change this.

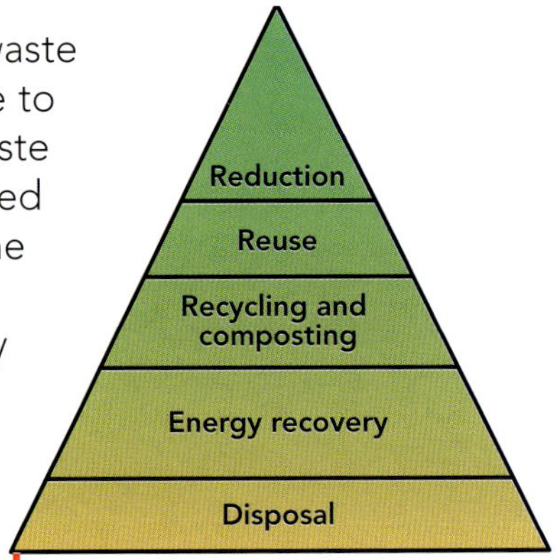

Reduction
Reuse
Recycling and composting
Energy recovery
Disposal

b This shows the government's preferred order for dealing with waste

c At the moment most of our waste ends up buried in the ground as landfill

CHALLENGE

1 Study figure a:
   a) What do you notice about where most waste goes?
   b) How would this create problems, be unsustainable, in the future if the trend was to continue?
2 Study figure b:
   a) What is the purpose of the waste hierarchy?
   b) How do you think the government could try and reduce waste?

What can local authorities do?

> I am Neil Ferris, Principal Waste Management Officer for North Lincolnshire Council. At North Lincolnshire Council we have a number of waste management schemes. For example, like many parts of the country, we have a recycling and waste collection scheme which requires residents to use different bins for different types of waste. This means that less rubbish goes to landfill. This helps make sure that we meet the target, set by central government, of reducing the amount of household waste not reused, recycled or composted by 45% by 2020.

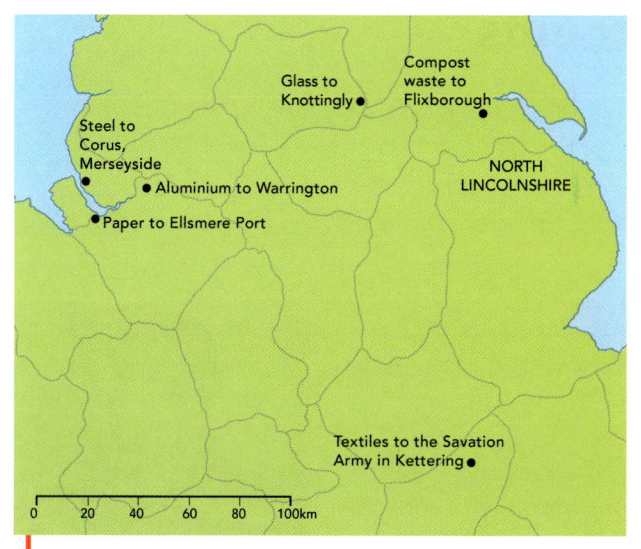

d A map showing where the rubbish collected through North Lincolnshire's recycling and waste collection scheme goes

The options

There are a number of methods that could be used to reduce the amount of waste going to landfill:

- Education: telling people about the problem and encouraging them to reduce, reuse and recycle.
- Charging for waste (pay as you throw).
- Providing different coloured bins for different types of waste to encouraging people to recycle and compost.
- Reduce the frequency of household bin collection.
- Introduce incentives to a recycling scheme, such as entry into a monthly prize draw when the blue box is put out.

Many of the methods that council can use to increase recycling rates cost money, but they may save money in the long term if central government increases the price of disposing of waste in landfill. The government charge local councils for every tonne that goes to landfill, and they are putting the price up to encourage other methods of waste disposal.

CHALLENGE

3 a) What are the advantages of North Lincolnshire's recycling and waste collection scheme?
   b) Can you think of any disadvantages to the scheme?

   HINT: Think about how the waste is collected and the distance it is transported. North Lincolnshire consists mainly of low-density housing and there are very few flats.

4 You have been appointed as the Principal Waste Management Officer for your local area and have been asked to develop a plan to reduce landfill waste. Develop your plan using the information on these pages.

5 Create a leaflet that could be given to residents in your local area to educate them about recycling and to encourage them to do more.

Are you doing your bit?

Previously we looked at the role national and local government plays in trying to reduce the amount of waste going to landfill and increasing the amount of waste reused or recycled. While government can do a lot, individuals have a part to play and in this lesson you will find out how you can help.

Every bit counts

You might feel as if your efforts won't have an impact but, if everyone does their bit, then together we will easily be able to achieve the targets set. And, as well as saving the environment you may also save money!

Paul's fact file

Paul is a second year student at university. He lives in a house with four other students. They all use the same bin and don't separate any of their waste. Paul shops at the local supermarket each day after he finishes his lectures. He has a busy life so usually eats quick snacks and canned drinks during the day. He also eats fruit on a regular basis. He throws all the waste he produces into the bin, just like the rest of his housemates.

The Gosal family's fact file

Mr and Mrs Gosal both have full-time jobs and live in a four-bedroom house with their two daughters who are aged 8 and 2. They believe in a healthy diet and buy ready-washed and prepared fruit and vegetables in packaging from their local supermarket. They are trying to recycle and collect their plastics and newspapers and take them to their nearest recycling centre. Mr Gosal doesn't have time in the morning to make lunch and buys a sandwich and drink from a corner shop near work.

The Gosal family

It's true!

- Every year, the average dustbin contains enough unrealised energy for 500 baths, 3500 showers or 5000 hours of television.
- Every eight months the UK produces enough waste to fill Lake Windermere (the largest lake in England).
- Every steel can is 100% recyclable. It can be recycled over and over again into products like bicycles and, of course, new cans.
- If all the aluminium drinks cans sold in the UK were recycled, there would be 14 million fewer full dustbins per year.
- On average, every person in the UK throws away his or her own body weight in rubbish every seven weeks.

Are you doing your bit?

a Many supermarkets now reward you for reusing old carrier bags or they have recycling bins for used plastic bags. This helps to reduce the energy wasted producing new carrier bags

b Some shops and supermarkets are reducing the packaging on products, but it is best to buy loose fruit and vegetables which come in just their own, natural, packaging

c Many local councils offer households free or reduced-price composters and wormeries. These turn organic waste into compost and liquid fertilisers. This reduces waste, saves money and the compost is more environmentally friendly than peat-based compost

d Reusing things that are normally thrown away, instead of buying new items, helps to reduce the amount of waste and saves you money. Try filling up an old water bottle before leaving home, rather than buying a drink and a new plastic bottle when you are out and about

e Try and separate your waste for recycling. You can take it to your nearest recycling centre or use the bins provided by your council

CHALLENGE

1. a) Look at Paul's fact file. What could he do to reduce the amount of waste he generates?
   b) Look at the Gosal family's fact file. What could they do to reduce the amount of waste they generate?
   HINT: Remember the 3Rs: reduce, reuse and recycle.

2. Think about your everyday life. Is there anything that you can do to help? Design your own waste management plan. Again, remember the 3Rs.

Is it easy to move within settlements?

Many people like to travel into and around cities like London by car because they want to travel independently and in comfort. They don't want to be left waiting for late trains, or get cold and wet at bus stops. But too many cars in narrow urban streets leads to congestion. In this lesson, we explore one city's attempt to solve the problem.

The London congestion charge

The London Congestion Charge began on 17 February 2003 as a fee of £8 to be paid by many motorists (but excluding motorcyclists) entering the central London Congestion Charging Zone between 7am and 6pm each day. The charge aims to:

- discourage the use of private cars and encourage people to use public transport
- reduce congestion so that public transport can move around more quickly
- provide money that can be used to invest in public transport.

In 2007 Manchester and New York voted to introduce the scheme, however, Edinburgh voted against the idea. Other cities such as Bristol, Cardiff and York are still discussing the controversial idea.

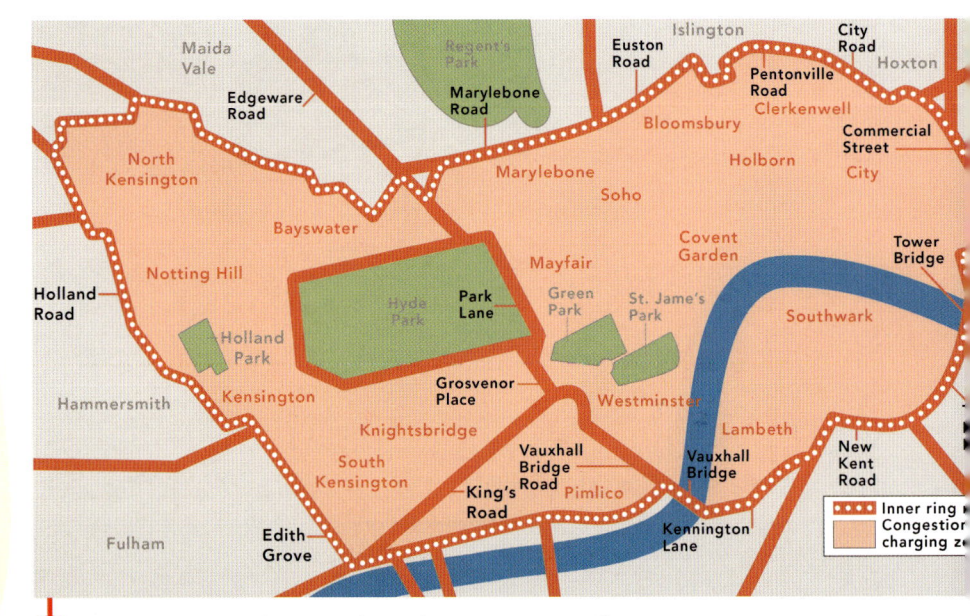

CHALLENGE

1 Table b shows how the London Congestion Charge has affected different forms of transport:
   a) Which form of transport has been reduced the most since the introduction of the congestion charge?
   b) Why has the number of motorcycles remained the same?
   c) What has happened to the number of buses inside the congestion charge zone?
   d) What effect has the congestion charge had on the differences between private and public transport?

   HINT: Refer to specific dates to illustrate the way situations change over time. Quote figures too. You could also draw graphs to illustrate your answers.

a A map showing the central London Congestion Charging Zone

Is it easy to move within settlements?

Public transport	1995	1996	1997	1998	1999	2000	2001	2002	2003	2004	2005
Surface rail	395	399	435	448	460	465	468	451	455	452	473
London Underground	348	333	341	360	362	383	377	380	339	344	342
Bus	63	68	68	68	68	73	88	81	104	116	115
Coach/mini bus	21	20	20	17	15	15	10	10	10	9	9
All public transport	827	819	863	892	905	935	935	929	909	929	939
Private transport											
Private car	145	143	142	140	135	137	122	105	88	86	84
Motorcycle	11	11	11	13	15	17	16	15	16	16	16
Pedal car	10	10	10	10	12	12	12	12	12	14	17
All private transport	166	164	163	163	162	165	150	132	113	115	118
All transport	993	983	1026	1055	1066	1100	1086	1061	1022	1036	1057

b A table (in 000s) showing different forms of transport in the London Congestion Charging Zone, 1995–2005

Different people have different feelings about the congestion charge. Here are some opinions:

A: Shops and other businesses have really suffered since the introduction of the congestion charge. Fewer people visit central London now and we have to pay more to receive deliveries.

B: Transport for London, the organisation that manages the congestion charge, have recorded falling levels of pollution within the congestion charge zone since the introduction of the scheme.

C: The congestion charge wasn't the only thing affecting the number of shoppers in London in 2005. The economic downturn, the SARS outbreak (influenza epidemic) and the threat of terrorist attacks all had a part to play.

D: A report in 2004 by Transport for London, the organisation that manages the congestion charge, showed that business activity within the congestion charging zone has been higher than before the charge was introduced, and that the charge has had a broadly neutral impact on London's economy as a whole.

CHALLENGE

2 Consider people's views about the London Congestion Charge then answer the following questions:
   a) Which of the opinions support and which are against the congestion charge? Explain your answers.
   b) How is the congestion charge affecting the environment in London?

3 Write a short letter to Bristol, York or Cardiff City Council giving the arguments for and against the introduction of a congestion charge and your opinion on whether or not they should introduce one.

4 Hybrid cars are exempt from the congestion charge. Find out what they are and why they are exempt.

Is it easy to move between settlements?

Increasing congestion isn't just a problem on London's roads. In this lesson we will discover how many of the country's main transport links are becoming increasingly congested, making travel between settlements more difficult. We will also consider a possible solution and its effects.

Congested network

Our transport infrastructure – our roads, railways and airports – finds it has to cope with more and more traffic. So, how can we improve our transport infrastructure for the future, so that movement between settlements becomes easier? We could continue to build more roads, increase the number of internal air flights and increase the number of trains on our railways, but perhaps we should be looking at new solutions. One possible solution is to develop a new high-tech, high-speed rail network, linking the major urban areas in the UK.

Ultraspeed UK

Ultraspeed UK is the company behind the hi-tech plan. It envisages a network that links Stratford in East London, Heathrow Airport, Birmingham, Liverpool, Manchester, Leeds, Newcastle, Glasgow and Edinburgh. The trains, called Maglev trains, would hover 1cm above a 3m-wide track on an electro magnetic cushion of air and accelerate to a maximum speed of about 510km/h. Maglev trains are already used in Japan, China and Germany.

a A map showing the proposed route of Ultraspeed's high-speed trains

b A map showing light pollution from the major conurbations (extended urban areas) in the UK

c A Maglev train in Japan, where they reach speeds of 510km/h

Is it easy to move between settlements?

d Likely journey times using Ultraspeed UK's proposed network

Origin	Intermediate calling points	Destination	Approximate journey time (minutes)
London or LHR (London Heathrow Airport)	-	M25/M1 Park and Ride	10
London/LHR	-	Birmingham	30
London/LHR	Birmingham	Manchester	50
London/LHR	Birmingham, Manchester	Liverpool	60
London/LHR	Birmingham, Manchester, Leeds, Teesside	Newcastle	100
Newcastle upon Tyne	Teesside, Leeds, Manchester	Liverpool	60
Manchester	-	Liverpool	10
Manchester	-	South Yorkshire	15
Glasgow	-	Edinburgh	15
Glasgow	Edinburgh, Newcastle upon Tyne, Teesside, Leeds, Manchester, Birmingham.	London/LHR	160
Edinburgh	-	Newcastle upon Tyne	35

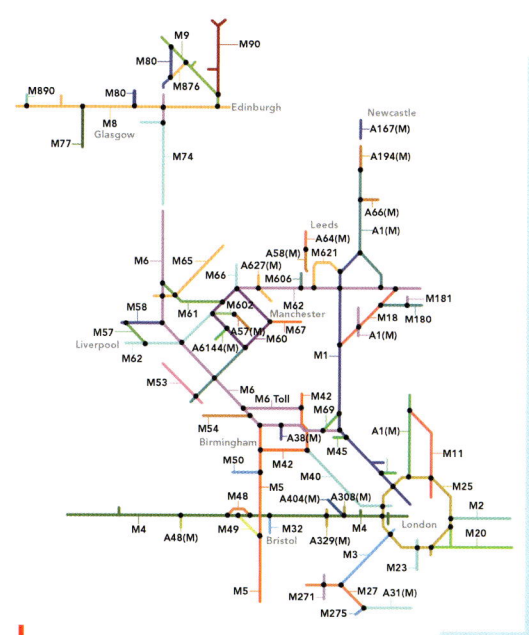

e The motorway network of the UK

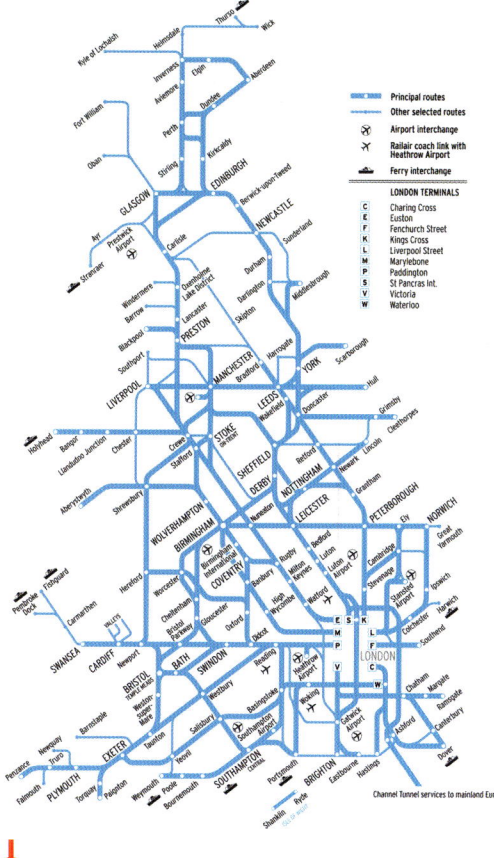

f The National Rail network of the UK

CHALLENGE

1. a) What impact would the high-speed train service have on your settlement? Would its route be close to you?
   b) Using maps a and b, explain why this route has been chosen.
   c) Would you move closer to the proposed route? If so, why?
   d) Using table d, how long would it take to get from London to Newcastle in the North East of England using the new high-speed train service?
   e) Using table d, how long would it take to get from Manchester to Liverpool using the new high-speed train service?

2. a) Using maps e and f, identify the following traditional routes from London to the:
   - North West
   - North East
   - South West
   - South East

   b) If Ultraspeed UK's proposed network went ahead, what do you think would happen to the traditional road and rail networks and their routes?

Is it easy to move between settlements?

The North–South divide

The 'North–South divide' describes a division between the wealthier South East of England, and the less wealthy parts of northern England, Wales, Scotland and Northern Ireland. The following maps show a variety of ways in which this division appears.

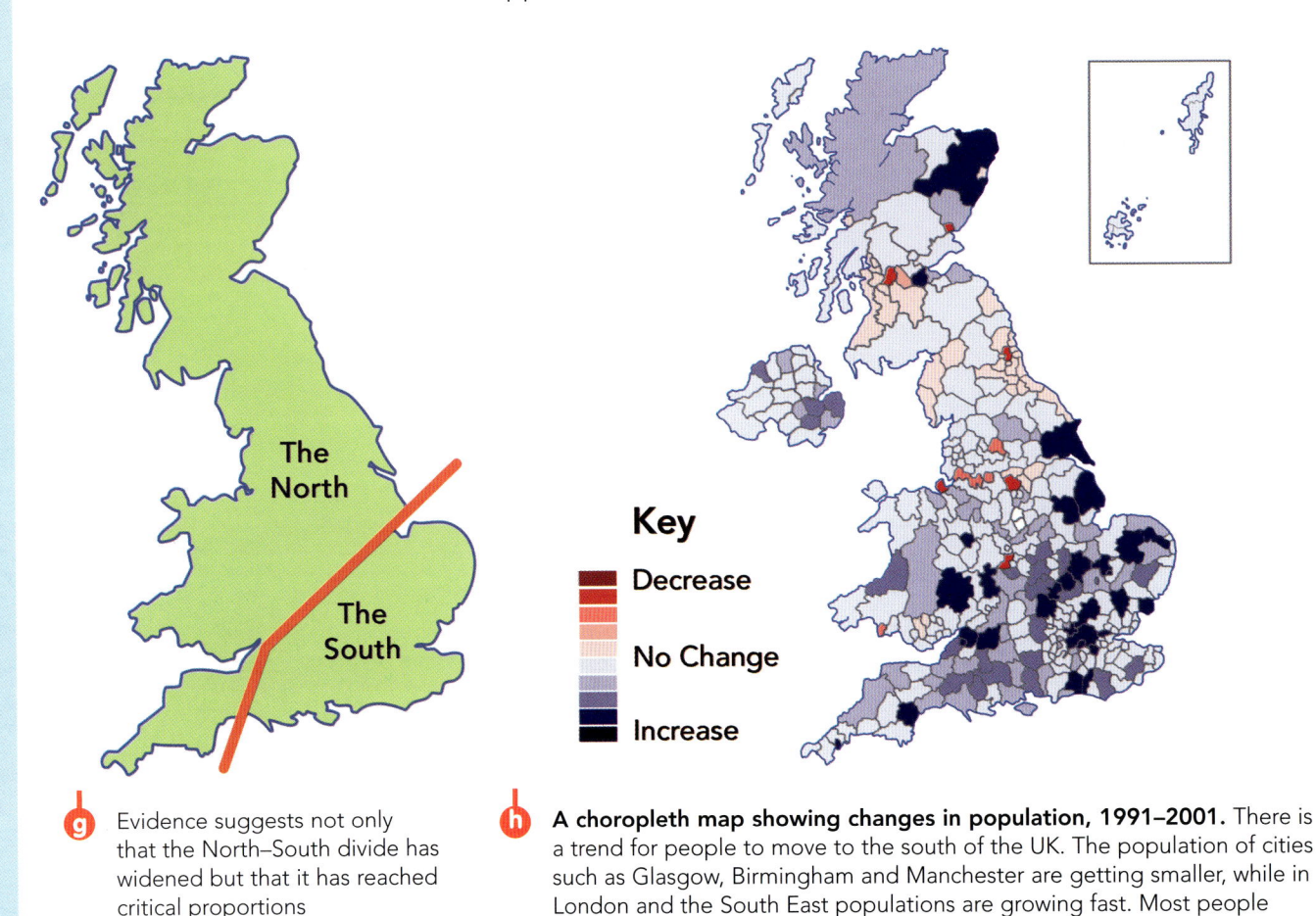

g Evidence suggests not only that the North–South divide has widened but that it has reached critical proportions

h A choropleth map showing changes in population, 1991–2001. There is a trend for people to move to the south of the UK. The population of cities such as Glasgow, Birmingham and Manchester are getting smaller, while in London and the South East populations are growing fast. Most people moving to the UK from abroad are staying in the South East

CHALLENGE

3 Consider maps g–k and explain what impact the high-speed rail network will have on the North–South divide. Will it help to reduce the divide? Explain your answer.

4 a) Find out the views of the UK Parliament and the Scottish Parliament about the new high-speed train network.
  b) Find out what people living in Wales and the South West of England think about the high-speed rail network.

Is it easy to move between settlements?

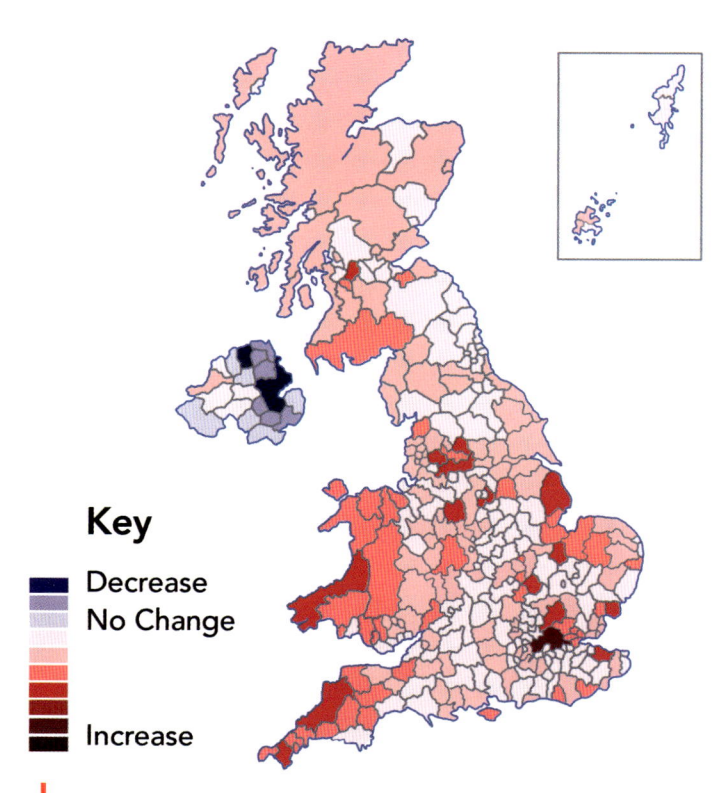

Key
- Decrease
- No Change
- Increase

A choropleth map showing changes in poverty, 1991–2001. Northern Ireland is the only part of the UK that has had a decrease in poverty between 1991 and 2001

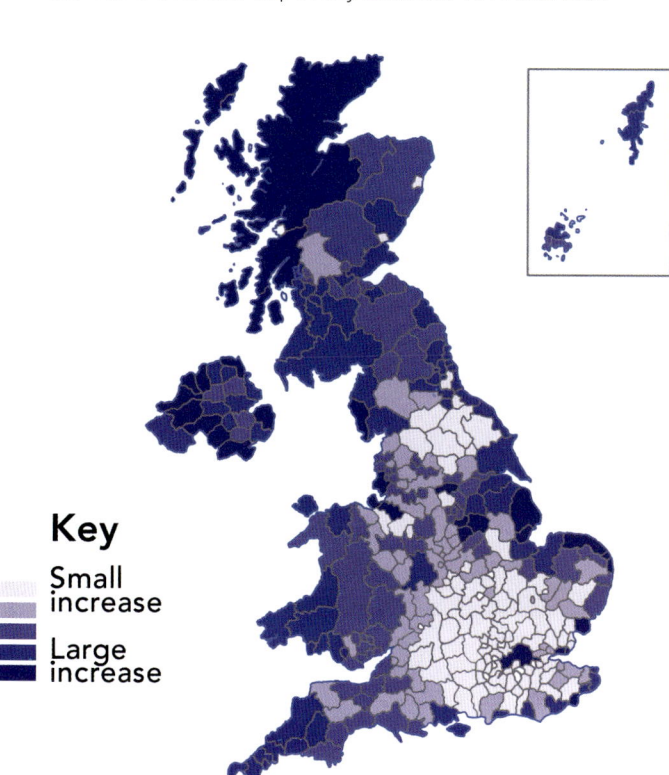

Key
- Less
- More

A choropleth map showing university graduates in 2001. The South East of England is attracting the people with degrees. The South East is rich and has lots of high-paid jobs that require high qualifications. This highly-educated population will enable more industry to locate in the South East, too

Key
- Small increase
- Large increase

A choropleth map showing changes in illness, 1991–2001. The rates of long-term illness vary dramatically between different regions. The old industrial areas in Wales, the North, and Scotland, have the largest increase in poor health. People living in the South East will live, on average, longer than people living in the North

117

How can we use our industrial heritage?

Your task is to design a development plan for Scunthorpe and submit it to the local council. The aim of the plan is to improve the environment surrounding the steelworks and create new job opportunities. This will mean land from our industrial past can become useful again in the foreseeable future.

a A map of Scunthorpe. The red area is the land to be redeveloped. It is 13km².

How can we use our industrial heritage?

Option 1: Energy from waste plant

An example of an energy from waste plant can be found on Richmond Hill, Douglas, Isle of Man. The idea behind the scheme is to prevent the Isle of Man from sending their waste to two landfill sites at Point of Ayre and Archallagan. It burns the rubbish and provides enough electricity for 4000 homes – that's 10% of the island's electricity during the day and 33% of night-time electricity. The plant has a chimney designed to look like a sail from a Viking ship.

Would energy from the waste plant be good for Scunthorpe? Could it be built within the designated redevelopment area?

"This is an excellent idea as it will reduce the amount of waste we have to put into landfill sites."
Local government officer

"The site of the new incinerator would be ideal as it would blend in with all the other chimneys and there is lots of noise and air pollution from the steelworks anyway."
Local resident

"I am worried about the possible effects of dioxins and furans."
Local resident

"We don't need an incinerator like the Isle of Man incinerator, as we can recycle our waste."
Member of a local environmental group

"There are seven times more dioxins in smoke from a barbecue than a waste incinerator. There are also safeguards in place to make sure that if pollution increases above a certain level, the plant would shut down."
Plant operator

b The energy from waste plant on the Isle of Man

How can we use our industrial heritage?

Option 2: Wind farm

"The wind farm would not create many jobs for our region."
Local council

"The noise from the wind turbines will affect our quality of life."
Local resident

c Coal Clough wind farm, Lancashire

Option 3: Theme park

"All the noise from people screaming day in day out will make our lives unbearable in our back gardens and homes."
Local resident

"I think the theme park will be excellent and it will bring in a lot of new jobs."
Local resident

"We will invest millions of pounds in landscaping the western side of the steelworks. The contaminated waste land will be renovated so that the visitors can enjoy their experience."
Theme park owner

"There are excellent links off Junction 4 of the M180. The road infrastructure could easily cope with the flow of traffic in the morning and the evening."
Local council member

"I think a new theme park, if opened, would have a dramatic effect on our theme park as visitors will pass the new theme park before they get to us on the coast. We may have to reduce our workforce."
Local competing theme park owner

d A theme park ride

How can we use our industrial heritage?

Option 4: The largest shopping complex in the North of England

"The proposed new shopping complex would probably close most of the retail parks in the area."
Local manager of out-of-town shopping complex

"Everything all under one roof, it's the future! I would enjoy going to the new shopping centre."
Local resident

"There will be a lot more jobs created in the new shopping complex. However, this may cause too much competition for our existing services, so we could also lose jobs."
Local council member

"I don't think we will be able to continue with our business in the high street. We will probably have to close down or move."
High street trader

e A large shopping complex

Option 5: Biofuel plant

Dr Rudolf Diesel built the first diesel engine in 1885 with the full intention of running it on any hydrocarbon fuel including gasoline and peanut oil. In 1912 Diesel stated, "… the use of vegetable oils for engine fuels may seem insignificant today but such oils may in the course of time become as important as petroleum and the coal tar products of present time."

f A biofuel plant

"We could grow crops such as sunflower, rapeseed or even jatropha if the climate gets a lot warmer on our set-aside fields and then send it to the biofuel plant."
Local farmer

"It would prevent us from having to use fossil fuels for transport. Biofuels are much cleaner and help reduce are carbon emissions."
Environmentalist

"It would reduce the amount of money we have to pay farmers."
Government official

"I don't like the smell of the rapeseed in the fields. It affects my breathing. We will have a massive increase in traffic into our area from lorries bringing the crops to the biofuel plant."
Local resident

"Biodiesel is completely sustainable. It is carbon neutral in that it releases the same amount of carbon dioxide into the atmosphere as it took out in the first place during the growth cycle."
Biodiesel plant spokesperson

How can we use our industrial heritage?

Option 6: New housing estate for first-time buyers

"This would be an ideal opportunity for us to own our own home. We are finding it difficult to get housing that we can afford."
Young couple, recently married

"There are already enough houses on the market within the area. Some of them have been on the market longer than six months. More new houses in this area are not required."
Local estate agent

"It is an opportunity to build new houses but I am concerned that the land will require a lot of work to remove the contaminated soil and to replace it with new top soil."
Local builder

"We have concerns about the contamination in the land from the heavy industrial activity of the past."
Member of local council

g A new housing estate made up of small houses

Option 7: New Airport

"Although there is a lot of flat land for an airport, we would need to spend a lot of money building new roads to the airport. Would we create enough demand from our region to make full use of it?"
Local council member

"We already have several airports in the region. Why do we need another one?"
Local airport manager

"I am worried about the noise and pollution caused by an airport."
Local resident

"We have access to Humberside, Doncaster, East Midlands, Sheffield and Leeds Bradford airports, and a bit further away Manchester, Liverpool and Newcastle airports. We don't need another airport."
Local resident

h Humberside airport

How can we use our industrial heritage?

Option 8: Country park golf course

A golf course

"The large holes in the ground could be used as landfill sites and then reclaimed and turned into a country park."
Local council member

"There would an excellent opportunity to create a golf course on top of the reclaimed land."
Private entrepreneur

"The area would create some new habitats and some new public footpaths for the local people."
Environmentalist

CHALLENGE

1 What are the advantages and disadvantages of each option? Don't forget to think about the site and situation of the land.
2 Write a detailed proposal to the local council stating how you would like to regenerate the land surrounding the steelworks. You could include a combination of options. Remember to fully justify your decisions and include a map showing where you would place your scheme.

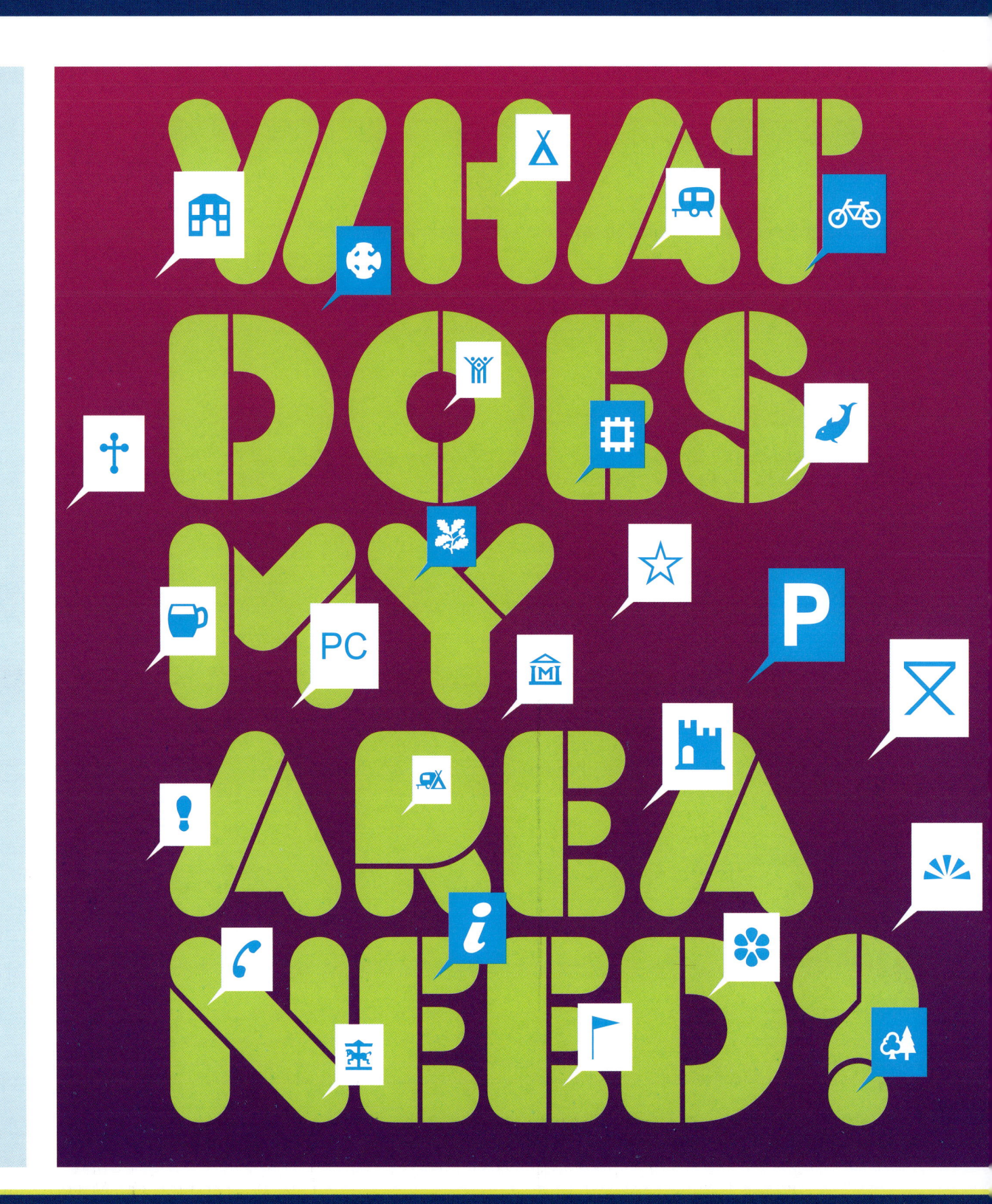

WHAT DOES MY AREA NEED?

Contents

Sue Jenkinson

1	What does my area need?	124–129
2	Why do we use different scale maps and plans?	130–133
3	How do we measure route distances and identify routes on a map?	134–135
4	How do we give directions?	136–137
5	How do we accurately locate places and features on a map?	138–139
6	How do we show the height, gradient and shape of the land?	140–143
7	How do we use photographs?	144–145
8	How do we carry out a geographical enquiry?	146–150

What does my area need?

To find out what your area really needs you will learn how to assess your surroundings, understand the differences and similarities between neighbourhoods and find out that people have different opinions about their surroundings. Planners use knowledge like this to shape the environment in which we live. You will discover and develop the map skills they use to help them, so that you can begin thinking and working as a planner does. You may even have the opportunity to make real changes to your school or your local community.

How do we view our neighbourhood?

a

b

c

d

e

What does my area need?

CHALLENGE

1. a) Which photograph is most like your neighbourhood? Why?
   b) Which photograph is least like your neighbourhood? Why?
   HINT: Think about the different aspects of a neighbourhood which support work, leisure and living.
2. a) What do you like about each photograph? Why?
   b) What do you dislike about each photograph? Why?
   By identifying what you like and dislike about each photograph you have classified, or grouped together, your observations.

What does my area need?

How do planners help to shape our neighbourhood?

I have to think about how my decisions affect people and businesses, and their environment.

Look out of the window. How has the view been affected by past planning decisions on what to build?

What a neighbourhood looks like reflects the decisions planners make about what people living and working there need. To make sure that a neighbourhood develops sustainably – that it supports not only people's needs now, but also the needs they might have in the future – planners have to understand the physical and human geography of the area.

Land is used for many things: housing, transport, recreation, shopping, education, hospitals, waste disposal and services like power, water and sewage. With all these demands on the land, planners also have to make sure that their plans care for the environment.

What does my area need?

Communities are made up of lots of people of different ages and different cultures, all with different interests. The decisions planners make play a big part in people's quality of life, so planners have to consult communities and businesses and try to make decisions which most people are happy about.

Planners have to 'read' maps and photographs. They use Geographic Information Systems (GIS) too. GIS are very powerful and can combine and display a lot of information visually, in layers.

Once planners have collected their data and presented it, they have to analyse it and interpret it to help them make their decisions.

CHALLENGE

3 a) Look out of your classroom window. What do you think about the view? To help you answer this question carry out an environmental assessment. Copy the scales below and decide where on each scale the view you are looking at should be placed.

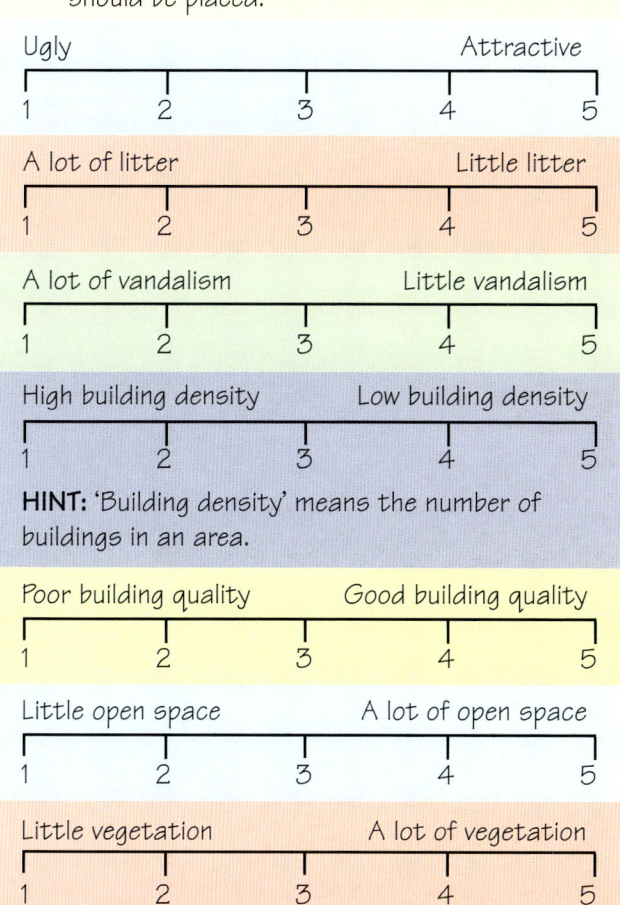

Ugly				Attractive
1	2	3	4	5

A lot of litter				Little litter
1	2	3	4	5

A lot of vandalism				Little vandalism
1	2	3	4	5

High building density				Low building density
1	2	3	4	5

HINT: 'Building density' means the number of buildings in an area.

Poor building quality				Good building quality
1	2	3	4	5

Little open space				A lot of open space
1	2	3	4	5

Little vegetation				A lot of vegetation
1	2	3	4	5

HINT: 'Vegetation' means plant life.

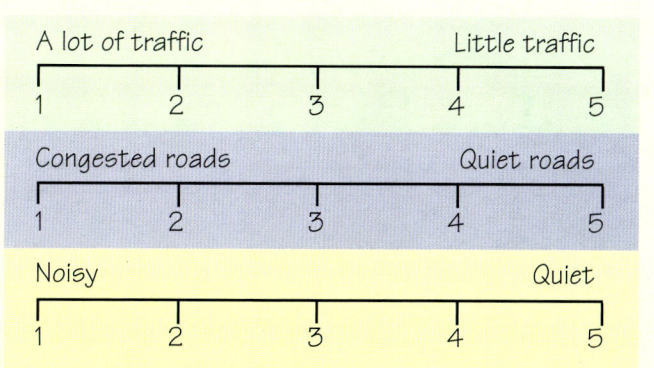

A lot of traffic				Little traffic
1	2	3	4	5

Congested roads				Quiet roads
1	2	3	4	5

Noisy				Quiet
1	2	3	4	5

HINT: You could go to http://maps.google.co.uk to find a map of the location you are looking at to help you complete the survey.

b) Which three aspects of the environmental survey received the lowest scores?

c) What are the *causes* of the lowest scores? Are the causes physical (natural) or human (man-made)?

d) What could planners do to help to improve the low scores?

4 a) Take three photographs or draw three pictures which you think best show what your neighbourhood is like.

b) Write a paragraph to accompany each photograph or drawing, explaining how and why you think it represents your neighbourhood. Use the terms from the environmental assessment to help you.

Why do we use different scale maps and plans?

We are going to find out what scale is and how using different scales in maps and plans helps us to do different things. We are also going to take our first look at a Geographical Information System (GIS).

I need to use scales to visualise how much space there is available for new developments.

This is central Cheltenham at a scale of 1:17 647

Maps a to e all show the same place, but at different **scales**.

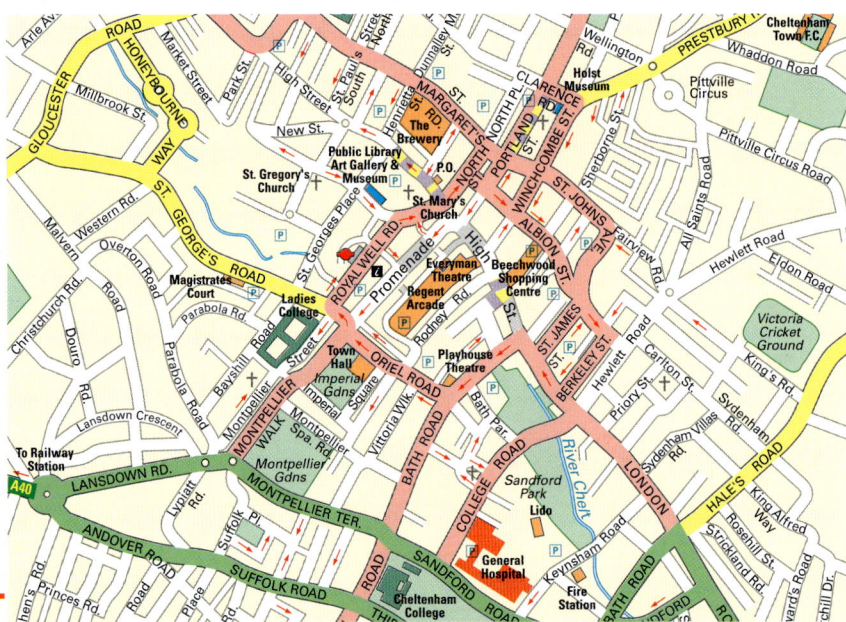

CHALLENGE

1. Look at maps a, b, c, d and e. What do you notice about the differences between the maps?
2. Which is the best map for:
   a) giving directions to someone visiting Cheltenham by car?
   b) arranging to meet a friend in town on a Saturday?
   c) explaining where Cheltenham is in the British Isles?
   d) finding a location to build a new school?

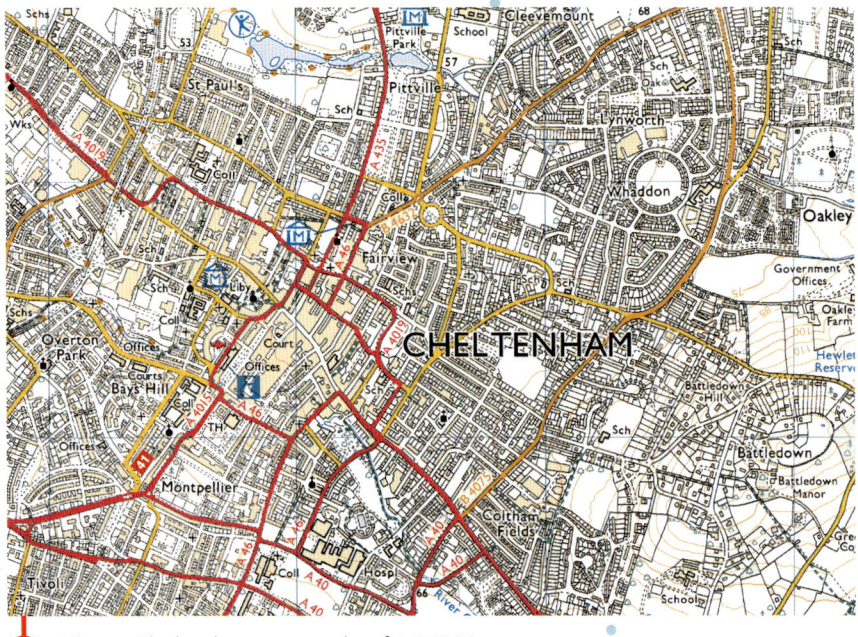

b This is Cheltenham at a scale of 1:25 000

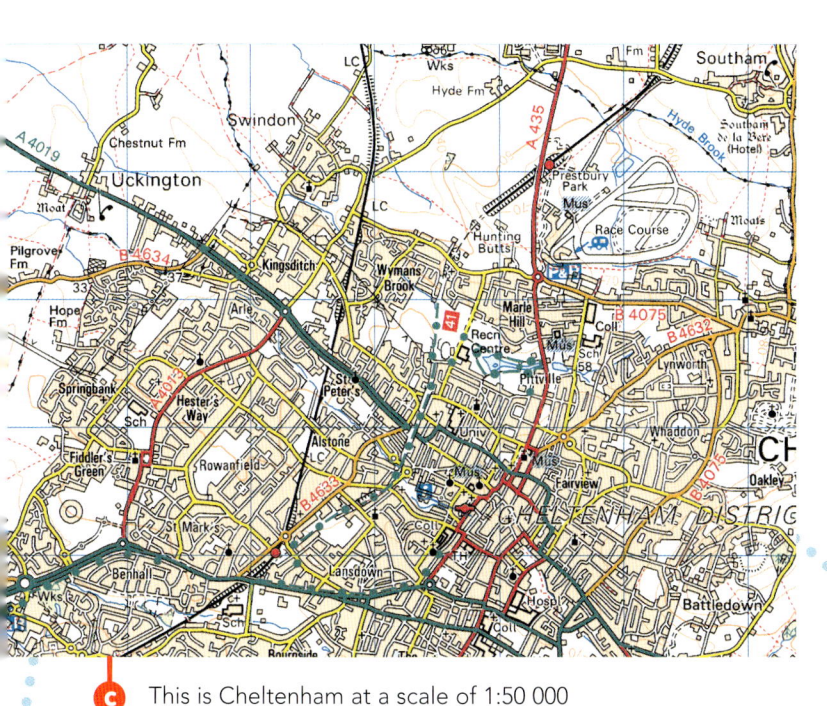

Why do we use different scale maps and plans?

c This is Cheltenham at a scale of 1:50 000

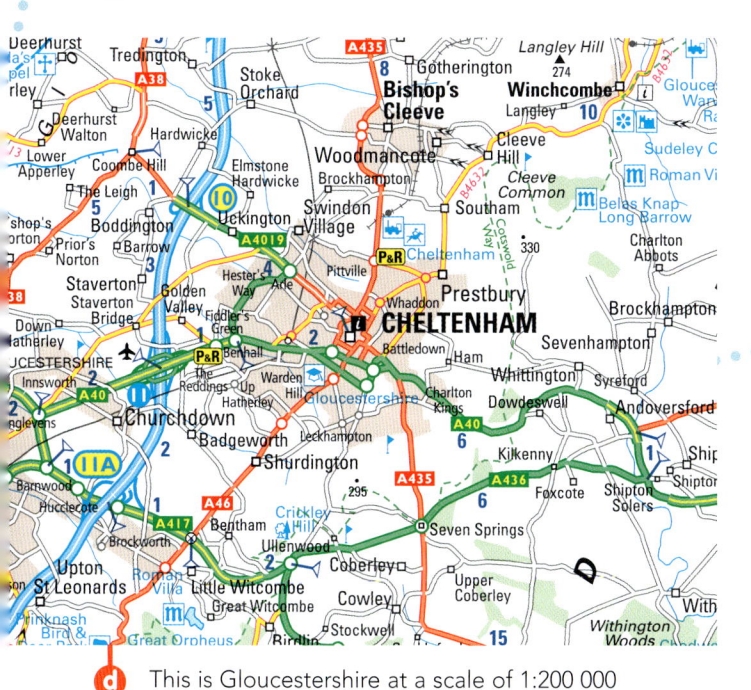

d This is Gloucestershire at a scale of 1:200 000

e This is a map of the British Isles showing Cheltenham

The maps on these pages show Cheltenham at different scales. Because we cannot show places at full size in a book we use a scale so that we can measure distances and areas on a map or plan and calculate, or work out, what they represent in real life on the ground.

On two pieces of paper the same size, a *large-scale* map would show a lot of detail but not much area, whereas a *small-scale* map would show a lot of area but not much detail.

CHALLENGE

3 Look at maps a, b, c, d and e:
   a) Which map is drawn at the largest scale?
   b) Which map is drawn at the smallest scale?
   c) Which map shows the most area and the least detail?
   d) Which map shows the most detail and the least area?

4 a) Give two examples of when you would use a map or a plan drawn at a large scale.
   b) Give two examples of when you would use a map or a plan drawn at a small scale.

Why do we use different scale maps and plans?

How do we represent distance and area on a map?

There are three main ways to show a scale:

1 As a line:
   This is called a **linear scale**.
2 As a **statement of scale**:
   2 cm represents 1 km
3 As a **ratio**:
   1:50 000
   This means that 1 unit on the map represents 50 000 of the *same units* on the ground.

GIS and scales

These two examples (f and g) show how a planner might use maps at different scales in a GIS.

Notice the different layers of information which can be added.

A planner can use the detailed information on the shape of individual buildings and plots of land to calculate their area.

A GIS showing data at a scale of 1:1250

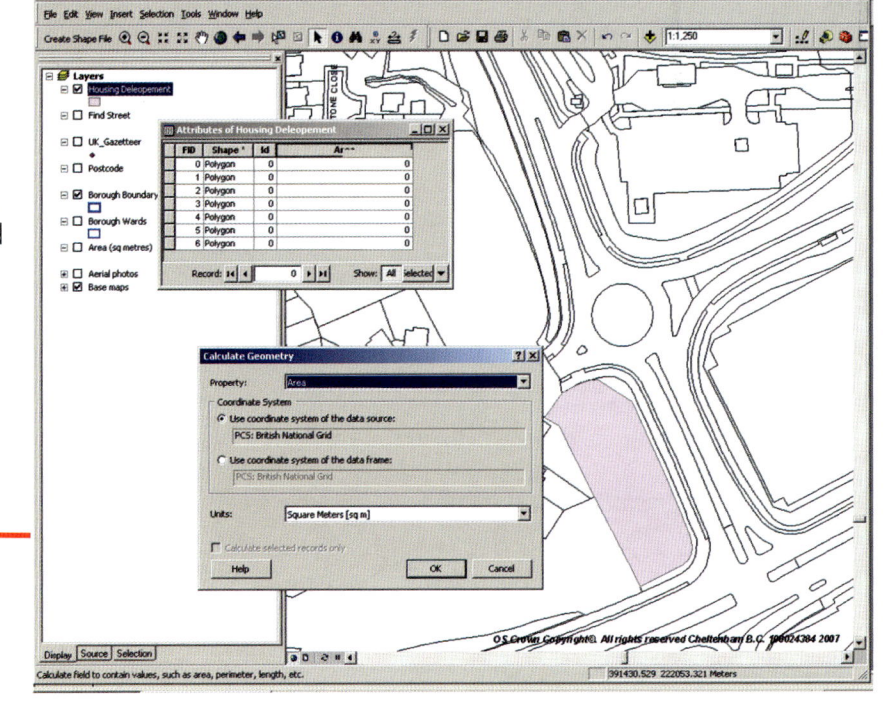

CHALLENGE

5 These three lines are drawn to a scale of 1cm to 20m. What distance do they represent in real life?
   a) _____
   b) _____
   c) _____

6 Draw a linear scale to represent the following distances at a scale of 2cm to 1km:
   a) 4km   b) 2.5km   c) 1.25km.
   Remember to label the lines. The real distances the scales represent should be labelled above the line and the distance on the map should be labelled below the line.

7 Look at Map c on page 131. It is a 1:50 000 scale map. This means that 1cm on the map represents 50 000cm or 0.5km on the ground.
   a) How many kilometres is it from the east (left) of the map to the west (right) of the map?
   b) How many kilometres is it from the south (bottom) of the map to the north (top) of the map?

8 If a map has a scale of 1:25 000 what distance in real life does each of the following represent:
   a) 1cm   b) 4cm   c) 8cm?

Why do we use different scale maps and plans?

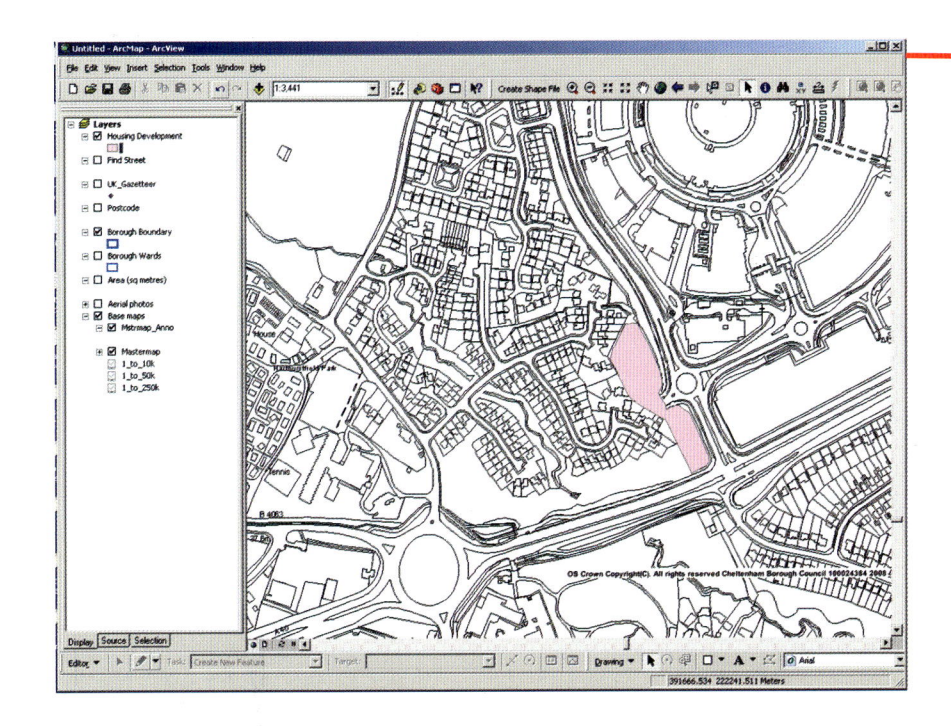

g The same GIS showing data at a scale of 1:3441

9 Using a 1:25 000 map of your local area:
   a) Find places which are 1cm, 4cm and 8cm apart.
   b) Use your home or school as a starting point and measure 2cm, 4cm and 8cm in a straight line. Where do you end up?

10 a) What is the scale of map f shown as a ratio?
   b) How many centimetres represents 1km on this scale?

11 This is the top of a desk drawn to scale, 1cm on the plan represents 10cm in real life.

   a) Draw a copy of the desk in your exercise book to the exact scale.
   b) Add a statement of scale.
   c) Draw a linear scale to go with the plan.
   d) Show the scale as a ratio.
   e) At the same scale, draw your exercise book, this textbook and your pencil case on the plan. Measure each item in real life, convert the measurements to the same scale as the plan and then draw them on your plan.
   f) What is the area of the desk in real life? Multiply the length by the width to find out the answer. Remember that the units will be m^2.

12 Create a scale plan of a room of your choice, remembering that the plan will only show the view from above – the bird's eye view – of the items in the room.
   a) Measure each item in the room.
   b) Choose a suitable scale and show this on your plan as a statement, a linear scale and a ratio.
   c) Add a key and a title to your plan.
   d) State the area of your chosen room.

How do we measure route distances and identify routes on a map?

There is a big difference between **straight-line distances**, distances which can be measured by placing a ruler between two points on a map, and **route distances**, which bend to follow roads and footpaths. Planners use route distances to work out how long it takes people to travel to places and to make sure that routes to school are safe.

a How to measure a route distance using a piece of paper

Measuring a route distance

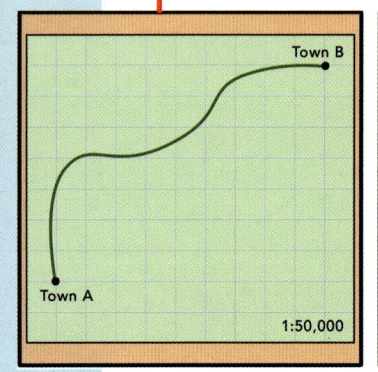

Do you want to measure the distance by road between Town A and Town B? Don't know how to because the road isn't straight?

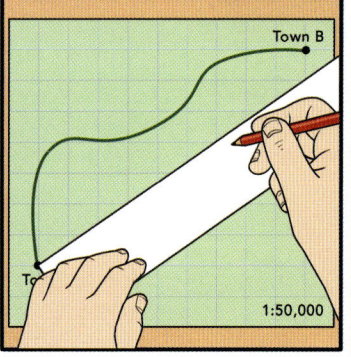

Use a piece of paper! Place the corner of the piece of paper at the beginning of the route…

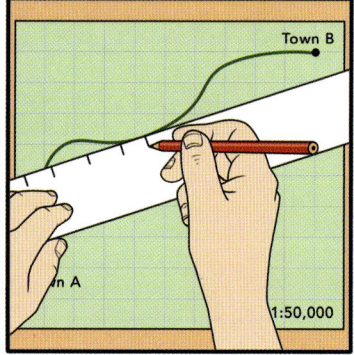

…and, at each change of direction in the road mark the paper and pivot it to measure the next section of road.

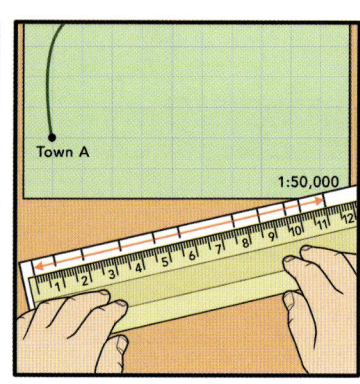

Then you measure the distance between the first mark on your piece of paper and the last mark on your piece of paper and work out the distance in real life using the scale on the map. It's easy!

CHALLENGE

1. a) Measure the straight-line distance between Town A and Town B on map b.
   b) Using the scale, work out the straight-line distance between Town A and Town B in real life.
2. a) Measure the route distance between Town A and Town B on map b.
   b) Using the scale, work out the route distance between Town A and Town B in real life.
3. Look back at map c on page 9:
   a) What is the straight line distance between Kingsditch and Hyde Farm?
   b) What is the route distance, by road, between Kingsditch and Hyde Farm?

   HINT: Don't forget to give the distances measured on the map (in centimetres) and the distances in real life (in kilometres).

b

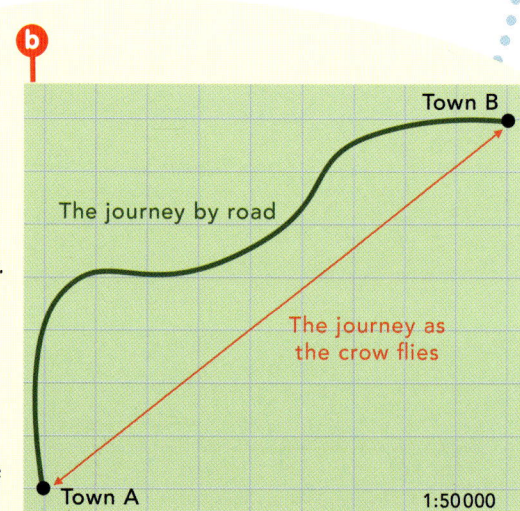

How do we measure route distances and identify routes on a map?

How do we measure safe routes on a map?

We know how important exercise is as part of a healthy lifestyle, and cycling or walking to school can provide us with daily exercise. But we have to take care on the roads, to keep ourselves safe and make sure we are not a danger to others. We need to be observant and to act sensibly.

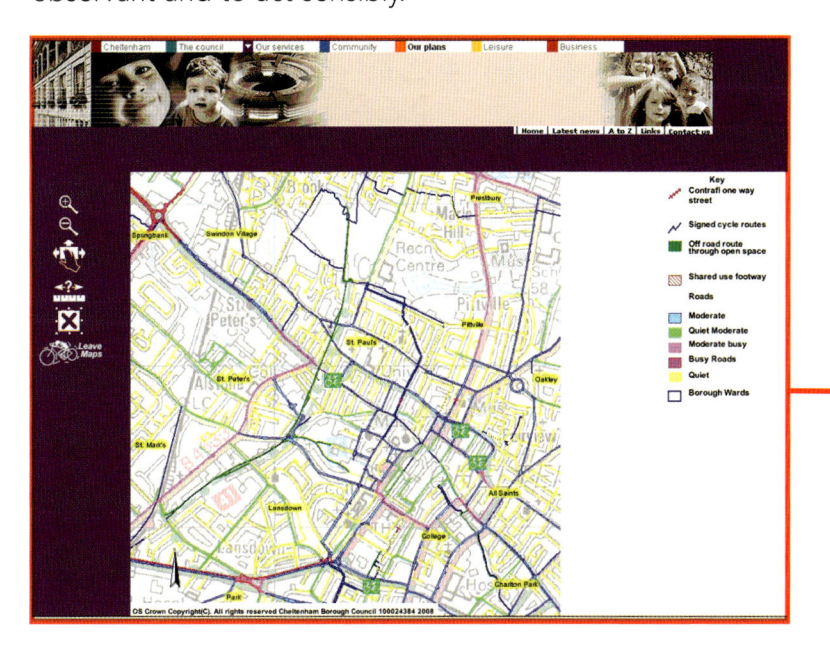

C On this map, cycle routes have been classified, according to the degree of skill needed to cycle on them. It is an interactive map and allows you to measure route distances. It is another example of a GIS at work

CHALLENGE

4 What factors influence the safety of a route?
5 How can the safety of a route be improved? List as many ways as you can think of.
6 a) Measure the straight-line distance of your journey to school using a map of your local area.
   b) Measure the route distance of your journey to school using a map of your local area.
   HINT: Be as accurate as you can, and don't forget to give the distances measured on the map (in centimetres) and the distances in real life (in kilometres).
7 a) Draw a map of your route to school. It has to fit in the space you have available, so choose your scale carefully and don't forget to show the scale on your map.
   b) Colour-code your route to show road safety, using different colours for sections which you consider to be:
   - Quiet
   - Moderately quiet
   - Moderate.
   - Moderately busy
   - Busy

   You may find that you do not use all five categories, but you must create a key so that anyone looking at the map will know what the different colours you do use mean.
8 How safe is your route to school?

How do we give directions?

Being able to give directions is an important skill. So is being able to read a map and work out where you are. Without knowing how to give accurate **compass directions** and make use of a key to give clear route descriptions you will find it difficult to get to places you have never been to before and to help others get to where they want to go.

I need to know in which direction new developments will be facing because it will affect how much sun they receive and how much shade they will create.

Giving directions

This is a sixteen point compass:

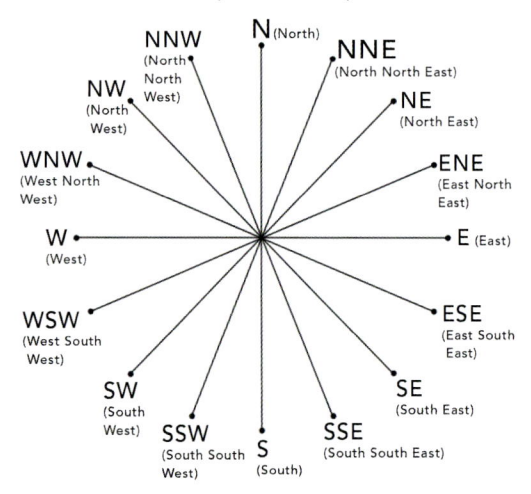

[Sixteen point compass diagram with points: N (North), NNE (North North East), NE (North East), ENE (East North East), E (East), ESE (East South East), SE (South East), SSE (South South East), S (South), SSW (South South West), SW (South West), WSW (West South West), W (West), WNW (West North West), NW (North West), NNW (North North West)]

A ───────► B
If you are travelling from A to B, you are travelling East.

A ◄─────── B
If you are travelling from B to A, you are travelling West.

a The scale of this map is 1:50 000

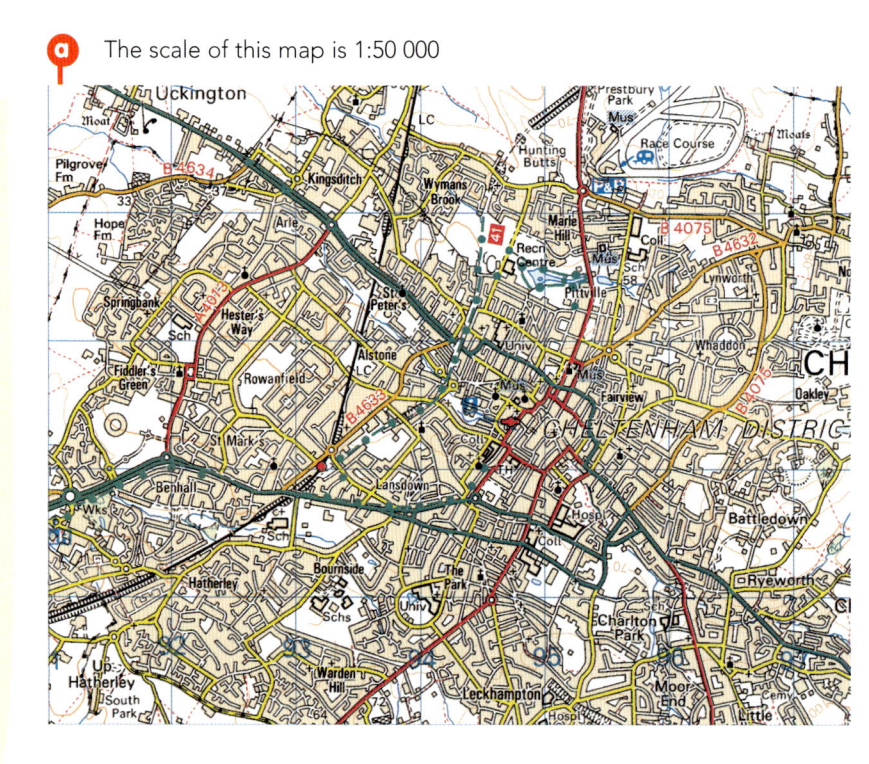

CHALLENGE

1. Look at map a and give the direction you would be travelling in if you were going:
   a) from Fairview to Charlton Park
   b) to Oakley from Fiddler's Green
   c) from Warden Hill to Kingsditch
   d) to Springbank from Pittville.
2. It is important to know where North is on a map. Add a compass to your 'My route to school' map to show where North lies.
3. How far and in which directions do you travel to get to school? Using your 'My route to school map' and your local map, write a brief set of instructions on how to get from your house to your school using only distances and directions.

How do we give directions?

> I have to be able to identify features and give exact location references of current and proposed developments.

How do we show features on a map?

Symbols are used on maps to help us identify features. The symbols used are shown in the **map key** and can help us work out where we are. Think about the many different symbols, such as road signs, that we see around us. They are there to give us information. In a similar way, a map key provides us with information using symbols.

P	Parking
PC	Public Convenience
🚐⛺	Camping and caravan site
✤	Cadw (Welsh heritage)
▦	English Heritage property

b A selection of map symbols. A full key for a 1:25 000 Ordnance Survey map can be found on the inside front cover of this book

CHALLENGE

4 a) Think about the features which you pass or which have an impact on your journey to school and add them to the key of your 'My route to school' map. These features might be buildings with particular functions, like a library, or a landmark, like a town square or a park.

You might use a symbol like this 🚦 to show a set of traffic lights.

Or a symbol like this |||| to show a zebra crossing.

b) Now, add the symbols from your key to your map.

5 a) Look back at the description of your route to school that you completed for Challenge 3 and re-write it making use of the information about features which you have added to your map.

b) How does this new information improve your description?

How do we accurately locate places and features on a map?

We now know how important it is to be able to give directions and identify symbols on a map. But how do we explain to other people which part of a big map they should look at to find what they are looking for? We use four and six figure grid references.

Using grid references to find out where something is

Grid lines divide maps into squares (see map b). Each line is numbered and these numbers are used to give a **grid reference**. If you tell someone the grid reference they will be able to work out exactly where on the map to look.

We can give a four figure grid reference for a whole square, or a six figure grid reference for a specific point within a square.

Four figure grid references

To give a grid reference for the shaded square in diagram a:

1. Start at the bottom left-hand corner of the map.
2. Read along the bottom of the map from left to right until you come to the number on the left-hand side of the square you want to reference, in this case 16. Because you are reading towards the East these references are called **Eastings**.
3. Read up the side of the map from the bottom to the top until you come to the number at the bottom of the square you want to reference, in this case 43. You are reading towards the North so references are called **Northings**.
4. Combine the two references into a four figure grid reference: 1643.

Six figure grid references

Imagine that each grid square is divided into tenths as in diagram a. (It would make the map too difficult to read if these were actually included.) Follow the same procedure to give a four figure grid reference, adding in the tenths.

The campsite has a six figure grid reference of 17**8**44**6**. It is 8 tenths further east of line 17 and it is 6 tenths further north of line 44.

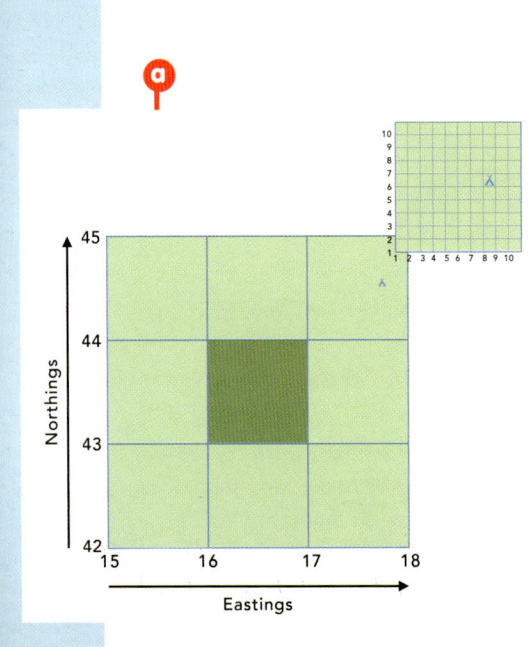

Scale 1:25 000

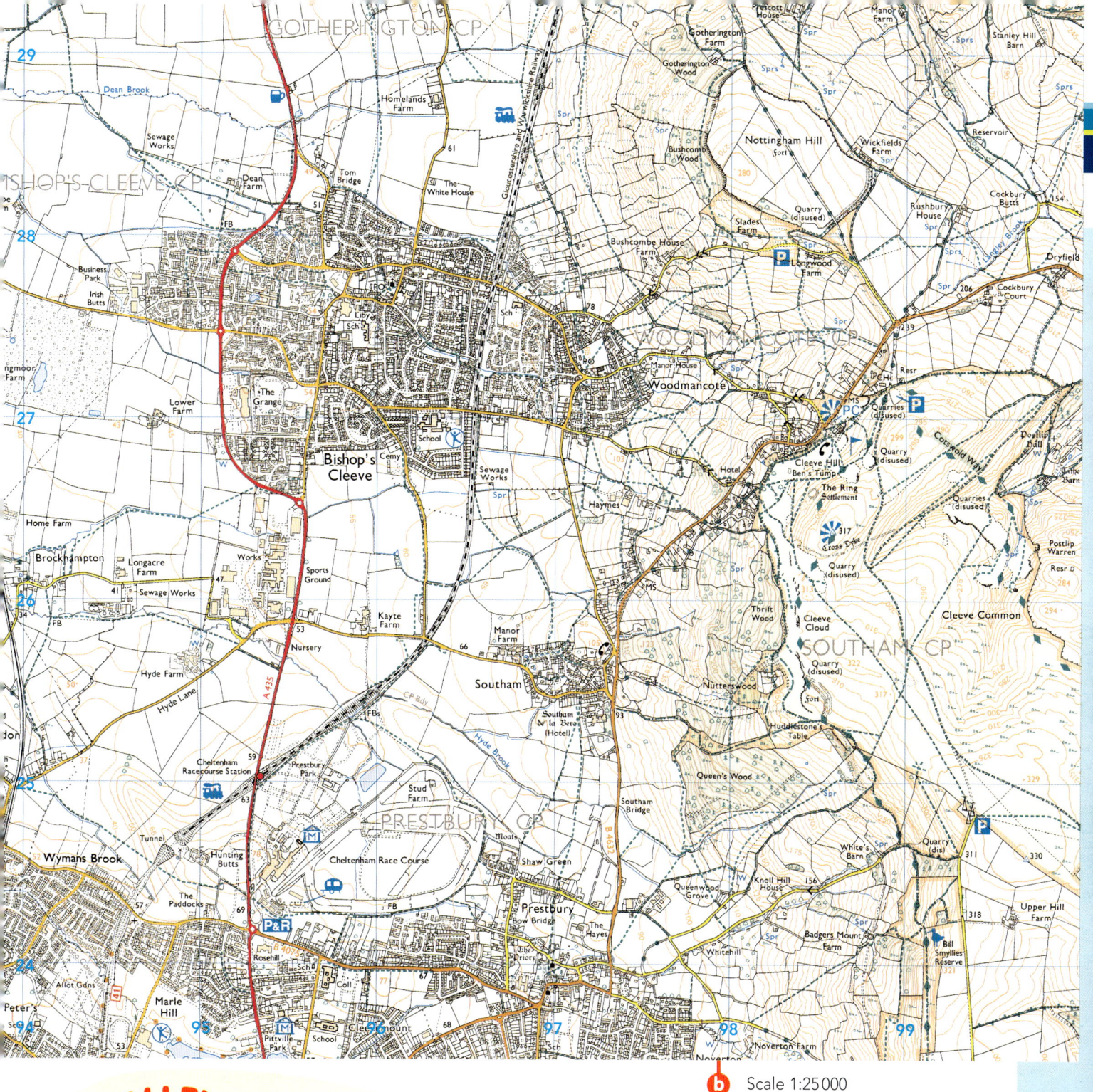

CHALLENGE

Look at map b and the key on the inside front cover of this book.

1. Give the four figure grid references for the squares containing the following:
   a) Queen's Wood   b) Nottingham Hill
   c) The Grange.

2. Give the six figure grid references for the following features:
   a) the public house on the A435
   b) the sports centre in Bishop's Cleeve
   c) the museum on Cheltenham race course.

3. What is the name of the National trail or recreational path which runs through squares 9824, 9825, 9826 and 9827?

4. Name the feature at each of the following locations:
   a) 962277   b) 956262   c) 969278.

5. Which type of vegetation is found in Thrift Wood, which can be found between 9825 and 9826?

How do we show the height, gradient and shape of the land?

As you move across the land there are changes in shape: it rises and falls. It is important that maps show these changes, so that they accurately represent the features of the landscape in front of you.

If I am going to choose a location for a wind farm, I need to know how high and how steep the land is.

How high is the land?

On an OS map **contour lines** are used to show the height of the land above sea level. A contour line joins together all the points of equal height. It is important to work out the **contour interval** (the difference in height between contour lines) before using a map.

a A contour line joins together all the points at 50m above sea level

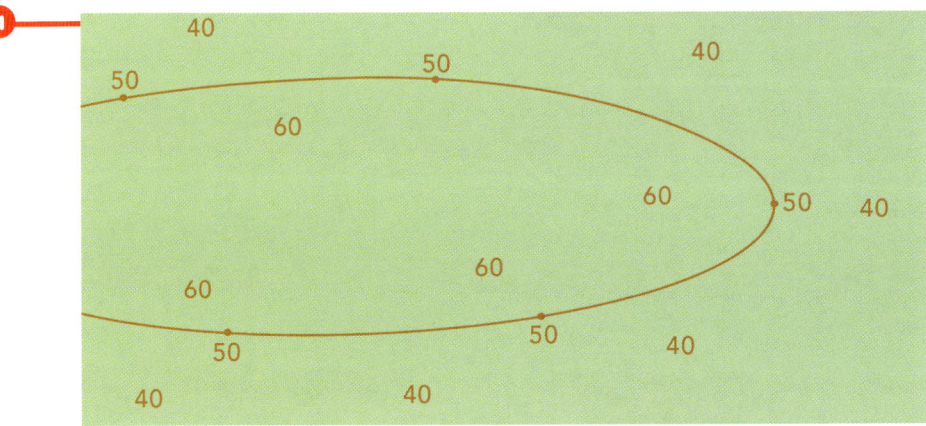

Another way of showing the height of the land is with a **spot height**. The height is shown in metres.

b This map extract shows a spot height of 282m. Can you identify any other spot heights?

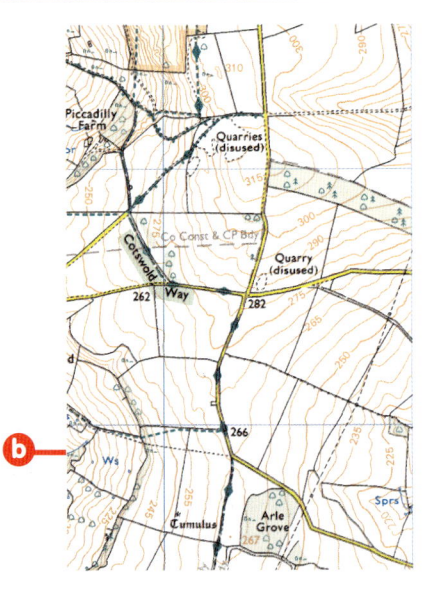

How do we show the height, gradient and shape of the land?

How steep is the land?

The spacing of the contours shows how steep the land is: what the gradient of the land is.

Closely placed contours show us that the land increases in height over a short distance, so it is steep. It has a steep gradient. **c**

Widely placed contours show us that the land increases in height over a longer distance, so it is gently sloping. It has a gentle gradient. **d**

What shape is the land?

The pattern of the contour lines shows the *shape* of the land.

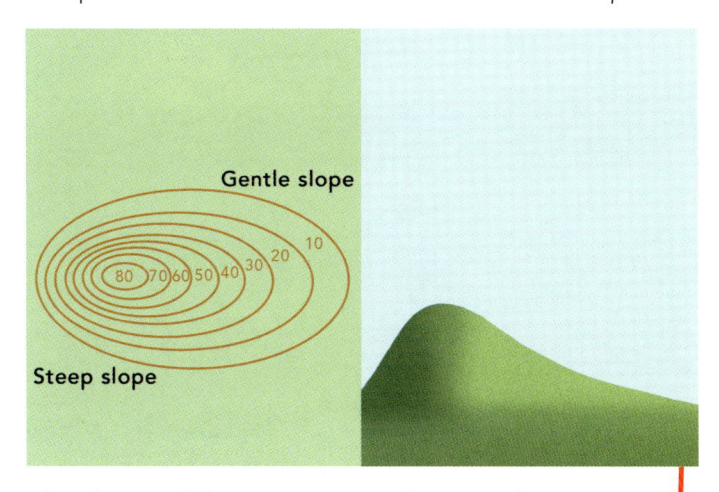

The shape of these contours show us that this feature is a hill and the spacing of the contours shows us that it has a steep slope on the western side and a gentle slope on the eastern side. **e**

The shape of these contours show us that this feature is a hill and the even spacing of the contours show us that it has uniform slopes. **f**

How do we show the height, gradient and shape of the land?

CHALLENGE

1. Add information on gradient to your 'My route to school' map by labelling the sections which are 'steep', 'gentle' or almost 'flat'. Think about how easy or difficult it is to walk along different sections.

2. Look at the four map extracts a, b, c and d, each showing different physical features. For each map:
   a) give the height of the highest point of the land
   b) note down any spot heights you can see.

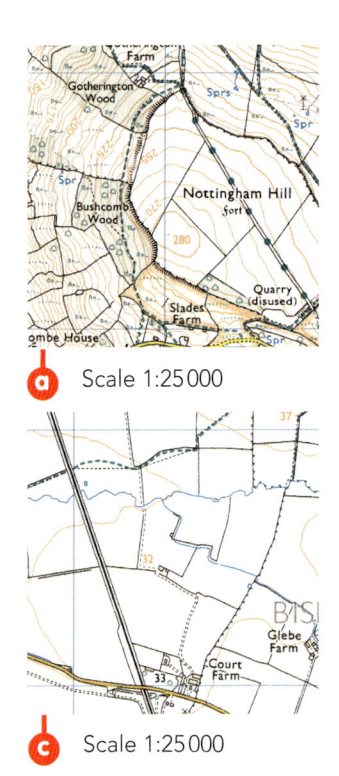

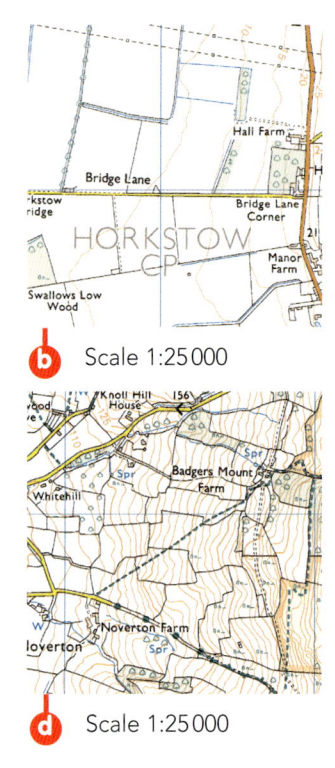

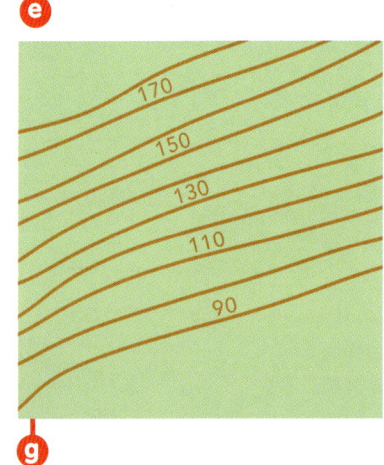

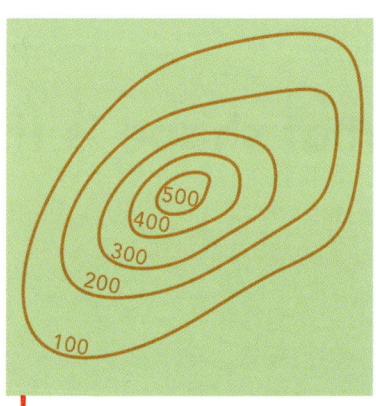

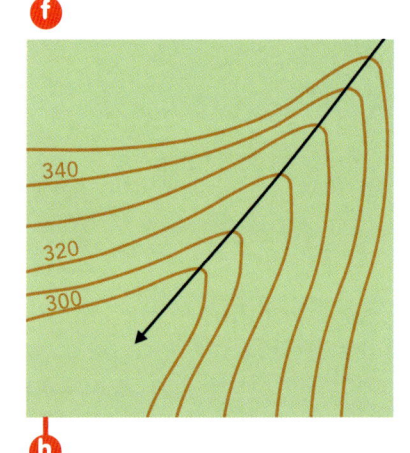

a) Scale 1:25 000

b) Scale 1:25 000

c) Scale 1:25 000

d) Scale 1:25 000

CHALLENGE

3. Which of the four contour patterns e to h represents:
   a) a hill?
   b) a valley?
   c) steep land?
   d) flat land?

142

How do we show the height, gradient and shape of the land?

Drawing an accurate cross-section

A **cross-section** shows us what land would look like if we could slice through it. Cross-sections help planners choose suitable locations for new developments.

STEP 1

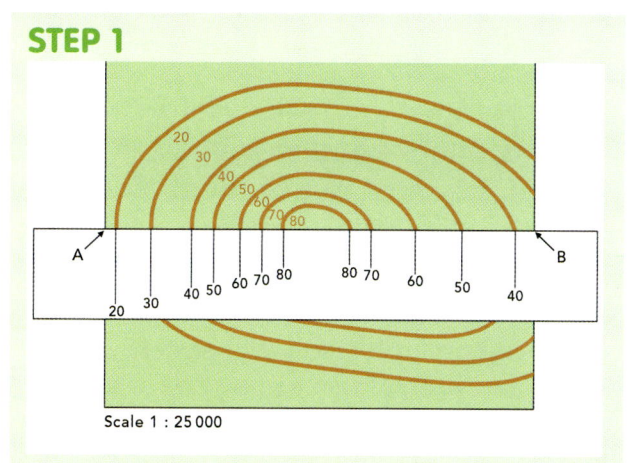

Scale 1 : 25 000

Place a piece of paper along the line of cross-section and mark each contour line.

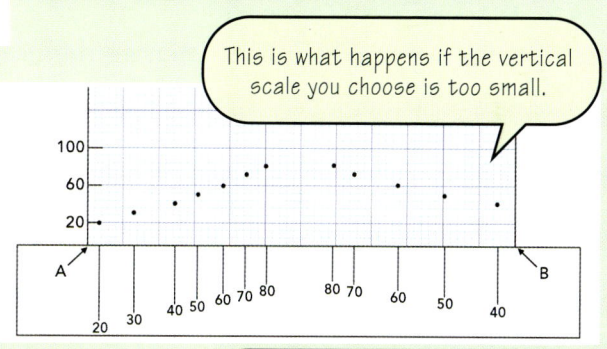

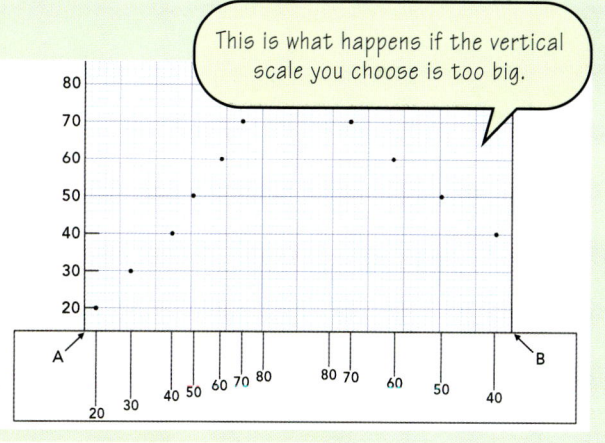

STEP 2

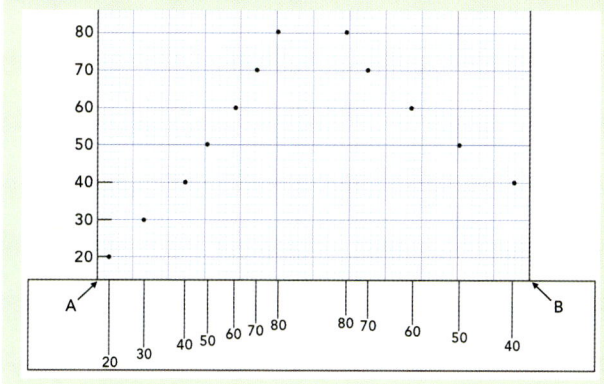

This is what happens if the vertical scale you choose is too small.

This is what happens if the vertical scale you choose is too big.

Place a strip of paper on a piece of graph paper and mark the heights on a vertical scale. Make sure you choose an appropriate vertical scale for your cross-section, otherwise a gentle hill can look like a steep mountain.

STEP 3

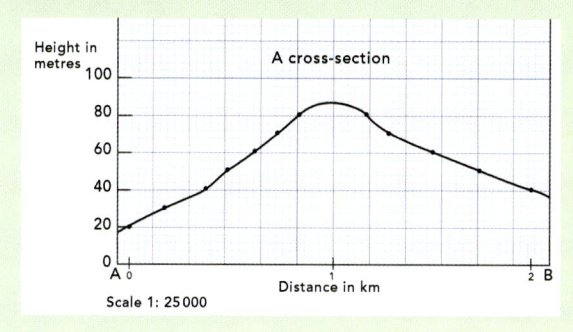

A cross-section

Scale 1: 25 000

Join the points together. Label your cross-section.

CHALLENGE

4 a) Draw a cross-section showing the land between 955263 and 986264 on the map on page 139.
   HINT: Don't forget to label your axes and give your drawing a title.
   b) Label the steep land and the flat land on your cross-section.
5 Draw a cross-section from your local area map.

How do we use photographs?

Photographs are really useful tools. And, like all tools, there are things you can learn to make sure you get the most out of them. For example, do you know the difference between an aerial photograph and an oblique aerial photograph? Do you know how to draw an annotated sketch based on a photograph? You will soon…

I need to know what an area looks like. Photographs can help me choose the best place for a new development.

Different views

Photographs can be taken from the ground, showing a ground view. Photographs can also be taken from the air. They can show a vertical aerial view, which means the photograph has been taken from directly above. Or they can show an oblique aerial view, which means the photograph has been taken from above but at an angle.

A planner can use vertical and oblique aerial views to see what an area looks like before any new developments are planned. They can also use computer software to see what an area will look like once the planned development has been built.

a A photograph of the Promenade in Cheltenham taken from the ground

b A vertical aerial photograph of Pershore

c An oblique aerial photograph of the Promenade in Cheltenham

d The vertical aerial view in b with possible new roads added to it

How do we use photographs?

Drawing an annotated sketch of a photograph

Photographs can be used as a base from which to draw an annotated (labelled) sketch.

e A photograph of Cheltenham race course taken from Cleeve Hill

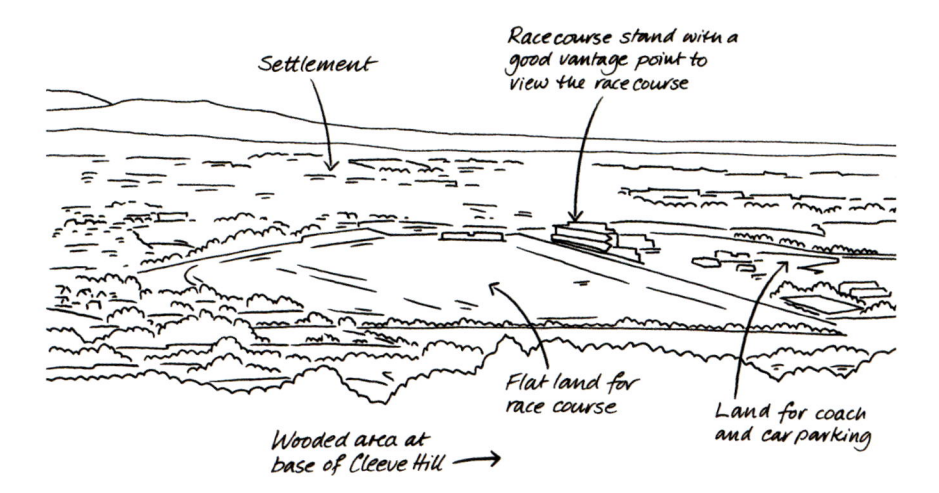

f An annotated sketch of photograph e

CHALLENGE

1 Choose a photograph from this book **or** a photograph of your local area or a place you have visited and make an annotated sketch of it, following the stages below.

STEP 1
Draw a box for your sketch. It might be the same size as the photograph or enlarged or reduced in scale.

STEP 2
Draw the outline of the main features, such as the roads, rivers and significant boundaries.

STEP 3
Include other features, such as buildings, to add more detail.

STEP 4
Label the sketch. What you choose to label will depend on the purpose of the sketch. Is it to show why a particular location has been chosen for a new building? Do you want to focus on physical geographical features? Or human geographical features? The labels shown in f focus on land uses around the racecourse.

How do we carry out a geographical enquiry?

You've learned a lot about your local area and how to create and interpret maps, plans and photographs. Now it is time to put all this knowledge and these skills to work. It is time to carry out a **geographical enquiry**: to think like a planner and find out what your area needs.

> I have to carry out local investigations in an ordered way. I have to collect information to find out what people think. Then I need to present that information clearly so that communities know what is being planned and how it might affect them.

CHALLENGE

1. Carry out a geographical enquiry into the viability of a proposal to change something within your school or local area.

    When something is viable it means that it is possible from all perspectives. You are going to find out if your proposed change is something that will be welcomed by the majority of people whom it will affect and if it is affordable. It is up to you to decide what the change you want to propose is, but it should be something that you think would improve your school or local area and make it more sustainable.

    Use the five stages of the enquiry process to structure your enquiry:

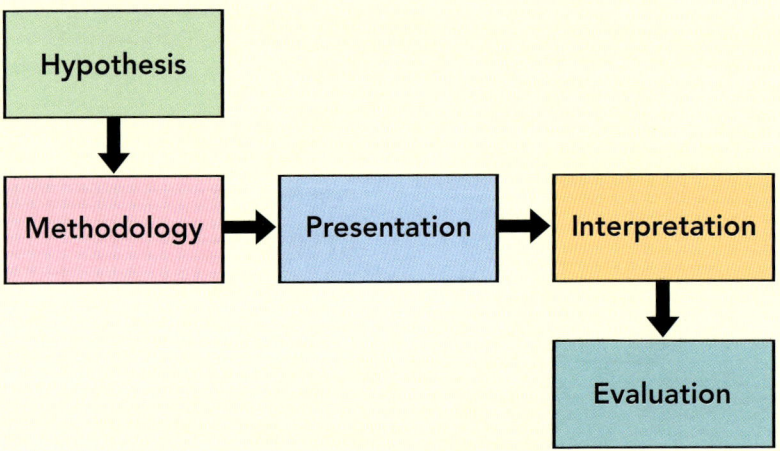

    Hypothesis → Methodology → Presentation → Interpretation → Evaluation

2. Prepare a five minute presentation to the rest of the class to explain your geographical enquiry and how you are going to use the results to support your proposal for change.

    From your idea for a proposed change, you should produce a hypothesis, which is a statement linked to your idea, which you can investigate to discover whether it is true or not.

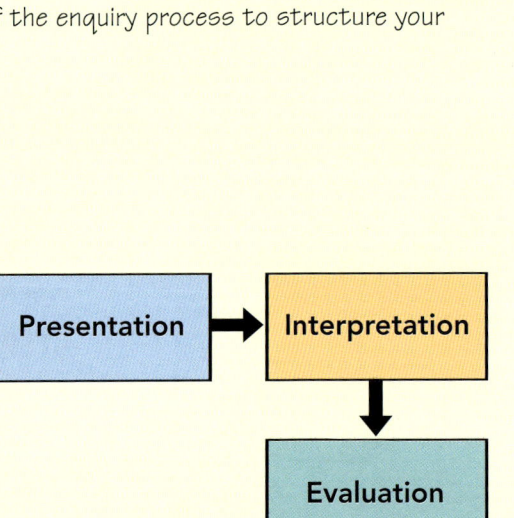

How do we carry out a geographical enquiry?

The enquiry process

Stage 1: Hypothesis

Decide on your proposal and state clearly what you intend to investigate.

Think back to the environmental assessment that you carried out. Could you develop one of the aspects you identified as needing improvement into a proposal for change? For example, you might have decided that your local park is untidy and full of rubbish, so your proposal could focus on who uses the park and how they could be encouraged to tidy up after themselves.

Your hypothesis might be:
'Providing extra litter bins and improving park facilities will encourage people using the park to keep it tidy.'

Or you might feel that the number of cars dropping students off at school in the morning and picking them up in the evening is too high; that it is dangerous for pedestrians. So you might develop a proposal to encourage more students to walk, cycle or travel to school by public transport, and decide that you are going to investigate whether or not this is viable.

Or, in your school grounds, you might identify the need for more litter bins, more benches or more shade. You might want to improve a neglected area, create a wildlife habitat, decide where to site a new bike shed or even build an extension to house purpose-built geography classrooms.

How do we carry out a geographical enquiry?

Stage 2: Methodology

Once you have decided on your enquiry you need to work out how you are going to collect the information you need to find out if your proposal is viable.

Methods of data collection that you could use include:

- administering a questionnaire
- finding or drawing a map of the area
- taking measurements
- making field sketches
- taking photographs
- using secondary sources such as the Internet or local newspapers

If you are using secondary sources you need to identify any bias in the opinions expressed. Look carefully at when the data was collected or the newspaper was written. Ask yourself who presented the information and why. Consider whether or not it is accurate, and presents a fair and balanced representation of views.

If you decided in Stage 1 that you want to try and reduce the number of students travelling to school in cars, then you need to find out *how* people travel to school at the moment and *why* they use that method of transport. To do this you could administer a questionnaire.

A questionnaire is a series of short questions that you ask people to obtain information. When you are writing a questionnaire – or working out any other data collection method – you must think ahead and consider people's possible answers.

For example, the following question will be difficult for a student who walks for ten minutes before travelling on a bus for twenty minutes to answer:

> Do you travel to school by:
>
> a) foot? ☐
>
> b) bus? ☐
>
> c) bicycle? ☐
>
> d) car? ☐

It might be better to ask:

> What is the main method of transport you use to get to school:
>
> a) walk? ☐
>
> b) bus? ☐
>
> c) bicycle? ☐
>
> d) car? ☐
>
> e) other? ☐
> Please give details
> _____

Stage 3: Presentation

Once you have collected your data you need to present it.

Here are some examples of ways in which you can present data:

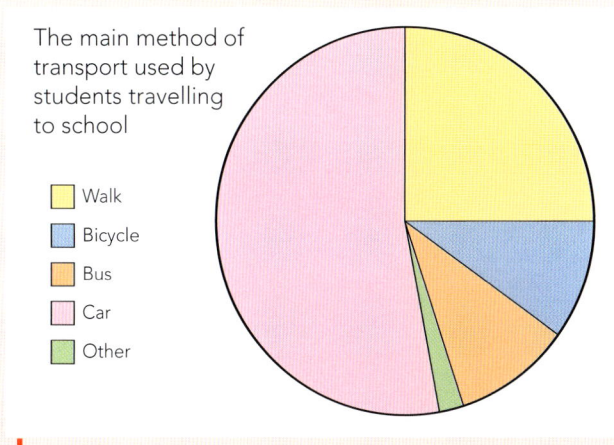

The main method of transport used by students travelling to school

- Walk
- Bicycle
- Bus
- Car
- Other

The main reasons students in Year 7 give for the method of transport they use to travel to school

(bar chart: Number of Students vs Reasons — Lives close to school, Lives far from school, Only method of transport available, Safest method of transport available, Parents' decision)

a This is a pie chart

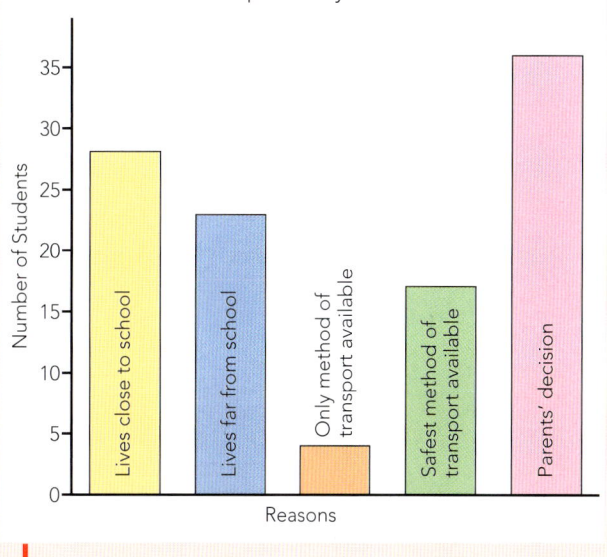

b This is a bar chart

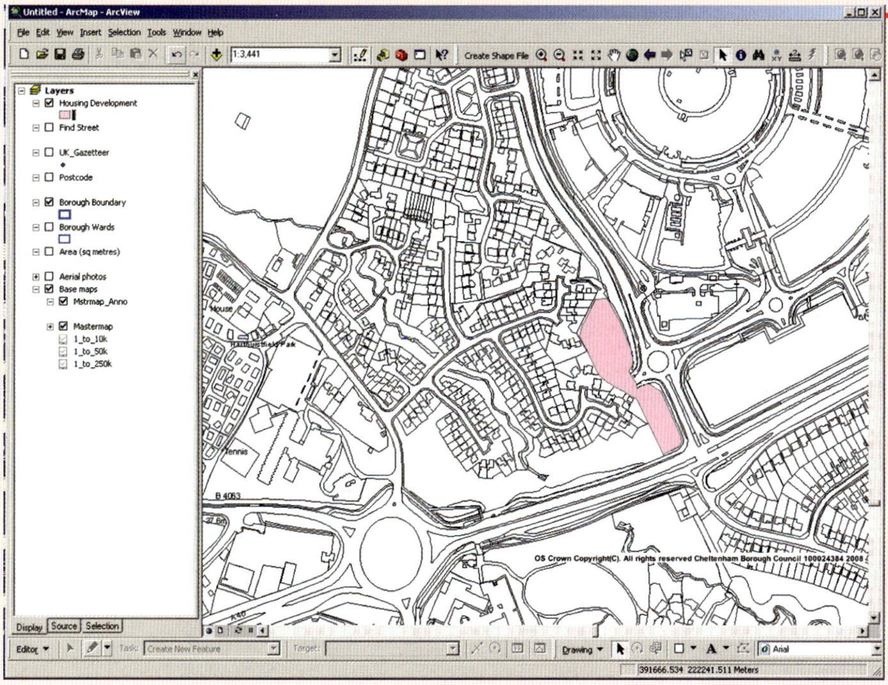

c A map shown through a GIS

You could also use text, data tables, photographs and sketches of photographs.

How do we carry out a geographical enquiry?

Stage 4: Interpretation

When you have collected and presented your data, you need to *analyse* and *interpret* it. You need to look at the information and data and ask yourself:

> What conclusions can I draw from my results?

> What do my results tell me?

Stage 5: Evaluation

This is where you ask yourself questions about the data you have collected, the results you have presented and the conclusions you have drawn.

> Were my methods of data collection accurate?

> Have I presented my results clearly and accurately?

> If not, why were they inaccurate?

> How would I change them if I did this enquiry again?

> Are my conclusions valid?

> Do I have all the information I need to support my proposal? What else do I need to know?

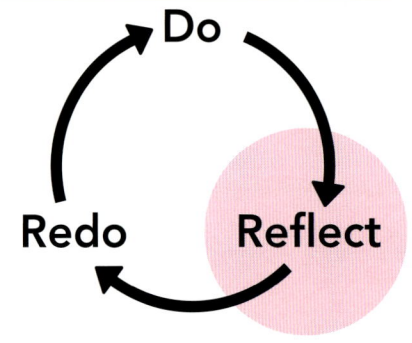

It is important to evaluate your geographical enquiry.

Success criteria levelling grid

Action	Level
I have suggested a geographical question and have used different geographical skills to answer it. I have used data I have collected myself as well as information from other sources and have used geographical terms in my presentation.	4
As Level 4 and: I have suggested geographical questions and have used different geographical skills relevant to my enquiry. I have been careful to think about different views and opinions. I have drawn conclusions and used graphs and geographical terms.	5
As Level 5 and: I have taken care to carry out my investigation in a logical order. I have used appropriate methods of presentation. I have used different sources of information and have explained where I think they may be biased. My conclusions are based on the information I have collected and I have used geographical terminology appropriately.	6
As Level 6 and: I have planned my investigation very thoroughly using my own ideas and have a range of geographical skills. I have questioned the evidence and have explained differences in opinions and bias. I have used geographical terminology accurately and have provided evidence to support my conclusions.	7
As Level 7 and: I have chosen my own question to investigate and have effectively sequenced the enquiry. I have used a wide range of skills very effectively and accurately. I have questioned sources of evidence before I have used them. I have provided a lot of evidence to support the conclusions I have made.	8
As Level 8 and: I have carried out my own enquiries at different scales. I have been careful to evaluate sources of evidence before I have used them. I have provided detailed evidence to support my conclusions, which I have accurately explained.	Exceptional performance

WHY ARE SOME COUNTRIES DRY WHILST OTHERS FLOOD?

Contents

Dawn Price

1	Why does the rain never stop?	154–155
2	Where does a river start and where does it go?	156–157
3	What happens in a river?	158–161
4	What does a river do to the landscape?	162–163
5	What is a flood?	164–167
6	Why are some countries wetter than others?	168–169
7	What is a drought?	170–173
8	Why are some countries drier than others?	174–177
9	What are NGOs and what do they do?	178–179

Why does the rain never stop?

Have you ever thought about how water gets to the tap? Or why there is so much water in the oceans? And why sometimes the rain keeps falling and falling? In this lesson we will find out what the water cycle is, how it works and how humans can affect it.

What is water like?

Before we think about how water moves, we need to think about what it is actually like. A water molecule is made up of oxygen and hydrogen. Its chemical formula is written like this: H_2O. Water exists in three states:

- **liquid water** (rivers, streams and oceans)
- **solid ice** (glaciers, snow and ice cubes)
- **gas or water vapour** (steam from a kettle).

a Water as a liquid

b Water as solid ice

c Water as a gas

What is the water cycle?

The amount of water in the world always stays the same. It just changes its state as it moves through the water cycle. There are four main processes in the watercycle: **evaporation**, **transpiration**, **condensation** and **precipitation**.

CHALLENGE

1. a) Look at pictures a–c. What is the link between them? Which is the odd one out, and why?
   b) What percentage of the world's water do you think is in each of these states?
2. a) The following changes in state are involved in the different processes of the water cycle:
      - liquid to gas
      - gas to liquid
      - liquid to gas via a plant

      Which change goes with which process? Use diagram d to help you.
   b) If precipitation is the only process that does not involve a change of state, what do you think it does involve and how could we define it?

Why does the rain never stop?

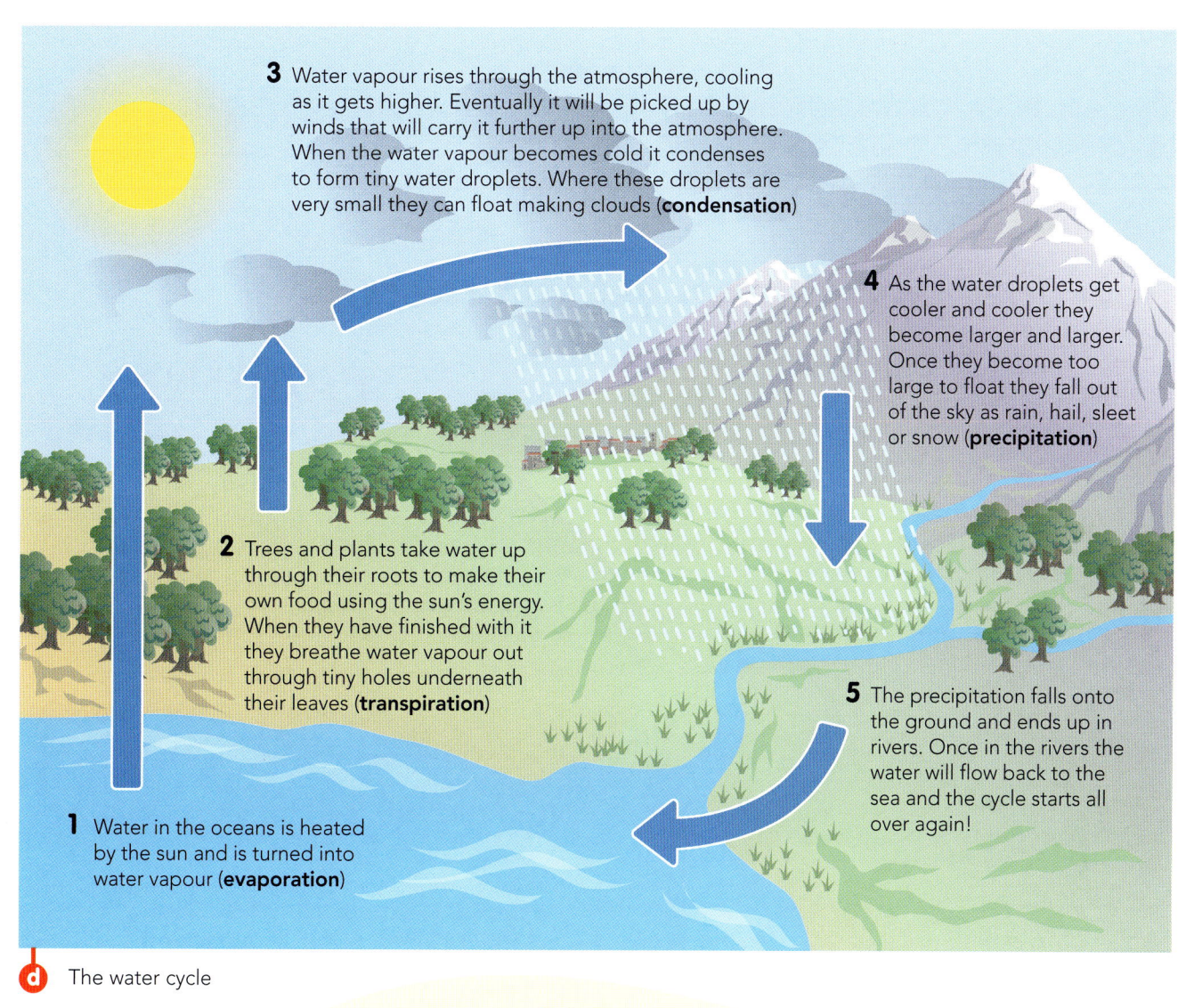

3 Water vapour rises through the atmosphere, cooling as it gets higher. Eventually it will be picked up by winds that will carry it further up into the atmosphere. When the water vapour becomes cold it condenses to form tiny water droplets. Where these droplets are very small they can float making clouds (**condensation**)

4 As the water droplets get cooler and cooler they become larger and larger. Once they become too large to float they fall out of the sky as rain, hail, sleet or snow (**precipitation**)

2 Trees and plants take water up through their roots to make their own food using the sun's energy. When they have finished with it they breathe water vapour out through tiny holes underneath their leaves (**transpiration**)

5 The precipitation falls onto the ground and ends up in rivers. Once in the rivers the water will flow back to the sea and the cycle starts all over again!

1 Water in the oceans is heated by the sun and is turned into water vapour (**evaporation**)

d The water cycle

CHALLENGE

3 Draw a simple diagram of the water cycle. Add the following labels to your diagram, and number them to show the order in which the processes happen.

- Rivers flow to the seas and oceans.
- Plants and trees breathe out water vapour through tiny holes in their leaves. This process is called transpiration.
- Warm air rises, then cools to form tiny water droplets that make clouds. This process is called condensation.
- The sun heats up the lakes and oceans, turning liquid water to water vapour. This process is called evaporation.
- The water droplets get bigger and bigger until they get too heavy and fall from the sky as precipitation.
- When precipitation hits the ground it can soak in or move across the surface, ending up in rivers.

4 Imagine that you are a water droplet. Look at all the information on pages 154 and 155 and draw a flow chart to show the different things that could happen to you in a day. You could think about what will happen to you if you travel to different places: water droplets in the Arctic will do different things to water drops in India!

Where does a river start and where does it go?

The water cycle showed us that water moves continuously around a system. We will now find out how precipitation gets into a river and how a river changes as the water in it flows towards the sea.

How does precipitation get into rivers?

When water hits the ground it can move in three different ways: over, through or under. Whichever way it goes, because of gravity, it moves downhill until it ends up in a river. Rivers are always at the bottom of a valley.

You can see this by pouring water onto a dry sponge on a plastic surface. Some of the water reaches the plastic surface quickly (the water moves underground). Some of the water is soaked up by the sponge and travels through it (the water moves through the ground). And, once the sponge is full the water moves across the surface of the sponge (the water moves over ground).

The diagram below shows the three ways water – or precipitation – flows into a river.

CHALLENGE

1 Look at diagram a.
   a) When it hits the ground, precipitation flows in three ways to reach a river. Which flow is the quickest and why? Which flow is the slowest and why?
   b) Do you think the water table stays in the same place all the time? Why?

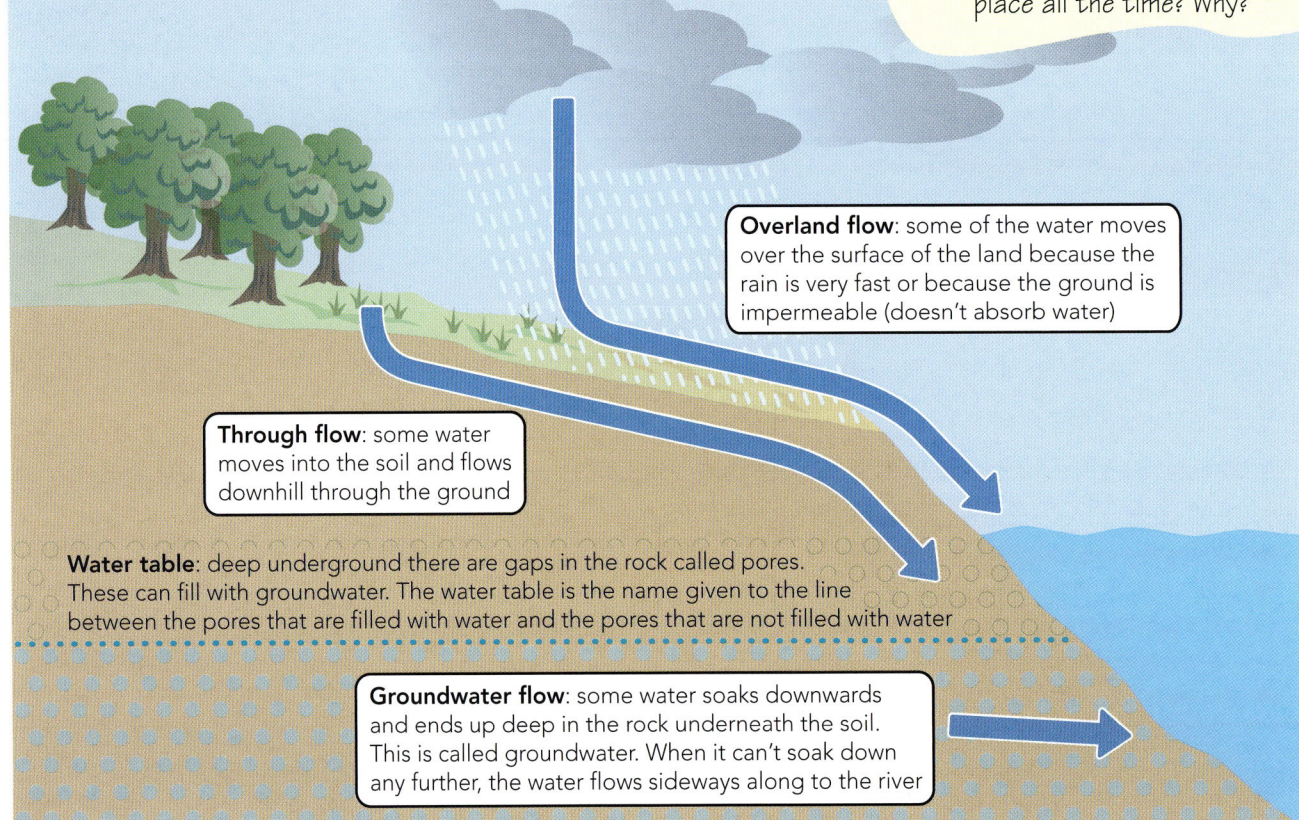

Overland flow: some of the water moves over the surface of the land because the rain is very fast or because the ground is impermeable (doesn't absorb water)

Through flow: some water moves into the soil and flows downhill through the ground

Water table: deep underground there are gaps in the rock called pores. These can fill with groundwater. The water table is the name given to the line between the pores that are filled with water and the pores that are not filled with water

Groundwater flow: some water soaks downwards and ends up deep in the rock underneath the soil. This is called groundwater. When it can't soak down any further, the water flows sideways along to the river

a The three different ways water flows into a river

What happens to the water in a river?

Every river flows through a **drainage basin**. A drainage basin is like a giant sink: any water that falls into it drains out through the 'plug hole', the river. Diagram b shows the features of a river on its journey from its source to the sea. Every river – large or small, long or short – has these features.

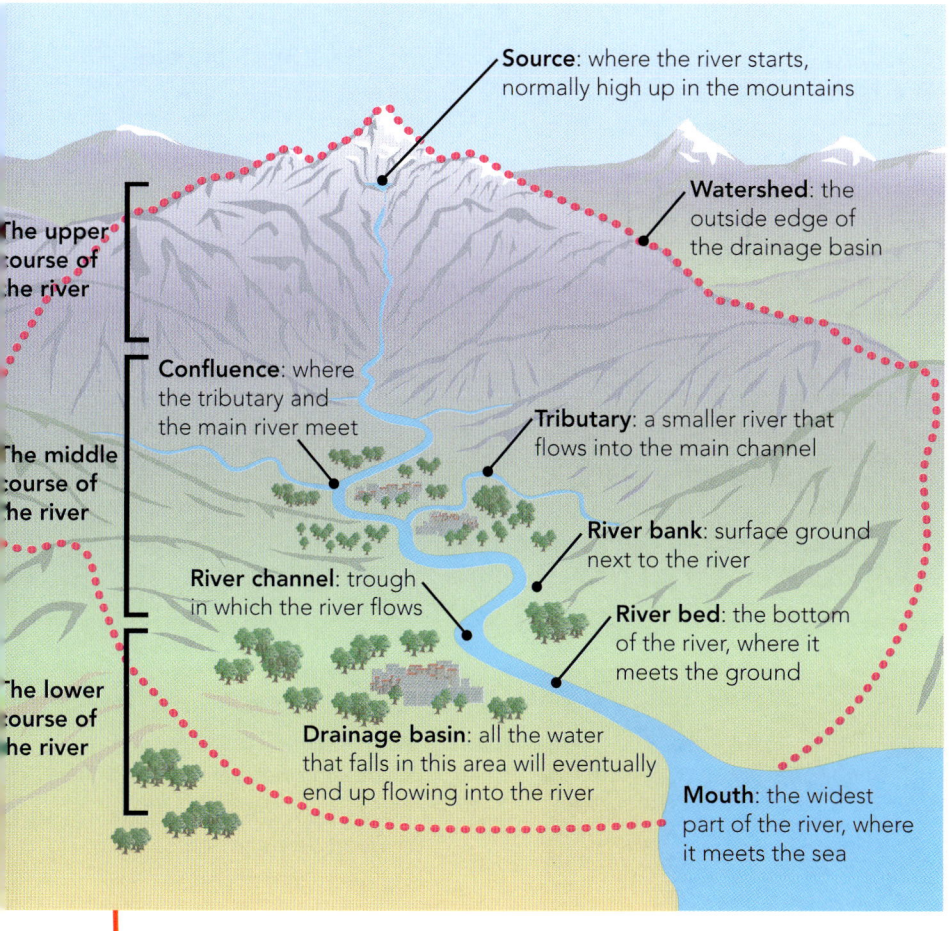

b Drainage basin, which shows a river's journey from source to sea

Labels on diagram:
- **Source**: where the river starts, normally high up in the mountains
- **Watershed**: the outside edge of the drainage basin
- **Confluence**: where the tributary and the main river meet
- **Tributary**: a smaller river that flows into the main channel
- **River bank**: surface ground next to the river
- **River channel**: trough in which the river flows
- **River bed**: the bottom of the river, where it meets the ground
- **Drainage basin**: all the water that falls in this area will eventually end up flowing into the river
- **Mouth**: the widest part of the river, where it meets the sea
- The upper course of the river
- The middle course of the river
- The lower course of the river

What is the long profile?

If you imagine that a river is straight and you cut it in half from the source to the mouth you get the **long profile**. It shows the height of the land along the length of the river. In the upper course the slope is steep; in the middle course the slope is gentle; in the lower course the slope flattens out at the river mouth.

CHALLENGE

2 Use diagram b to help you to answer these clues:
   a) The line around a drainage basin (9)
   b) It's a bit like a sink! (8, 5)
   c) The point where two rivers meet (10)
   d) The river doesn't sleep here! (5, 3)
   e) Where the river flows (5, 7)
   f) Where the river starts (6)

3 Draw a diagram to show the long profile of a river and label the upper course, the middle course and the lower course.

4 The River Severn is Britain's longest river. Find a map of the River Severn in an atlas or on Google Earth. Now see if you can find out the following:
   a) Where is the source of the River Severn and how high is it?
   b) Where is the mouth of the River Severn and what is it called?
   c) What are the names of six towns along the river?
   d) What are the names of six major tributaries?
   e) How long is the River Severn?
   HINT: Think back to your lessons on map skills.

What happens in a river?

We have seen how a river moves from its source to the sea. In this lesson we are going to learn about the processes that happen in a river, and how the amount of energy in the water influences them.

Where is the energy in a river?

Have you ever tried to stand up in a fast-moving stream or held your hand under a waterfall? It's difficult to keep still, isn't it? This is because of the force of the moving water.

All moving things, including water, have energy. The faster the water is moving, the more energy it has. People sometimes use this energy for their own purposes, and so does nature.

a Moving water has energy!

CHALLENGE

1. a) How many examples can you think of where people have made use of the energy in water?
   b) What examples can you think of in nature where the energy in water has caused damage to people, buildings, roads, and so on?
   c) How important do you think harnessing the power of water will be in the future to provide us with energy? Why?
   d) Do you think that water power will be more important than wind power or solar energy? Why?

What happens in a river?

What happens when water has lots of energy?

Fast-moving water can be seen in waterfalls, mountain streams, flood waters and in turbulence around obstructions in the river. In these places you can see evidence of the river banks and river bed being worn away. This is called **erosion** and it happens in four ways: abrasion, attrition, hydraulic action and solution.

CHALLENGE

2 Which process of erosion will:
   a) be best for making rocks smoother?
   b) be best at making banks weaker?
   c) have the biggest effect in an area where the river banks are made of soluble rock?
   d) help to increase the surface area of the load?
   Remember to explain your answers fully!

Erosion

1 Abrasion

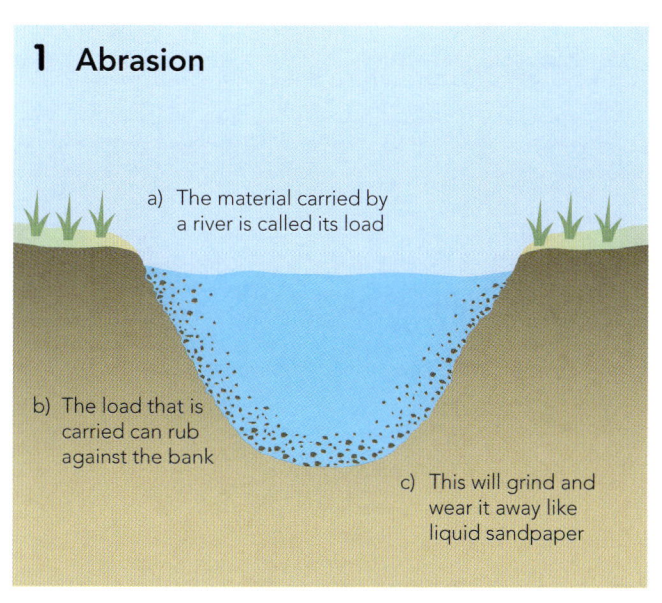

a) The material carried by a river is called its load
b) The load that is carried can rub against the bank
c) This will grind and wear it away like liquid sandpaper

2 Attrition

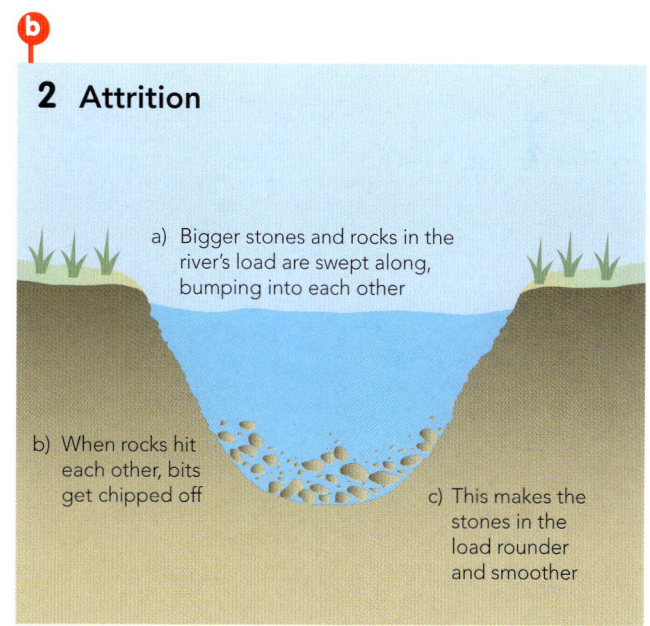

a) Bigger stones and rocks in the river's load are swept along, bumping into each other
b) When rocks hit each other, bits get chipped off
c) This makes the stones in the load rounder and smoother

3 Hydraulic action

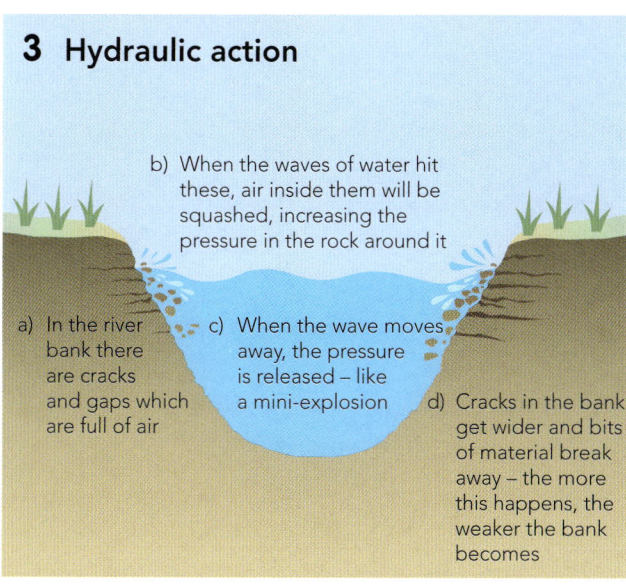

a) In the river bank there are cracks and gaps which are full of air
b) When the waves of water hit these, air inside them will be squashed, increasing the pressure in the rock around it
c) When the wave moves away, the pressure is released – like a mini-explosion
d) Cracks in the bank get wider and bits of material break away – the more this happens, the weaker the bank becomes

4 Solution

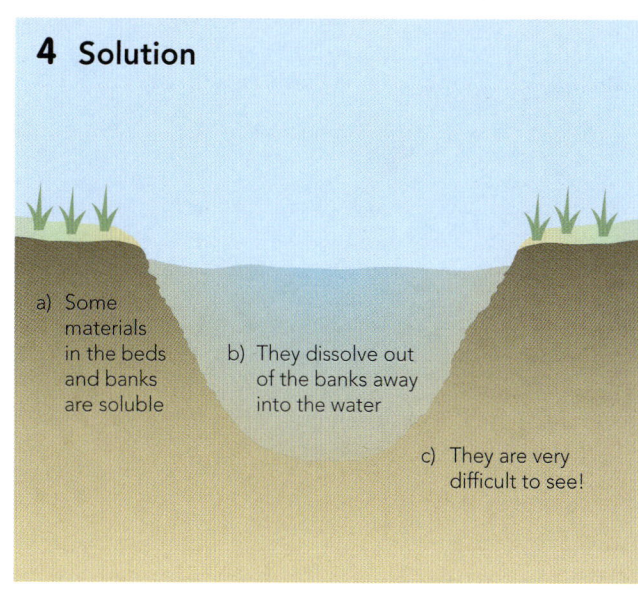

a) Some materials in the beds and banks are soluble
b) They dissolve out of the banks away into the water
c) They are very difficult to see!

What happens in a river?

CHALLENGE

3 Which method of transportation will:
a) move the load furthest?
b) use the most energy?

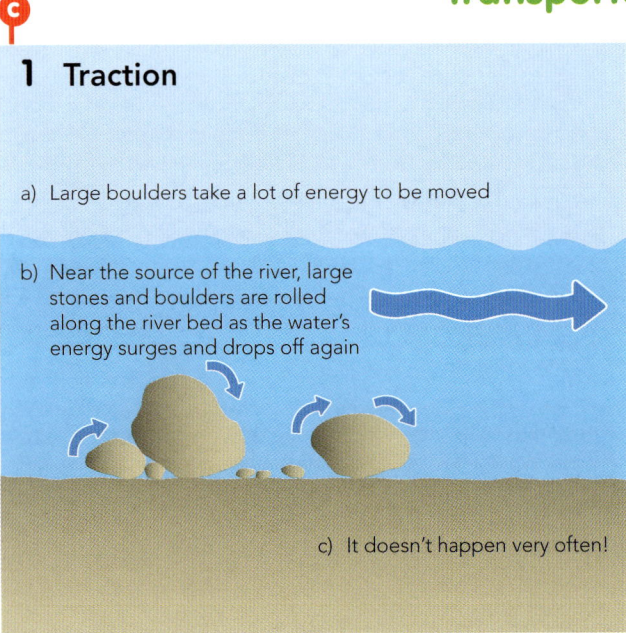

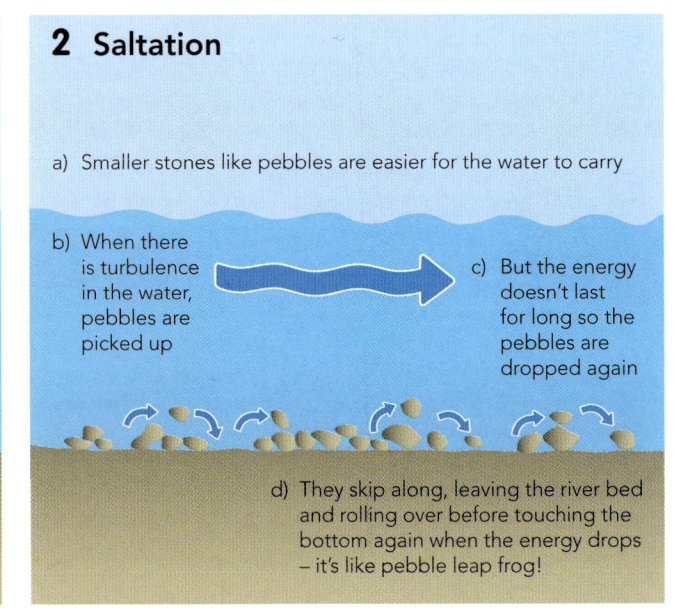

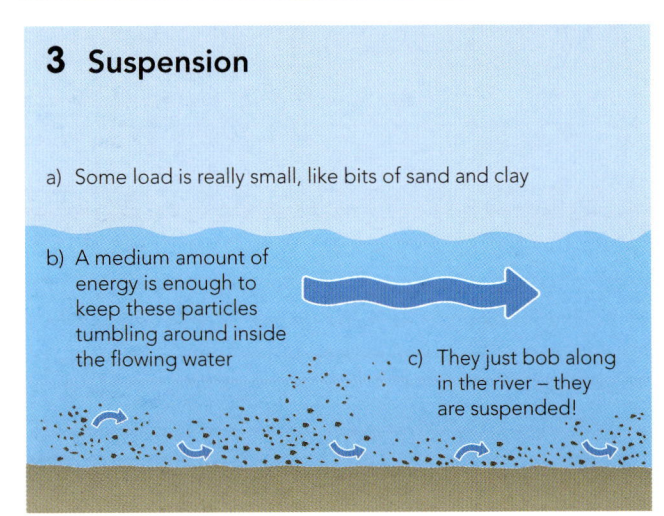

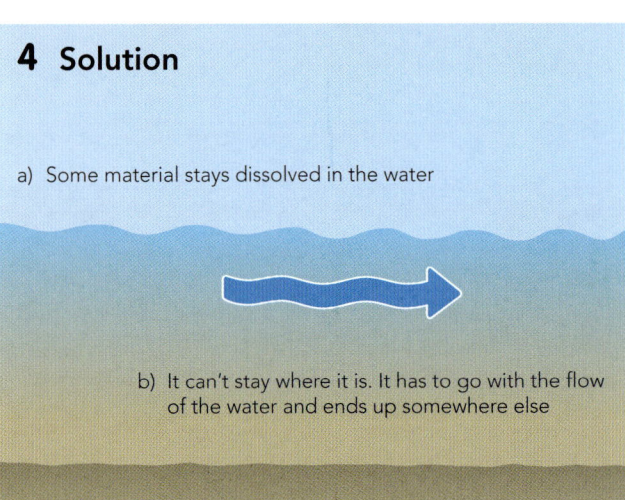

What happens when water has a medium amount of energy?

Just like us, rivers cannot be very energetic all the time. Even a bustling mountain stream doesn't have the same energy as a waterfall. When the water has a medium amount of energy it doesn't cause erosion but the energy is still strong enough to keep stones and particles moving along in the water. This process is called **transportation** and again there are four ways in which it happens: traction, saltation, suspension and solution.

Transportation

1 Traction

a) Large boulders take a lot of energy to be moved

b) Near the source of the river, large stones and boulders are rolled along the river bed as the water's energy surges and drops off again

c) It doesn't happen very often!

2 Saltation

a) Smaller stones like pebbles are easier for the water to carry

b) When there is turbulence in the water, pebbles are picked up

c) But the energy doesn't last for long so the pebbles are dropped again

d) They skip along, leaving the river bed and rolling over before touching the bottom again when the energy drops – it's like pebble leap frog!

3 Suspension

a) Some load is really small, like bits of sand and clay

b) A medium amount of energy is enough to keep these particles tumbling around inside the flowing water

c) They just bob along in the river – they are suspended!

4 Solution

a) Some material stays dissolved in the water

b) It can't stay where it is. It has to go with the flow of the water and ends up somewhere else

What happens when water only has a little energy?

Even in faster sections of the river there are places where the water slows down: after obstructions or steep drops, or on the inside of a bend. At these points, and especially in the lower course near the sea, water has less energy. It has trouble creating any erosion, except in the very softest soils, and even transportation becomes a bit of a chore. All the bits of the river bed that have been swept along in transportation start falling to the bottom in a process called **deposition**.

Deposition

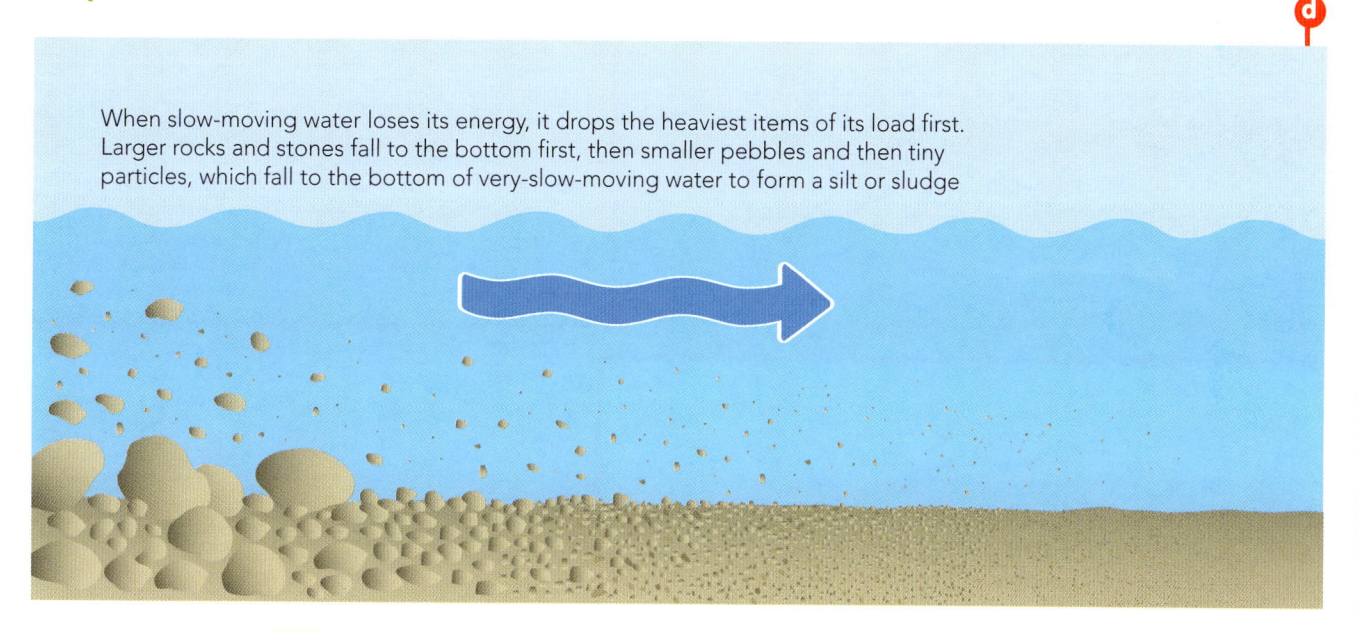

When slow-moving water loses its energy, it drops the heaviest items of its load first. Larger rocks and stones fall to the bottom first, then smaller pebbles and then tiny particles, which fall to the bottom of very-slow-moving water to form a silt or sludge

CHALLENGE

4 Imagine that you have a bottle half-filled with water, you add some soil and some gravel, put the lid on and shake it up. Then put the bottle on the table. What do you think will happen next? In what order will the materials drop to the bottom? Remember to use as many geographical terms to explain your answers as you can.
5 Think back to the long profile of a river. Where is it most likely that erosion, transportation and deposition will take place?

What does a river do to the landscape?

Three processes take place in all rivers: erosion, transportation and deposition. Depending on how much of each process happens, different landforms are formed. And, because the water in a river is always moving, the landforms constantly change.

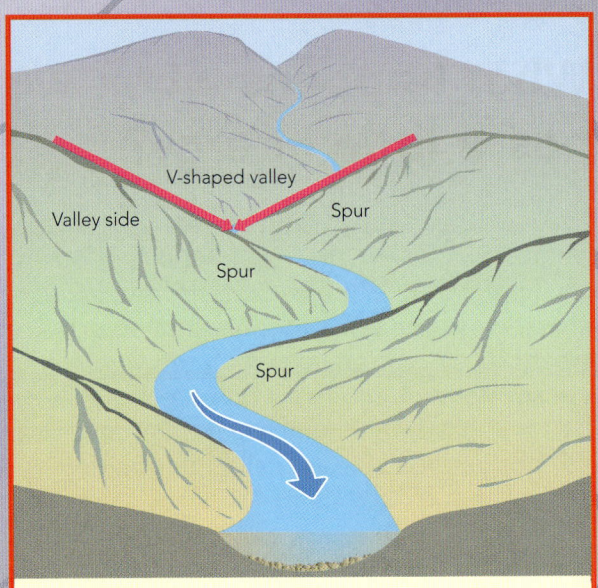

V-shaped valley, Valley side, Spur, Spur, Spur

The upper course
In the upper course of the river, although there is a lot of energy, there is not a lot of water. This means there is not enough power for the river to expand sideways, so it cuts downwards. As it keeps cutting downwards over time, a V-shaped valley is created. The water also does not have enough power to cut through obstacles such as hills, so it ends up flowing around them, leaving a spur of land that juts out from the valley side. Over time, interlocking spurs are formed as the river zig-zags from side to side around the spurs.

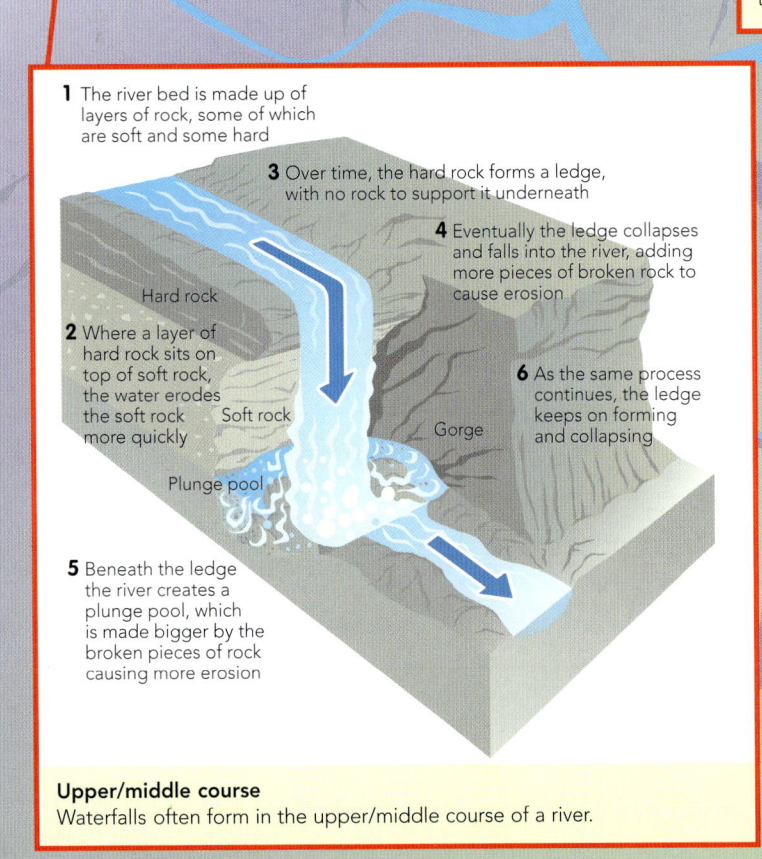

1. The river bed is made up of layers of rock, some of which are soft and some hard

2. Where a layer of hard rock sits on top of soft rock, the water erodes the soft rock more quickly

3. Over time, the hard rock forms a ledge, with no rock to support it underneath

4. Eventually the ledge collapses and falls into the river, adding more pieces of broken rock to cause erosion

5. Beneath the ledge the river creates a plunge pool, which is made bigger by the broken pieces of rock causing more erosion

6. As the same process continues, the ledge keeps on forming and collapsing

Hard rock, Soft rock, Plunge pool, Gorge

Upper/middle course
Waterfalls often form in the upper/middle course of a river.

What does a river do to the landscape?

1 When a river flows around a bend, the fastest water is on the outside. It uses its energy to erode the banks

The slowest water is on the inside bend. It has less energy, so it deposits material

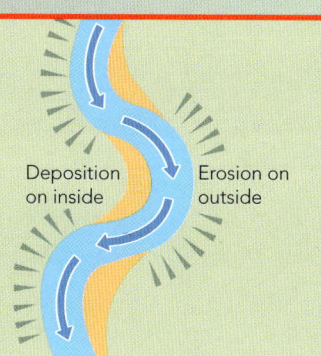

Deposition on inside   Erosion on outside

2 Over time the curve of the bend gets deeper and deeper, forming a meander

Eventually the meander forms a loop with a narrow gap (neck) between the two ends of the loop

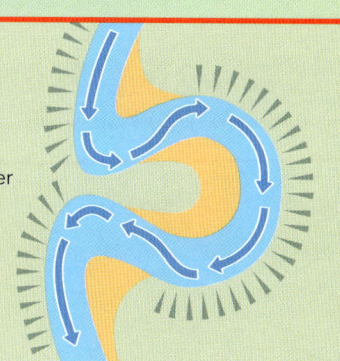

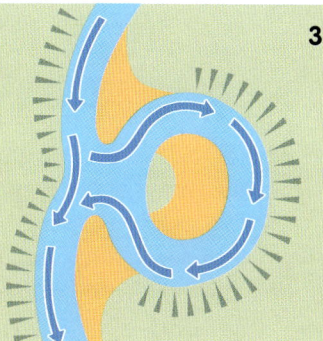

3 The neck gets smaller and smaller. Eventually the water pressure breaks through the neck, forming a complete loop

4 When the river has two paths, the straight one becomes dominant, so the loop is abandoned, leaving an oxbow lake

Over time, sediment will fill in the lake, leaving a banana-shaped area of greener grass

The middle/lower course
In the middle course, the land is a bit flatter and the river forms meanders and oxbow lakes.

Lower course
In the lower course, where the river finally meets the sea, the river runs out of energy and drops all the material it is carrying. The sand and gravel are deposited more quickly than the tide can remove them, so this sediment clumps together to form a delta at the mouth of the river. This is flat land which grows out from the shore, forming a triangular-shaped piece of land added on to the coastline.

CHALLENGE

1. Draw a simple sketch of each of the following features and explain in 15 words how it is formed:
    a) a V-shaped valley
    b) interlocking spurs.
2. a) Look at the waterfall diagram. What will happen to the position of the waterfall over time? What impact would this have on a map of the area?
   b) Draw a flow chart to explain how a waterfall is formed.
3. A cross-section is the image you get if you slice downwards through the landscape. Draw a cross-section of a meander loop (from bank to bank). Annotate your diagram with labels to show what is happening.
4. Why do you think a delta is a triangle shape?

What is a flood?

In June and July 2007, the UK saw some of the worst flooding in living memory. In this lesson we will explore some of the reasons why this extreme weather happened and what the human impacts were.

What is flooding?

Flooding and droughts are part of a natural system, the water cycle. We only view them as hazards because of the effects they have on people. When we understand why floods and droughts occur, we will be better geographers who are more able to predict which areas are more at risk.

Rivers are natural routes for water flowing across land. Provided that the amount of water entering a river system roughly matches the system's ability to get rid of it at the other end, everything will be fine. Flooding is what happens when too much water enters the system or something stops it from following its natural course.

What might cause too much water to enter the system?

1. **Heavy rainfall** Large amounts of rain in short periods of time make it difficult for the water to be absorbed into the ground quickly enough. It therefore moves downhill above ground, as surface run-off.
2. **Rapid snow-melt** When temperatures are cold enough, precipitation falls as snow. While temperatures are low, the snow stays above ground. When the temperature rises, the snow melts and large amounts of water are released.
3. **Dam failure** Dams are man-made structures used to hold back the flow of a river. If a dam breaks, a small leak can rapidly become a major collapse and all the water is released in one big surge.

a Dam failure in 2007: firemen pumping water out of Ulley Dam, which is at breaking point, to relieve pressure

What is a flood?

What might stop the water following its natural course?

4 **Saturated ground** Where land is already waterlogged, as it might be after long periods of sustained rain, it won't be able to absorb any more water.
5 **Deforestation** Trees slow water down. They use some of it to help them grow. They also catch some of it as it lands and hold it up as it flows downhill. Deforestation – cutting down large areas of trees – stops this. Water hits the ground harder, moves more quickly and can wash away soil.
6 **Urbanization** Built-up areas are very different to rural areas. They have many more impermeable surfaces (surfaces that don't absorb any water). Drains, rather than natural processes, are responsible for taking water away. If there is a lot of rain and the drains can't cope with all the water, then flooding can occur.

b Urbanization: overflowing drains can't cope with all the water

c Deforestation: cutting down large areas of trees means water can move more quickly

CHALLENGE

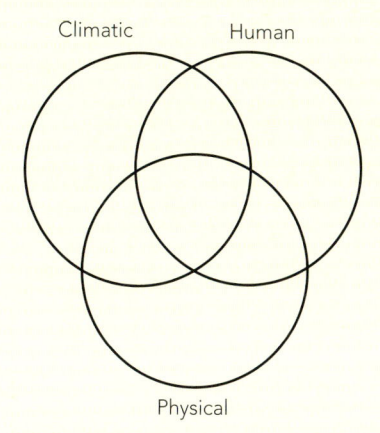

1 Very often in geography things are easier to talk about if you can put them into categories. We can split the six main causes of flooding into three categories:

- Climatic – weather related causes
- Human – the causes that people create
- Physical – caused by features of the land.

Copy the Venn diagram and add the six main causes of flooding to your diagram.

HINT: Remember to think about which causes fit into more than one category and put them into an overlapping part of the diagram.

What is a flood?

Why did central England flood in Summer 2007?

Rainfall in central England in June and early July was much heavier than average in 2007. Some places saw rainfall almost every day for six weeks and the ground became saturated. A lot of this rain fell on built-up areas.

Rain is often associated with low pressure systems. Think back to the water cycle:

when there is low pressure air rises → as air rises it condenses → condensation results in precipitation

On Monday 16 July, a large area of low pressure got stuck over central and western England. Map e shows this band of low pressure. It rained heavily for four days. Friday 20 July was the worst day. 150mm of rainfall was recorded officially in some areas, and amateur weather reporters recorded rainfall of up to 220mm. Rainfall was less from Saturday 21 July.

d Extreme amounts of rainfall meant the ground became saturated

e A weather map showing low pressure across central and western England. If low pressure moves slowly and gets stuck, all the rain will fall in one place

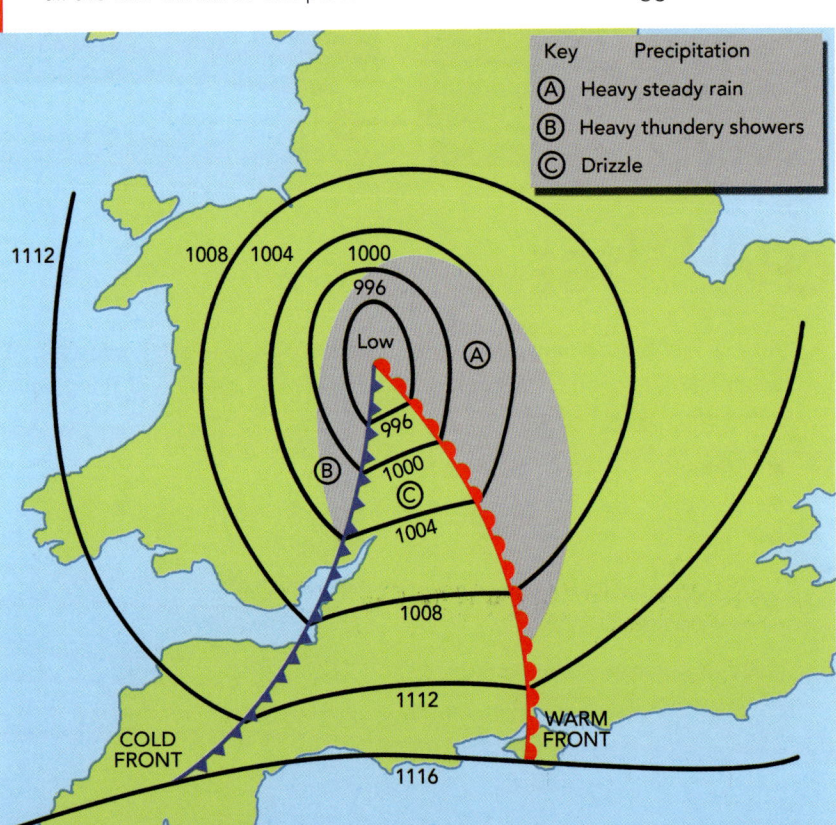

f Mobile pumping stations were sent to clear water from waterlogged roads

Key — Precipitation
- (A) Heavy steady rain
- (B) Heavy thundery showers
- (C) Drizzle

CHALLENGE

2 Explain, in three sentences, why central England flooded in the summer of 2007. Think about:
 a) Climatic causes
 b) Human causes
 c) Physical causes
Use your Venn diagram and figures d to i to help you.

What is a flood?

The impacts of the flooding

Geographers make sense of events by judging their impact.

- Localized floods are recorded across the Midlands, centred on Evesham in Worcestershire.
- The River Avon rises to more than five metres above its normal level.
- The M5 is closed and 10 000 people spend the night stranded on the motorway.
- Holiday parks are evacuated by Air Sea Rescue helicopters.
- Bridges are closed as debris builds up and they threaten to collapse.
- Tewkesbury is worst affected as the Rivers Severn and Avon meet, creating a huge lake. Tewkesbury is completely cut off.
- Roads collapse as streams that run underneath them become swollen with water.
- Tewkesbury's water pumping station is flooded and the water supply is contaminated. 350 000 homes are without water for more than a week.
- Gloucester electricity station is within centimetres of being swamped. Emergency pumps and sandbags keep it open and power to 25 000 homes is maintained.
- The cost of the flooding was unknown at the time, but it is estimated that insurance claims will run to £1.5 billion.
- 900 water bowsers (tankers) are sent to Gloucestershire.
- The rain eases but the problem moves downstream to Abingdon and Oxford as the floodwater begins to flow down the River Thames.

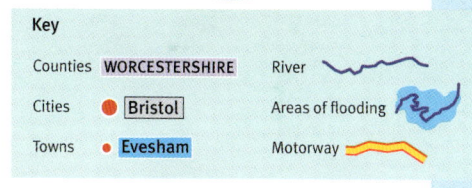

g People are airlifted to safety

h The worst affected areas

Key
- Counties: WORCESTERSHIRE
- Cities: ● Bristol
- Towns: ● Evesham
- River
- Areas of flooding
- Motorway

CHALLENGE

3. Some of the impacts of the floods were more significant than others.
   a) Choose the nine most significant impacts of the summer floods of 2007.
   b) Complete a 'diamond nine' with your chosen impacts. Put the most important impact at the top, the next two most important impacts underneath and so on until you come to the least important impact at the bottom of the diamond. How are you going to choose where each impact should go? What makes an impact more or less significant? Be ready to explain your ideas.
4. There have been many floods in the UK throughout the twentieth century. What criteria could we use to decide which were the worst? **HINT:** Think about the impacts of the floods in central England in the summer of 2007.

i Residents sandbag their homes to try to keep the water out

Why are some countries wetter than others?

Some parts of the world are more likely to experience flooding than others. Using what we know about some of the causes of flooding, we will explore why this is and how these countries cope with floods.

Why do countries flood?

- Countries at or below sea level are more likely to flood because there is nowhere for the flood water to go.
- Countries with climates that often have extreme weather events – such as tropical cyclones, hurricanes and monsoons, which all bring huge amounts of rain – are more likely to flood.
- In some countries, people have tried to manage flood risk but have made it worse, making these areas more likely to flood.

Countries which are at greater risk of flooding need to take measures to manage the impacts of flooding.

We are going to look at two places in the world that have suffered serious flooding in recent years and the impact this has had.

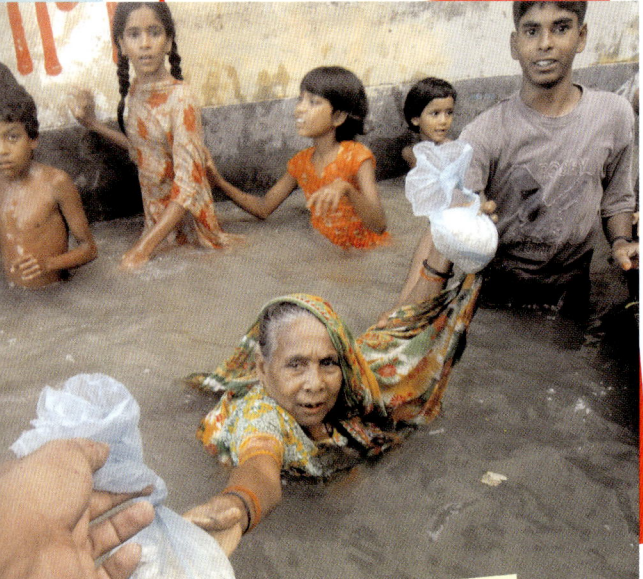

a Bangladeshi struggle through flood water

Bangladesh, July 2007

In July 2007, Bangladesh, in South East Asia, experienced some of the worst flooding for several years. Some physical reasons contributed to the flooding:

- Bangladesh is very low lying, with 70% of the land area less than 1m above sea level.
- Tropical cyclones travel up the Bay of Bengal. This causes large amounts of rain to fall.
- Melting snows in the Himalayas add to water levels in the summer monsoon season.
- 80% of the country is flood plain and delta.
- Bangladesh is at the confluence of three major rivers: the River Brahmaputra, the River Meghna and the River Ganges.

Bangladesh is also a less economically developed country (LEDC), where the standard of living is low, and it is one of the most densely populated countries in the world. To feed the growing population, parts of the forested areas in Bangladesh have been cut down and turned into agricultural land. Unfortunately this deforestation makes the land even more likely to flood.

Impacts of the floods

- 14 million people suffered.
- Over 100 people were killed.
- One million acres of crops were destroyed.
- 1000km of roads and highways were flooded.
- Many embankments that protected coastal areas from flooding were damaged.

Why are some countries wetter than others?

New Orleans, August 2005

In August 2005, Hurricane Katrina hit south-eastern America. One of the worst impacts of the hurricane was the flooding of New Orleans in the state of Louisiana. The flooding occurred for a mixture of human and physical reasons:

- 80% of the bowl-shaped city of New Orleans is below sea level.
- The storm surge (a surge of sea water caused by the hurricane) ripped across Lake Pontchartrain and damaged the levees (embankments) that protected New Orleans.
- Because of the damaged levees, once the water got in it was very difficult for it to drain back out again.

Impacts of the floods
- The hurricane cost America $84 billion.
- 1836 people are thought to have died, 1577 from Louisiana.
- 80% of all properties in New Orleans were damaged by water.
- Nearly one million people were without electricity for several weeks.
- One million people fled New Orleans following evacuation advice; around 80 000 stayed.

Most of the city of New Orleans lies beneath sea level and is protected from the water by levees (embankments)

Lake Pontchartrain — Levee — Sea level — New Orleans — Levee — Mississippi River

CHALLENGE

1. Compare the flooding in Bangladesh and New Orleans. Think about:
   - Where was the flooding?
   - Did the flooding happen in an MEDC (a more economically developed country) or an LEDC (a less economically developed country)?
   - Why did the flooding happen?
   - What were the impacts of the flooding?

2. Write a short paragraph discussing which was the more serious disaster, and explaining why you made the decision you did.

New Orleans under water in 2005

What is a drought?

Just as too much water can be disastrous, too little water can also have extreme effects. Not having enough water can cause droughts and droughts have serious impacts on both LEDCs and MEDCs.

What is a drought?

A drought is a continuous period of time where less precipitation falls than expected. The definition changes for different parts of the world. In the UK a drought is defined as 15 continuous days where less than 0.25mm of rain falls in any 24 hours. But some parts of the world have naturally dry climates. So in parts of Africa, for example, a drought is defined as two years or more in which there has been less than average rainfall.

What causes droughts?

Severe droughts occur when two or more of the following factors are combined.

1. **Lack of rainfall** If it doesn't rain, you expect the land to be dry.
2. **Lack of snowfall** Many places at higher altitudes rely on snowmelt from mountains for water.
3. **Ridges of high pressure** If a high pressure stays still for a long period of time, then the normal process of air rising and water vapour condensing will stop. There may be rain occurring either side of the high pressure but not under it.

If we understand weather patterns we can attempt to predict where droughts will occur.

a) The remains of the Haweswater reservoir in the village of Mardale Common, Cumbria which was affected by drought in 1995

b) Animals which have died because of drought

CHALLENGE

1. On a blank world map, shade all the places that you think suffer from droughts.
2. In an atlas, find a world map which shows very dry (arid) areas. These areas suffer droughts.
   a) How do the dry areas match with your map?
   b) On another blank world map:
      - shade the places that do suffer from droughts.
      - label at least six countries which suffer from droughts.

What is a drought?

What are the impacts of droughts?

Droughts have very serious impacts. Geographers like to put the impacts that share similar features into groups; this is called classification. Impacts of drought can be classified as direct or indirect:

- **Direct impacts** are things that happen as an inevitable consequence of not having enough water, such as crops not growing.
- **Indirect impacts** happen as a result of the direct impacts – they are the 'knock-on' effects. For example, the indirect impact of crops not growing is an increase in the price of food because it is in short supply.

Impacts can also be classified as social, environmental or economic:

- **Social impacts** affect people and their quality of life.
- **Environmental impacts** affect the habitats and ecosystems of an area.
- **Economic impacts** are things that prevent the normal economic cycle. They might stop people earning money or mean that people have to pay more for certain goods.

Some impacts fall into more than one group.

c A woman looks for water in a dried up well

d Local residents travel long distances to find water

CHALLENGE

3 Copy the circle diagram and add these impacts to the correct part of the diagram. Add any others that you can think of.

- Crops can't grow well
- Ships can't travel on waterways
- Clay soils shrink, causing structural damage to buildings
- People suffer mental and physical stress
- Endangered species are wiped out
- There is little or no fresh drinking water
- There is an increased risk of disease as food and water run short
- People move from the country to towns
- Without crops to sell, farmers struggle to earn a living
- Farmers need to spend more money on irrigation

HINT: Remember that some impacts may fit into more than one category.

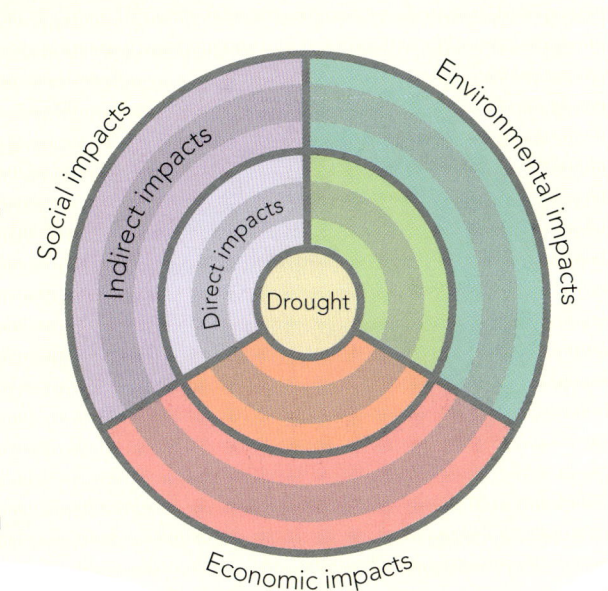

What is a drought?

Drought in Australia, 2000–2007

FACT FILE: Australia

Population: 21 million
Area: 7.7 million km²
Life expectancy: 78 (male)
 83 (female)
Exports: metals, wool, fuel

Australia has a varied landscape and climate. In southern Australia, the Murray–Darling drainage basin normally has a moderate climate but rainfall is erratic. The area has a mixture of scrubland, desert and farmland.

From 2000–2007 this area suffered from a drought, which Australians call the 'the big dry'. The rainfall was lower than at any time since records began in the 1850s.

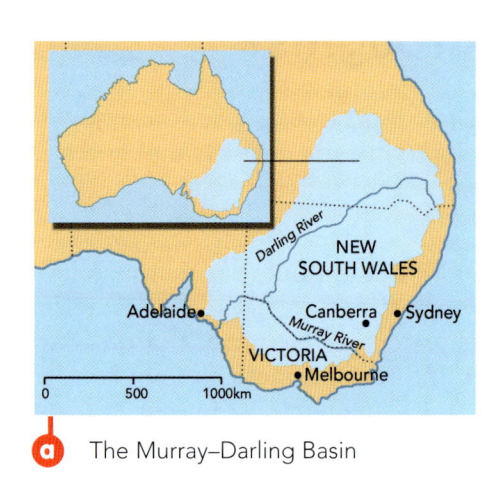

a The Murray–Darling Basin

b The Murray–Darling Basin before the drought

c The Murray–Darling Basin during the drought

CHALLENGE

4 a) Draw a circle diagram like the one on page 171 and use it to help you classify the impacts of the drought in Australia. Note that not all the sectors will be completed.

 b) Add any other impacts you can think of.

Impacts of the drought:

- Crop yields are massively reduced.
- The government has to subsidise farmers to stop them going out of business. In 2007, this cost $1.7 million a day!
- Suicide rates rise because of stress and anxiety.
- Australia's total economy is reduced by 1%.
- The government has to take control of states to co-ordinate drought action.
- The koala bear's natural habitat is damaged.

What is a drought?

Drought in Afghanistan, 1996–2007

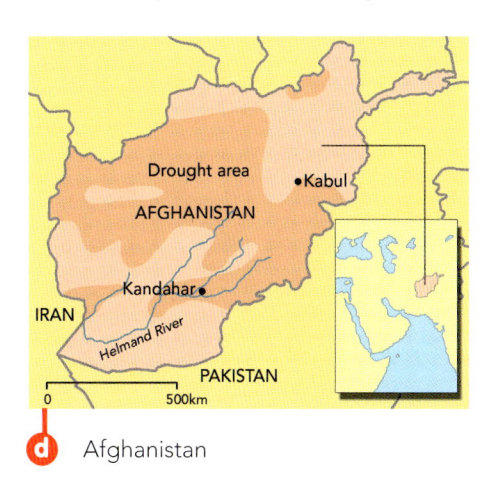

Under normal climatic conditions, Afghanistan has fertile soil irrigated by snowmelts and spring rains. The farmland produces wheat, melons, vegetables and pomegranates. However, between 1996 and 2007, Afghanistan experienced eight years that were classed as drought years due to low snowfall and rain levels.

FACT FILE: Afghanistan

Population:	26 million
Area:	652 000km^2
Life expectancy:	46 (male and female)
Exports:	fruit, nuts, carpets, wool, opium

d Afghanistan

e Afghanistan before the drought

f Afghanistan during the drought

Impacts of the drought:

- Crops fail on a large scale.
- The range of crops produced is much less than normal.
- Food prices rise by 50%.
- The poppy crop increases because it does well in drier climates. Opium, the key ingredient in heroin, is made from poppies.
- Hot sand is blown across previously farmable areas and desertification increases.
- People move to urban areas from the country.
- People suffer starvation and homelessness.

CHALLENGE

5 Draw a circle diagram and use it to help you classify the impacts of the drought in Afghanistan.

6 Look at the similarities and differences between the impacts in Australia and Afghanistan. Where do you think drought has had more impact: Australia or Afghanistan? Why?

Why are some countries drier than others?

Water is not always in plentiful supply but it is essential for our survival. In this lesson, we will discover why water is a key element in enabling a country to develop economically. We will also look at the serious effects of not having water.

Access to water around the world

a The world map shows that different areas have different levels of access to water.

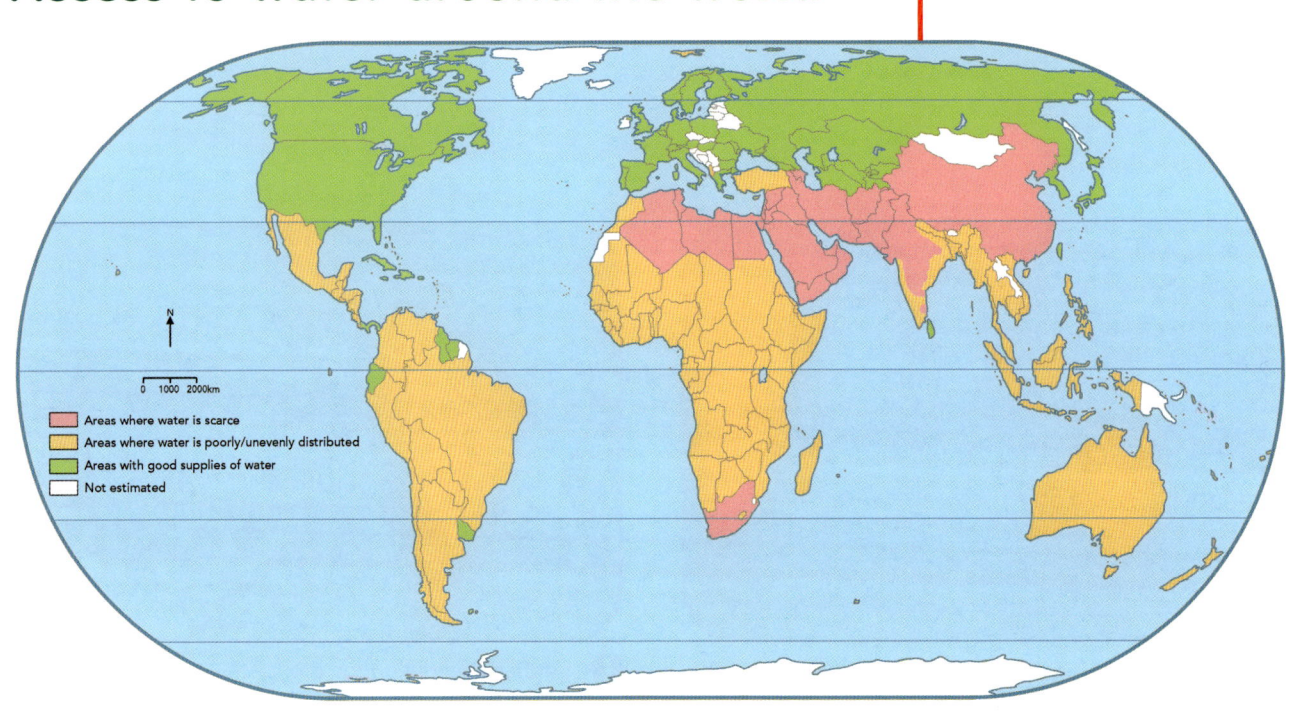

- Areas where water is scarce
- Areas where water is poorly/unevenly distributed
- Areas with good supplies of water
- Not estimated

What causes different amounts of water around the world?

- **Where you are in the world** Different areas have different climates. Brazil's tropical rainforest has more than 2000mm of rain each year; northern Africa has less than 250mm.
- **How concentrated the rainfall is** In India, most of the rain falls during the monsoon season, from June to September, when heavy rainstorms can lead to flooding. The flood waters come quickly but also leave quickly, meaning the water can't be stored or used.
- **How reliable the rainfall patterns are** In some places the rainfall is unreliable: it just doesn't arrive when it's supposed to.
- **How many people live in the area** More water is needed to support growing populations. Mexico City's population grew from 15 million in 1990 to over 19 million in 2005. Parts of the city are sinking by 40cm a year because extra water has been drawn from underground rivers.
- **Climate change** Scientists know that the world's climate is changing and that this is affecting weather patterns. Places that already have unreliable rainfall could receive even less rain. Areas with a Mediterranean climate could become like deserts.

Why are some countries drier than others?

What is the link between water and economic growth?

MEDCs such as the UK would not have developed economically without water.

Everything we do revolves around water. This is because it is a basic resource and we couldn't survive without it. Below are just some of the ways that water has allowed MEDCs to develop:

- **Industrial revolution** The late eighteenth century was a time of major technological and social change, as industry developed. Many manufacturing processes needed water for cooling, and for energy.
- **Hygiene** A successful country needs a healthy workforce. Clean piped water and sanitation help to make this possible.
- **Agriculture** The climate of the UK is temperate, which means we have a balance of reliable rain and sunshine. This means we can grow a range of crops so that we don't have to spend money on importing food if we don't want to.
- **Recreation** Many pastimes such as sailing, surfing and fishing rely on water. They provide jobs and the money made from them can be ploughed back into the economy.
- **Energy** Increasingly, water is becoming more important as a renewable energy source, through methods such as hydro-electric power and tidal power. In the past, water wheels generated energy.

b How much water do you use every day?

c How many of your pastimes involve water?

CHALLENGE

1 There are many other ways in which water has helped MEDCs to develop. How many can you think of? Try to think of groups that you could use to classify them.

Why are some countries drier than others?

What are the impacts of a lack of water on LEDCs?

The map on page 174 shows that many of the places with poor access to water are LEDCs in the developing world. How does that affect their development?

- **Health** Dirty water causes 80% of diseases in developing countries. These diseases include cholera, typhoid, diarrhoea and dysentery. Children are especially at risk.
- **Education** Many LEDCs have no access to piped water, children are sent to collect it. Collecting water is physically stressful and very time consuming and, as a result, girls are often too busy to attend school.
- **Agriculture** Lack of water makes it difficult for plants to grow and animals to stay healthy and productive. Without water, crops fail, animals die and people suffer from malnutrition.
- **Family life** Because children have to collect water, they have little time to enjoy family life and have to grow up very quickly.
- **Social unrest** People may fight over the few water resources available, leading to social problems.

When you add all of these effects together they have a very big impact on how a country can develop.

As long as the levels of development remain low, the quality of life will remain poor – all because of a lack of water.

d Women washing clothes in a river in Mgeta District in Tanzania

CHALLENGE

2 Imagine that you live in an LEDC. You are appalled at how people in MEDCs waste and pollute their water supplies. Write a speech to explain to people in MEDCs how lucky they are and why they should use their water supplies more carefully.
HINT: Remember to use as many different pieces of geographical evidence as possible.

e Slum dwellers scramble for water in Kusumpur Pahari, Delhi, India

Why are some countries drier than others?

Why do we need to use water more sustainably?

The water cycle shows that there is only so much water on the planet. But the world population is growing. It will reach over nine billion by 2045. And all these people need water. Without it, a person can live for only ten days!

How much water do we use?

In MEDCs, each person uses about 153 litres of water a day. In LEDCs, each person uses less than 25 litres. So how do MEDCs manage to use so much water? Even the most basic activities use large amounts of water:

- Brushing teeth with the tap running – 1 litre
- Having a bath – 80 litres
- Flushing the toilet – 8 litres
- Having a shower – 35 litres
- Using the washing machine – 65 litres
- Using the dishwasher – 25 litres

So by using a dishwasher once we are using the same amount of water that a person in the developing world has to live on for an entire day!

It's not just how much we use; it's also what we're doing to the quality of the water. Human activities such as farming, industry and transport are spoiling the quality of water by polluting it with insecticides, fertilisers and industrial waste.

If you use something sustainably it means that you are using it now while making sure that there is enough for future generations. The amount of water we are using, wasting and polluting is going to make life for future generations difficult, so it is clearly not sustainable. What can we do to improve things?

We can all make a difference. Try some of these:

- Turn off the tap when you're brushing your teeth.
- Wash the car with a bucket, not a hosepipe.
- Get a waterbutt to collect rain-water and use it to water the garden.
- Only flush the toilet when you really need to.

CHALLENGE

3 There is a limited amount of water in the water cycle. With people using so much water and a rapidly rising world population, will we have enough water in the future? Come up with an action plan of what we could do to improve the situation. Your action plan should include:

- the reasons why we need to reduce the amount of water we use
- the main factors that have led to people using so much water
- the actions we can take to use water more carefully.

What are NGOs and what do they do?

As responsible global citizens we should know what we can do to help people who don't have access to enough water. One of the ways in which we can help is to support Non-Governmental Organisations (NGOs). In this lesson we will find out about one of these: WaterAid.

WaterAid

WaterAid charity reg no 288701

What is an NGO?

An NGO is a voluntary group that works at a local, national or international level, but not for profit. NGOs are involved with a range of issues, from human rights to the environment and health. The International Red Cross, Greenpeace, Oxfam, Amnesty International and Doctors without Borders (Médecins Sans Frontières) are all NGOs, as is WaterAid, an NGO that deals specifically with water.

What is WaterAid?

WaterAid is an international charity. Its mission is to overcome poverty by helping the world's poorest people gain access to safe water, sanitation and hygiene education. These basic human rights underpin health, education and livelihoods. They are the essential first steps in overcoming poverty.

Working with people and organisations already in the country, WaterAid supports communities by helping them to gain the skills to set up and manage their own sustainable projects. This will help them to meet their real water needs.

The technology used by WaterAid is always low-cost and appropriate to the locations. It depends on the community's needs and water sources in the area. Knowledge of weather patterns is also a vital part of finding solutions. For example, countries which experience low amounts of rainfall during certain times of the year may not find rainwater harvesting useful. Two different methods are:

- **Rainwater harvesting** Falling rainwater is some of the cleanest water available. Water is collected from pre-cleaned rooftops where it runs, via guttering, into a storage tank.
- **Hand-dug wells** Hand-dug wells are the most common method of extracting water in LEDCs. WaterAid helps communities to develop wells that can quickly become the centre of village life.

a A hand-dug well

What are NGOs and what do they do?

WaterAid in Ethiopia

Ethiopia is in East Africa and although it is has a rich history it is best known for the droughts it experienced in the 1980s. Today, Ethiopia still faces serious problems:

- Only 22% of the population have access to safe water.
- Only 6% of the population have adequate sanitation.

WaterAid has been supporting projects in Ethiopia since 1983. These have included building toilets for houses and organisations, hygiene education, especially hand washing, and involving women and minority groups in helping with future projects. By 2010 it aims to help 100 000 people gain access to water and 95 000 gain access to sanitation and hygiene education every year.

FACT FILE: Ethiopia
Population: 71 million
Area: 1 128 000km^2
Life expectancy: 47 (male and female)

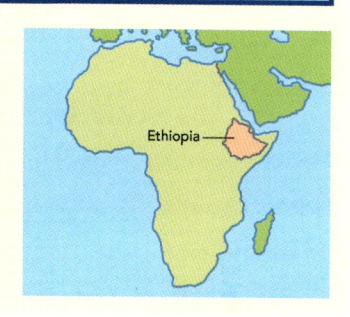

b A WaterAid worker explains how to practice hygiene safely

How can campaigns make a difference?

WaterAid role uses geographical knowledge to determine how best to use technology in LEDCs. It is also important for WaterAid to work in the UK to raise awareness of its work through the media, in order to raise money.

A WaterAid campaign officer's main responsibilities are to communicate with and support those who wish to take action on behalf of the organisation. A campaign officer has to stay informed about the latest policy on water and sanitation in the developing world.

CHALLENGE

1 Imagine that you are a campaign officer for WaterAid. Design a leaflet to communicate the issues about water and developing countries. Include the following information:

- why access to clean water is important for development
- what WaterAid can do to help change things
- a case study, including maps, diagrams, graphs and photos.

More information about WaterAid can be found at www.wateraid.org/uk.
HINT: Use as many different sources as possible.

Glossary

Abrasion The erosion process by which river load wears away the bed and banks like sandpaper

Active volcano A volcano which is still erupting

Annotated sketch A sketch of a photograph, or other diagram, which has been labelled to show information about features

Apartheid The racial segregation and discrimination in South Africa from 1948

Ash Molten rock thrown into the air from a volcano, which cools back into bits of solid rock

Attrition The erosion process by which material carried in the river collides causing pieces of the material to be chipped off

Bedrock The rock on which a building is built

Biofuel Fuel that comes from organic materials (plants - sunflower, rape, sugar cane)

Bridging points A settlement site where a river is narrow or shallow allowing a bridge to be built

Brownfield site Areas that were once built on and are now derelict

Building materials The matter from which something is made

Campaign officer A person who believes in and alerts other people to important causes

Cartographer A trained person who draws accurate maps

Central Business District (CBD) The central region of an urban area where most businesses are found

Community All the people living in a particular place

Commuter settlement A separate settlement close to the urban area, from which people travel to their place of work in the urban area

Compass directions Directions linked to the compass points, North, East, South, West, NE, SW, NNE, etc.

Condensation The process by which water vapour becomes a liquid when cooled

Cone The typical shape of a volcano. A large circular base tapering to a pointed top

Conflict This is a clash, fight, quarrel between countries

Confluence The location where two rivers meet

Congestion Overcrowding or excessive amount of people or traffic in a certain place

Continent A very large area of land. The continents include Africa, America, Antarctica, Australia and Eurasia

Contour lines Lines on a map which join together land of equal height above sea level

Convection current The movement of molten rock deep within the Earth

Cooperative A form of multiple ownership of a business

Counter-urbanisations People moving from urban areas to rural areas

Crater The bowl-shaped hole at the top of a volcano

Cross-section A drawing which shows us what land would look like if we could slice through it

Crust The outermost layer of rock surrounding the Earth

Defensive site The site of a settlement usually on an upland area or surrounded by water

Deforestation The cutting down of forested areas for agriculture, industry or homebuilding

Delta The landform created by the deposition of sediment where a river meets the sea

Glossary

Demand The amount of people willing to buy goods

Deposition The process by which material is dropped by moving water, usually because of a fall in energy levels

Desertification The process by which desert landscapes are extended to a larger area because of drought conditions and climate change

Development The process of improving a country and its standard of living

Dormant volcano A volcano which is not currently active but that might erupt again ('sleeping')

Drainage basin The area of land around a river which drains into it

Drought A continuous period of time where little precipitation falls in comparison with what is expected

Dry point site A settlement site located on high ground away from the risks of flooding (also making it a good defensive site)

Dynamic The way in which places and settlements can change

Earthquake A sudden movement of the earth which can be felt at the Earth's surface

Earthquake zone A place where earthquakes are likely or possible

Earth tremor A slight earthquake

Eastings The vertical grid lines on a map, which are read from left to right

Economic base The industry within a certain geographic area that provides jobs which are essential to support the community

Economic environment The jobs and money found in an area

Economically sustainable service A business which is able to continue into the future

Energy from waste plant A large incinerator which burns household and industrial refuse. The heat produced is used to produce electricity

Entrepreneurship The development of a new business by a private individual

Epicentre The point on the Earth's surface above the focus of an earthquake

Erosion The process by which worn material is removed by an agent such as ice, water or wind

Eruption A sudden ejection of lava, rock and steam through a volcano

Evaluation The fifth stage of the enquiry process, where you ask yourself questions about the data you have collected, the results you have presented and the conclusions you have drawn

Evaporation The process by which liquid water which has become heated turns into water vapour

Extinct volcano A volcano which is no longer active

Fault line A long crack in the Earth's crust.

Fertile soil Soil which contains lots of nutrients. Plants can grow in the fertile soil

Flooding The over-spilling of water when there is too much to be contained within the normal channel

Fold mountains Rocks that have folded, under pressure from two colliding tectonic plates, into mountain ranges

Food supply A regular amount of food which is available

Foreshock A mild tremor that comes before an earthquake

Glossary

Fuel supply A location where you can get fuel. A petrol station or an oil well or a country which has oil, gas, coal reserves. Nuclear supply or alternative energy supplies

Fumaroles A crack in the Earth's crust which lets gases emerge from the magma chamber

Function The purpose of a settlement

Geographical enquiry An enquiry that asks geographical questions

Geographical Information Systems (GIS) An information system that deals with geographically-referenced information, which can be used for storing, analysing and sharing data about the Earth

Geologist Someone who studies the rocks and structure of the Earth

Geyser A spring heated by molten rock to send steam into the air when it boils

Globalisation How people around the globe are more connected to each other. Goods and services produced in one part of the world are increasingly available in all parts of the world, e.g. McDonalds, international travel is more frequent and international communication is commonplace

Global Positioning System (GPS) A system that shows exactly where you are, based on information from satellites

Global warming The increase in the average temperature of the Earth's air and oceans in recent decades

Global village The world, shrunken into a village by communication technology

Gorge A steep-sided river valley

Gradient The relationship between vertical distance and horizontal distance. Hills can have a steep gradient, which means they are more difficult to walk up, or a gentle gradient, which means they are easier to walk up

Great Rift Valley The long, steep-sided valley where East Africa is splitting from the rest of Africa

Green belt An area of land that is protected from development, found on the edge of an urban area to stop urban sprawl

Greenfield site An area of land that previously has not had any urban development take place on it

Grid lines The horizontal and vertical lines used to divide a map into squares

Grid references Sequence of numbers used to locate places on a map linked to numbered grid lines; they can be four figure grid references or six figure grid references

Ground view The viewpoint of photographs taken from ground level

Groundwater flow The movement of groundwater towards the river channel

Habitats The natural conditions or environment in which a plant or animal lives

Hot spot A point where a thin stream of magma rises up from deep within the Earth to the surface

Hydraulic action The erosion process by which fast-flowing water in rivers forces air in gaps to become compressed and act like mini-explosions on the river bank

Hypothesis The first stage of the enquiry process; the hypothesis is the idea you want to investigate

Identity Who a person is; the qualities which make a person or group different from others

Infrastructure The roads, bridges and rail lines needed to keep an industrial economy going

Inner city The older part of an urban area, usually containing high-density housing from the industrial past. The area has mixed land use with residential and industrial buildings

Glossary

Inner suburbs A mainly residential area made up of housing, built between the First and Second World Wars, mixed with a range of services

Integration A set of personal characteristics which makes an individual part of a group

Interlocking spurs The landform created by a river following the V-shaped valley in the upper course of a river – like a giant zip

Interpretation The fourth stage of the enquiry process, where you analyse and interpret your data

Island arc A curved chain of volcanic islands along the edge of a tectonic plate

Landfill The burial of waste material

Landslide A sudden movement of tons of soil and rock down a slope

Lava Magma (molten rock) which pours out of a volcano during an eruption

Lava flow A stream of molten rock that pours out of a volcano during an eruption

LEDC Less economically developed country – a country where the standard of development and quality of living are low

Less sparse settlement A settlement which has a high density of households surrounding it

Levee The humped looking landforms formed either side of a river by flooding events. These can also be a man-made river management technique

Linear scale A line to show how units on a map represent distances on the ground, for example:

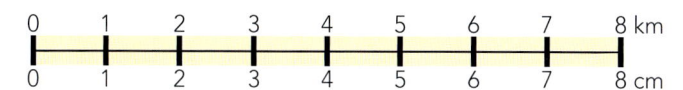

```
0    1    2    3    4    5    6    7    8 km
|----|----|----|----|----|----|----|----|
0    1    2    3    4    5    6    7    8 cm
```

Long profile The cross-section of a river's gradient from the mouth to the source

Lower course The generally flat lower section of the river

Maglev trains High-speed trains which run on a magnetic field

Magma chamber A reservoir of molten rock below a volcanic area

Magnitude The amount of energy released by an earthquake

Mantle The area of plastic rock (molten but under pressure) between the Earth's core and its crust

Map key A key to show the meaning of symbols used on a map

Meander A bend in a river

MEDC More economically developed country – a country where the standard of development and quality of living are high

Mercalli scale A 12-point scale for measuring the damage caused by an earthquake

Methodology The second stage of the enquiry process; the methodology describes the way you collect your data

Micro-loan This is a small loan of money to an individual to start a business

Middle course The middle section of a river

Mid-ocean ridge A long, volcanic underwater ridge in the centre of an ocean

Molten rock Rock heated up in the Earth until it becomes liquid magma

Glossary

Mouth The end of a river where it flows into the sea

Mudflow A river of mud, usually formed when a volcano suddenly melts snow

Mudpool A pool of hot mud found in volcanic areas, where hot water mixes with soil

Multi Use Centre Provides a dwelling where a number of services are available for the local community. The Centres are funded by the local council

Natural disaster An event like a volcano, earthquake, drought or storm, which leaves people dead, injured or homeless

Neighbourhood The area in which we live and which is shared by the local community

New Town A settlement that was planned rather than developed over time, and was built to create a socially mixed settlement for the excess population of other urban areas

NGO Non-Governmental Organisation

Northings The horizontal grid lines on a map, which are read from bottom to top

North–South divide This division can be observed on the global scale between rich and poor countries. The global South is poor and the North is rich. Some believe it can be observed within the UK. Regional differences in wealth exist. The North is generally poorer than the South of England

Oblique aerial view The viewpoint of photographs taken from above at an angle

Ocean Great sheets of salt water which make up 71% of the Earth's surface

Outer-city council estate Council-built housing on the fringe of an urban area

Outer suburbs The area on the fringe of an urban area, with residential land use and large modern properties

Overland flow The movement of water across a surface due to heavy rainfall or saturated ground

Oxbow lake The lake formed when the neck of the meander becomes so small it is cut through

Pangaea The ancient super-continent which broke up to form the world's continents

Physical environment This relates to the natural environment and also the land use found there

Planner Someone who shapes the physical and human geography of a community through the decisions they make about developments

Plunge pool A deep pool created by the erosion from a waterfall

Poisonous gases Fumes given off by a volcano that can injure or kill animals

Precautions Actions taken before a problem to lesson its effects

Precipitation Any form of moisture in the atmosphere falling to earth – hail, rain, sleet, snow

Presentation The third stage of the enquiry process, where you present your data in a variety of ways: using maps, graphs, diagrams, tables

Productivity How much output from a company or an individual can be completed in a specified time (e.g. output per worker)

Pyroclastic flow An outpouring of hot gas, steam and rock rushing down a volcano during an eruption

Quality of life The degree to which things about life are positive

Glossary

Racial segregation A division of people by their race

Ratio The relationship of one unit on the map to the number of similar units on the ground. For example: 1:25 000

Raw materials Raw materials are first extracted from the earth, e.g. coal, limestone, iron, ore. They are processed to produce 'semi-finished materials' and then 'finished materials' such as steel

Recycle To re-process an item into something new to be reused

Reduce To make smaller, either in size or quantity

Relief The height and shape of the land. The topography of the land

Relief agency An organisation which helps people affected by natural disasters, for example, the Red Cross and Red Crescent charities

Renovation To bring back a property to a former better state by cleaning, rebuilding, replacing equipment, painting

Retail park A retail park is a grouping of many retail warehouses with car parks. Retail parks are found on the fringes of most large towns and cities

Reuse To make use of something which would have been discarded or thrown away

Richter scale A scale for measuring the magnitude of an earthquake: one is small, eight is huge

Risk The likelihood of something dangerous happening

River bank The sides of the river

River bed The bottom of the river channel

River channel The trough shape which the river flows through

Route distance The actual distance between two points, following the available route

Saltation The transport process by which pebble-sized particles leapfrog over each other

Scale Used to show the distance on a map or plan in relation to the distance on the ground

Sea Shallow parts of oceans that are near continents, for example, the North Sea, and large inland lakes, like the Caspian Sea

Sea level The average level of the surface of the sea

Segregation To separate from a group

Seismograph An instrument that measures and records vibrations from inside the Earth

Seismologist Someone who studies earthquakes

Settlement A place where people live

Sirens Devices that make a long, loud noise

Site The characteristics of the land a settlement is built on

Situation A description of a settlement in relation to other settlements and the physical factors (the landscape) around it

Social environment This relates to the types of people in an area and the services available

Socio-economic segregation To be separated into different socio economic groups. Rich people living in one area and poor people living in another region

Glossary

Solution The process by which certain chemicals are dissolved out of the bed, banks and load of rivers. This can be both a form of erosion and transportation

Source The area high in the mountains where a river starts

Sparse settlement A settlement which has a small number of households surrounding it. The settlement is surrounded mainly by open countryside

Spring-line settlement Settlements occur along the spring line so that people originally had a supply of water. Building too low may have risked the settlement being flooded

Spot height A dot with a figure on a map to show the height of the land in metres above sea level

Statement of scale A scale represented as a statement, for example: 2cm represents 1km

Storm surge A rise in offshore water associated with hurricanes and tropical storms caused by winds pushing on the ocean surface

Straight-line distance The distance between two points as the crow flies

Subduction One tectonic plate plunging slowly underneath another

Suburbs/suburban A residential area around a major city

Superswell The swelling of the earth above a magma chamber, which is rising upwards

Supervolcano A big volcanic area sited over a huge magma chamber, which could lead to a massive explosion

Supply To make a product available for use

Suspension The transport method by which very small particles are carried along in the river's flow

Sustainable Able to meet our current living and resource needs without spoiling the ability of future generations to meet theirs. Sustainability means using resources sensibly

Sustainable development Development that meets the needs of the present generation without compromising future generations

Sustainability Something which is capable of being continued in the future with minimal long-term effect on the environment

Symbols Small diagrams used on a map to represent features

Technology The application of science to help develop an industrial or commercial idea

Tectonic plate An enormous moving block of the Earth's crust

Tenureship The relationship between a property and the person or people who live in it

Tephra All the bits of rock ejected into the air during a volcanic eruption

Throughflow Water in the soil which moves sideways through the spaces (pores)

Traction The transport process by which large boulders at the start of the river are rolled along the river bed irregularly

Transect A line, along which the changes that take place in an area can be seen

Transpiration The process by which liquid water is breathed out as water vapour by plants

Transportation The process by which river load is moved from one area of a river to another

Trench A very deep part of the ocean, usually arc-shaped, where a plate is sinking

Glossary

Tributary A small river which joins a larger river

Tsunami A long, massive wave caused by an earthquake

Underwater mountain chains Mid-ocean ridges formed by the sea floor splitting

Upper course The upper section of a river

Urban A word that describes an area that contains lots of buildings. Towns and cities are urban

Urbanization The process by which locations become more city like

V-shaped valley The steep-sided valley shape seen in the upper course of a river

Vertical aerial view The viewpoint of photographs taken from directly overhead

Viable Possible from all perspectives

Volcano A cone-shaped mountain formed by molten rock from deep within the Earth

Volcanologist (vulcanologist) Someone who studies volcanoes

Waste management The collection, transport, processing and recycling of all waste materials from homes and businesses

Waterfall The landform made when a river flows over a steep drop

Watershed The imaginary line around a drainage basin

Water cycle The continuous cycle of water on a global scale which involves evaporation, condensation, precipitation and transpiration

Water table The boundary between the underground rock spaces which are saturated with water and rock spaces which are not

Wet Point Site A settlement site located near to a water source e.g. a river. Or near a spring emerging from a slope, sometimes called a spring-line settlement

Index

abrasion 159
accuracy 150
active volcanoes 26, 27
aerial photographs 144–145
Afghanistan 173
Africa 6, 26, 28, 30–31, 49
Africa-splitting volcanoes 28
agriculture 168, 175, 176
AIDS 90, 91
airports 122
America 6, 20, 28, 30–31, 33, 46–48, 50, 58–59
annotation 145
Antarctica 6, 33
apartheid 86–89
Arctic Ocean 6, 41
ash 24, 55
asphalt 71
Atlantic Ocean 6, 17
atmosphere 155
attrition 159
Australia 6, 33, 172

Bangladesh 168
bedrock 53
bin collection 109
biofuel plants 121
Bonby 69
bridging points 69
Brigg 66–67
brownfield sites 78
building new communities 62
buoys 23
bus services 76, 77
business parks 81
business, starting 90

Cambourne 81
campaign officer 179
car parks 77
cartographer 30–31
CBD (Central Business District) 76, 83, 84–85, 88
charts 149
Chile 20, 46
classification of rural settlements 98

climate change 174
clouds 155
Commission for Rural Communities 99, 101
communities 129
commuter settlements 77
compass 136
compost 108, 109, 111
conclusions 150
condensation 155, 166, 170
cone 24
conflict 93–97, 101
confluence 157, 168
congestion 112–115
consultation 129
continents
    definition of 6
    movement of 31–33
    number of 6
contour lines 140–142
conurbations 114
convection currents 40
co-operatives 104–105
core 7
cost 146
counter-urbanisation 101
crater 24
cross-section 143
crust 7

dams 164
data 129, 132, 148–150
    collection 148
    evaluation 150
    interpretation 150
    presentation 149
declining industries 78
defensive site 69
deforestation 165, 168
delta 163, 168
density of population 98–99
dependence on industry 74–75
deposition 161, 163
development of LEDCs 176
development plans 100, 118–123
directions 136–139

docks 78–79
dormant volcanoes 26, 48
drainage basin 157
drains 165
droughts 164, 170–173, 179
    causes of 170
    impacts of 171, 172–173
dry point site 69
Durham 69

Earth
    core 7
    crust 7
    mantle 7, 16, 36
earthquake zones 14–15, 50, 52–53
earthquakes 7, 10, 11–23, 34–35, 36, 46, 49, 50, 52–53, 56–57, 60–63
    causes of 16–17, 36
    measuring of 18–19
    patterns of 14–15
    protection against 52–53
Eastings 138
economic base
    changing 75
    wide 90
economic growth 175
ecosystems 171
electricity 90–91, 113
electronic sensors 23
emergency services 53, 60–63
employment 74, 75, 79, 81, 90, 120, 121
energy 158–161, 162, 163
    from waste plant 119
    source 175
England 166–167
English Partnerships 80
enquiry process 146
entrepreneurship 90
environmental assessment 128, 147
epicentre 20, 60
Epworth 68
equator 39
erosion 159, 160, 162, 163

Index

eruption 10, 24–25, 48, 51, 56–57, 58–59
Eurasia 6
European Regional Development Fund (ERDF) 103
evaluation 150
evaporation 155
expedition 34
extinct volcanoes 26

fatalistic 50
fault line 53
fertile land 67, 68
field sketches 148
fire 53
fishing industry 78
flash points 94
flooding 164–169
    causes of 166
    impacts of 167, 168–169
focus of earthquakes 53
fold mountains 42–45, 46
foreshocks 20
fossils 44
fumaroles 58
future needs 128

gases 47, 54
Geographic Information Systems (GIS) 129, 132, 149
geographical enquiry 128, 146–151
geologists 10, 40
geysers 58, 59
ghost town 71
GIS maps 56
globalisation 92–93
golf courses 123
gorge 162
GPS (Global Positioning System) 42, 56
gradient 141
granite 70
graphs 149
gravity 156
Great Rift Valley 49

green belts 77, 80
greenfield sites 80
grid
    lines 138
    references 138–139
ground view 144
groundwater flow 156

heat 7, 36, 48
Hess, Harry 35
Himalaya mountains 42–45
HIV 90, 91
home delivery 107
hot smoker vents 37, 39
hot spot volcanoes 28, 58
house prices 100, 101, 122
housing 76, 77, 83, 88–89, 122
    high density 76
    low-cost 80, 90
    shortages 80–81
human rights 92–93
hurricane 169
hydraulic action 169
hydrogen 164
hypothesis 147

Ickham 100–101
impacts, types of 171, 176
impermeable 165
Indian Ocean 6, 15, 22, 25
industrial areas 83
injury 52–53, 62–63
insurgents 94
integration 88–89
interconnection 92
interlocking spurs 162
International Federation of Red Cross and Red Crescent Societies (IFRC) 61, 62
Internet 107
interpretation 150
Iran 63
iron production 72–73
island arcs 39, 41

jobs *see* employment

Kashmir 93–97
key 137
Kingston upon Hull 76–79

labour intensive 73
land, demands on 128
landfill sites 53, 108, 109, 119, 123
landforms 162–163
landscape 66
landslides 18, 48, 54
lava 24–25, 36, 47, 54
layers of information 129, 132
LEDCs (less economically developed countries) 82, 168, 176, 177, 178–179
levees 169
light pollution 114
limestone 72
linear scale 132
location of settlements 66–69
long profile 157
lower course 157, 163

magma 24, 46, 58
    chamber 58
magnitude 12, 19, 20, 50, 60
mantle 7, 16, 36
map
    drawing 143, 148
    key 137
    land shape, showing 140–143
    references 138–139
    symbols 137
mapping 30–31, 38–39, 56
markets 66, 89
meander 163
measuring distances 134–135
MEDCs (more economically developed countries) 175, 177
Mercalli Scale 18–19
methodology 148
micro-loans 90
microplate 39

Index

Mid-Atlantic Ocean Ridge 34–35, 40
middle course 157, 162, 163
Mid-Indian Ocean Ridge 34–35
Mid-Pacific Ocean Ridge 36–37
modernising 75
molten rock 24, 36, 37
Mount Everest 42–45
Mount Qomolangma 42; *also see* Mount Everest
Mount St Helens 48
Mount Vesuvius 51
mountains 7, 17, 34–35, 42–45
   fold 42–45, 46
   underwater chains 34–35
mudflows 10, 47, 48, 54
mudpools 58
Multi Use Centres 103

Namibia 82–91
Nant Gwrtheyrn 70–71
national grid 91
natural disasters 60
neighbourhoods
   differences between 126–127
   needs 128
New Orleans 169
New Towns 80–81
NGO (Non-Governmental Organisations) 178–179
North Sea 21
Northings 138
north–south divide 116–117

objectives of Namibian government 90–91
oblique aerial view 144
ocean
   definition of 6
   floor 17, 35, 36, 38, 40
   names of 6
   ridges 28, 34–36, 40
   sizes of 6
Ortelius, Abraham 30–31
overland flow 156
oxbow lake 163

Oxfam 91
oxygen 154

Pacific Ocean 6, 9, 17, 28, 35–37, 40, 46, 47
Pakistan 60–61
Pangaea 32, 33
pattern of earthquakes 14–15
photographs 144–143, 148
physical factors 66
planners 126, 128–129, 132, 146
planning applications 100, 118–123
planning decisions 128–129, 146
plates *see* tectonic plates
plunge pool 162
pollution 177
populations, changes in 99, 116–117
Port Nant Quarry 70–71
post offices 102, 103
poverty 91, 117
precipitation 155, 156, 164, 166
preparing for disasters 52, 62
presentation 149
pressure 7, 24, 159, 163, 166, 170
productivity, increasing 74
proposal 147, 148, 150
pyroclastic flows 47, 54, 55–56

quality of life 129
quarries 70–71
questionnaire 148

race separation *see* apartheid
radioactivity 7
rail network 114–115
rain 155, 156, 164, 166–167, 168, 170, 172, 173, 174, 178
rainwater harvesting 178
rapid growth 72
ratio 132
raw materials 72, 74
recycling 108–111

Red Crescent 61
Red Cross 60–61
redevelopment 78–79, 118–123
refugee camps 95
relief agencies 60–63
religion 94
reservoir 49
responding to disasters 62
results 150
retail parks 77, 121
reuse 108, 111
Richter Scale 18–19
rift valley 49
risk of earthquakes 13, 50
river
   bank 157, 159
   channel 15
   course 157, 162–163
   crossing point 66
   load 159, 160, 161
   mouth 157, 163
   source 157
route distance 134
rural
   homes 90–91
   settlements 98–107

safe routes 134–135
salt water 6
saltation 160
San Francisco 50
satellites 23
saturation 165
scale 130–132, 143
Scunthorpe 72
sea level 168, 169
sediment 163
segregation 86–89
seismologists 11, 34
services 76, 77, 84–85, 97, 99, 102–107
   Multi Use Centres 103
   supply and demand 102
settlement
   definition of 66
   modernising 75
   rapid growth 72

Index

services 76, 77, 84–85, 97, 99, 102–107
   site of 66
   situation of 66
shape of land 141
shelter 62, 63
shield volcano 27
shopping complexes 121
sirens 23
solar power 91
solution 159, 160
Southern Ocean 6, 15
spot height 140
statement of scale 132
steel production 72–74
storm surge 169
straight line distance 134
stratovolcano 27
subduction 40, 41
suburbs 76, 77, 88
success criteria 9, 151
sulphur 51
supermarkets 104, 107
supernova 58
superswell 49
supervolcanoes 58–59
suspension 160
sustainable 177, 178
   development 128, 146
symbols 137

tarmac see asphalt
tectonic plates 17, 24, 38–49
   collision 43, 45, 46
   definition of 38
temperature changes 164
tephra 47, 51, 55
   plumes 47

theme parks 119
through flow 156
Tokyo 50
townships 86
traction 160
trains 114–115
transpiration 155
transport 76, 77, 80, 102, 112–115, 122
transportation 160, 161
trench 40
tributary 157
trillions 50
tsunami 18, 19, 20, 21, 22–23
turbulence 160

Ultraspeed UK 114
United Nations 92
upper course 157, 162
urban
   development 76–77, 80–81
   settlements, definition of 98
urbanization 165
US Geological Survey (USGS) 12, 46

vapour 154, 155
vertical aerial view 144
viable 146
Victoria Dock redevelopment 79
village shops 104–106
ViRSA (Village Retail Services Association) 105
volcanic blasts 47
volcanic soil 51
volcanoes 7, 10, 23, 24–29, 35, 39, 40–41, 46–48, 51, 54–57, 58–59, 60–63
   causes of 24, 39, 40
   hazards 54–55
   predicting eruptions 56–57
volcanologists 10, 46, 54
voting 92, 96
V-shaped valley 162

waste 108–111
water
   access to around the world 174
   amount used 172
   and economic growth 175
   and health 176, 179
   chemical formula 154
   cycle 154–155, 166
   flow 155, 156–157, 165
   molecule 154
   states 154
   supplies 62, 63
   table 156
WaterAid 178–179
waterfalls 160, 162
watershed 157
weather patterns 170, 174, 178
wells 178
Welsh Language and Heritage centre 71
wet point site 69
wind farms 120
Windhoek 82–91

Yellowstone National Park 58–59

Acknowledgements

Why are South America and Africa two pieces of the same jigsaw?

© ABC Ajansi/Corbis Sygma: 11; AFP/Getty Images: 53; Andrew Woodley/Alamy: 44; © Archivo Iconografico, S.A./Corbis: 30 (both); © Arctic-Images/Corbis: 26 (left); Arlan Naeg/AFP/Getty Images: 10; Asif Hassan/AFP/Getty Images:52; © Arzu Ozsoy/International Federation of Red Cross and Red Crescent Societies: 61 (bottom); Beth Wald/ Aurora/Getty Images: 49 (top); Chad Ehlers/Alamy: 50; © Charles O'Rear/Corbis: 18 (bottom); C. Newhall/USGS/ Volcano Hazards Program: 55 (top centre left); © Colin Chapman/American Red Cross: 61 (middle); © Corbis: 24; © Dadang Tri/Reuters/Corbis: 23; Douglas Peebles Photography/Alamy: 27 (bottom left); E. Endo/ USGS/Volcano Hazards Program: 55 (top centre left); Emmanuel Lattes/ Alamy: 27 (top left); Harry Glicken/USGS/Cascades Volcano Observatory: 48 (top and bottom); © Hashimoto Noboru/ Corbis Sygma: 14; Image courtesy of Haymon et al. NOAA-OE, WHOI: 37 (left); Image courtesy of Spiess, Macdonald, et al, 1980/NOAA Ocean Explorer: 37 (right); © International Federation of Red Cross and Red Crescent Societies: 63 (bottom): John Russell/AFP/Getty Images: 22; Jon Arnold Images Ltd/Alamy: 26 (right), 27 (bottom right), 57; © Lester Lefkowitz/Corbis: 59; Liz Leyden/iStockphoto: 27 (top right); Marco Longari/AFP/Getty: 49: (middle); Mauro Carraro/ Rex Features: 54 (middle); Miguelito Parcero/AFP/ Getty Images: 51; M. Mangan/USGS/Volcano Hazards Program: 55 (top left); NASA Jet Propulsion Laboratory (NASA-JPL): 56; NASA Johnson Space Center - Earth Sciences and Image Analysis (NASA-JSC-ES&IA): 41; © Nathan Cooper/American Red Cross: 61 (top); Orlando Sierra/ AFP/Getty Images: 18 (top); Paula Bronstein/Getty Images: 42 (top); Pierre St. Amand/National Geophysical Data Center (NGDC)/NOAA Satellite and Information Service: 20; © Reuters/Corbis: 54 (top); Reuters/Raheb Homavandi: 63 (top); Richard Bouhet/AFP/Getty Images: 25; R. Hoblitt/USGS/Volcano Hazards Program: 55 (top right); Suolang Luobu/AP/PA Photos: 42 (bottom); T. Casadevall/ USGS/Volcano Hazards Program: 54 (bottom); Tom Casadevall/ USGS/Cascades Volcano Observatory: 55 (bottom right); TopFoto/ AP: 48 (middle); © Ulises Ruiz/epa/ Corbis: 47; Ulrich Doering/ Alamy: 49 (bottom); W.E.Scott/ USGS/Volcano Hazards Program: 55 (top centre right, bottom left, bottom centre left and bottom centre right)

What does my area need?

Elmtree Images/Alamy: 126 (top right); Holmes Garden Photos/ Alamy: 127 (top left); Neil McAllister/Alamy: 126 (bottom left); By Ian Miles-Flashpoint Pictures/Alamy: 127 (bottom left); David Newham/ Alamy: 127 (top right), 144 (top left); The Photolibrary Wales/Alamy: 126 (bottom right), 147; Christopher Pillitz/Alamy: 127 (centre left); Realimage/Alamy: 127 (bottom right); David Robertson/Alamy: 126 (bottom centre); Stephen Shepherd/Alamy: 126 (top left); © Fly Fernandez/zefa/Corbis: 128, 130, 136, 137, 140, 144 (top right), 146; Digital Mapping Solutions from Dotted Eyes © Crown Copyright 2008. All rights reserved, licence number 100019918: 130 (top right and bottom right), 131 (top left and bottom left), 136 (bottom left), 139 (top right), 150 (bottom right), 142 (top right, top left, second row left and second row right); OS Crown Copyright ©. All rights reserved Cheltenham Borough Council: 132,133, 135 (left), 149 (bottom); © Digital Nation/Photofusion: 135 (top right); educationphotos.co.uk/Walmsley: 148; Skyscan: 144 (bottom centre); Supplied by Skyscan; Imagery copyright Getmapping PLC: 144 (bottom left and bottom right); Skyscan/© M Leighton: 145

Do you really know where you live?

Jon Arnold Images Ltd/Alamy: 114 (bottom right); Bildarchiv Monheil GmbH/Alamy: 83 (bottom right);Mark Boulton/Alamy: 108, 111, back page (top left); britpik/Alamy: 123; Dinodia Images/Alamy: 95 (middle); Steve Hamblin/ Alamy: 121 (bottom); John Henshall/ Alamy: 71 (top); David Hoffman Photo Library/Alamy: 111 (middle left); Horizon International Images Limited/Alamy: 94; David Hosking/Alamy: 88; Images of Africa Photobank/Alamy: 91 (top); Vincent Lowe/Alamy: 78 (bottom right); Ed Maynard/ Alamy: 122 (top); M. Timothy O'Keefe/Alamy: 120 (bottom); PCL/Alamy: 121 (top); Chuck Pefley/Alamy: 111 (top right); Photofusion Picture Library/Alamy: 77 (top right), 120 (top); Magdalena Rehova/Alamy: 95 (top); Fredrick Renander/Alamy: 95 (bottom); Sami Sarkis Collections/ Alamy: 93, back page (top right); Neil Setchfield/Alamy: 89 (top); Charlotte Thege/Alamy: 89 (bottom); Redrawn with kind permission of BBC News: 96, 97; courtesy Cambourne Project Director David Chare, Bovis Homes and Taylor Wimpey www.cambourne-uk.com: 81; © Bettmann/Corbis: 87 (bottom); © William Campbell/Sygma/Corbis: 87 (top); © Louise Gubb/Corbis Saba: 90; Digital Mapping Solutions from Dotted Eyes © Crown Copyright 2008. All rights reserved, licence number 100019918: 67 (top), 68 (bottom), 69 (bottom left and top right), 72; courtesy Jim Downes: 104, 105; Tony Page/Ecoscene: 111 (bottom middle); Image courtesy of Christine Edwards: 75 (top right); Image courtesy of Neil Ferris: 109; Fox Photos/Getty Images: 70; www.francisfrith.com: 101; Image courtesy of Saskia Gwinn: 111 (bottom right); Images courtesy of Simon Howe: 76 (all), 77 (top left, middle left, middle left, bottom left, bottom right); Courtesy Iceland Foods Ltd.:107;
© iStockphoto.com/Wouter van Caspel: 102 (left);
© iStockphoto.com/Amy Dunn: 113 (bottom left);
© iStockphoto.com/Sheryl Griffin: 113 (bottom right);
© iStockphoto.com/Marie-Lise Laplante: 102 (right);
© iStockphoto.com/Nancy Louie: 113 (top left);
© iStockphoto.com/Linda & Colin McKie: 110 (bottom);
© iStockphoto.com/Vikram Raghuvanshi: 113 (top right);
© iStockphoto.com/Jacom Stephens: 110 (top); Mary Evans Picture Library:78 (bottom left); Photo reproduced by courtesy of Nant Gwrtheyrn Welsh Language and Heritage Centre: 71 (bottom); Reproduced by kind permission of North Lincolnshire Council Image Archive: 73; NRSC Ltd/Science Photo Library: 114 (left), back page (bottom left); Logo courtesy of Oxfam: 91 (bottom); Rex Features: back page (bottom right); Patrick Frilet/Rex Features: 83 (bottom left); Scunthorpe Telegraph: 75 (bottom), 122 (bottom); Courtesy SITA (IOM) Ltd www.sita.co.im: 119; Skyscan/© Imagery copyright Getmapping plc: 67 (bottom), 68 (top), 69 (top left and bottom right), 100; Skyscan/© J Webb: 75 (middle); Courtesy The Ruby Hunt Trust: 103

Why are some countries dry whilst others flood?

Mark Boulton/Alamy: 177 (bottom); Ron Buskirk/Alamy: 163 (left); Chad Ehlers/Alamy: 165 (left); m c photography/Alamy: 166 (top); Jenny Matthews/Alamy: 171 (top); Ace Stock Limited/Alamy: 175 (top); Charlotte Thege/Alamy: 176 (top); Realimage/Alamy: 177 (top); The Photolibrary Wales/Alamy: 175 (bottom); Mark Sykes/Alamy: 166 (bottom); Paul Glendell/Alamy: 163 (right); Andrew Brown; Ecoscene/Corbis: 158; Kyle Niemi/U.S. Coast Guard/ZUMA/Corbis: 169; Jim Winkley; Ecoscene/Corbis : 170 (top); spotlight-studios - Fotolia.com: 154 (top); Oleg Ivanov - Fotolia.com: 154 (centre); Peter Galbraith - Fotolia.com: 154 (bottom); Daniel Berehulak/Getty Images: 167 (top); Robert Cianflone/ Getty Images: 171 (left), 172 (right; Francoise De Mulder/ Roger Viollet/Getty Images: 173 (left); Chris Jackson/Getty Images: 170 (bottom); Adi Shah/AFP/Getty Images: 168; David Silverman/Getty Images: 167 (bottom); Edmond Terakopian/AFP/Getty Images:165 (right); Amir Shah/AP/PA Photos: 173 (right); Lewis Whyld/PA Archive/PA Photos: 164; Stuart Freedman/Panos: 176 (bottom); Dieter Telemans/ Panos: 171 (bottom); WaterAid 178 (top); WaterAid/Caroline Irby 179; WaterAid/Caroline Penn: 178